PSYCHODYNAMIC GROUP PSYCHOTHERAPY
Second Edition

PSYCHODYNAMIC GROUP PSYCHOTHERAPY

Second Edition

J. SCOTT RUTAN, Ph.D.
WALTER N. STONE, M.D.

THE GUILFORD PRESS
New York   London

©1993 The Guilford Press
A Division of Guilford Publications, Inc.
72 Spring Street, New York, NY 10012

Printed in the United States of America.

This book is printed on acid-free paper.

Last digit is print number: 9 8 7 6 5 4 3

Library of Congress Cataloging-in-Publication Data
Rutan, J. Scott
    Psychodynamic group psychotherapy / J. Scott Rutan, Walter N.
    Stone.—2nd ed.
          p.   cm.
    Includes bibliographical references and index.
    ISBN 0-89862-096-1
    1. Stone, Walter N. 2. Title.
      [DNLM: 1. Psychotherapy, Group.   WM 430 R972p 1993]
    RC488.R88   1993
    616.89′152—dc20
    DNLM/DLC
    for Library of Congress   93-15055
                                                        CIP

Preface to the First Edition

The idea for this book took form in 1981 when we were cochairmen of the American Group Psychotherapy Association's Institute Committee. The Institute is a remarkable event that occurs each year prior to the Association's annual conference. The purpose of the Institute is to enable mental health professionals to learn about therapy groups by participating in experiential learning groups. During the many years we were associated with the Institute, we had the marvelous opportunity of meeting, observing, and appreciating the skills of the Institute faculty—men and women from around the world who practice a wide variety of types of group psychotherapy.

Out of this experience we learned a great many things. We learned anew how very powerful groups are as change agents. We also learned that therapists with widely diverse philosophical, theoretical, and technical points of view can be immensely helpful to their patients.

As psychodynamic psychotherapists, we were particularly impressed with the differing approaches that live under the rubric of psychodynamic group therapy. Some practitioners focus on the dynamics of the group itself, rarely speaking to individual members. Others rarely seem to note the group processes, choosing to focus on the specific interpersonal interactions. We found that some of our colleagues listen only for material relevant to the group, while others are avidly curious about members' personal histories or their out-of-group lives. There are leaders who love a good dream, and others who view dreams as resistances. It became difficult to determine what might represent an orthodox psychodynamic approach to groups!

This led us to the realization that, though there are many fine books on group therapy, there is no book dedicated to a consistent, thoroughgoing psychodynamic approach to group therapy. That is what this book is about.

We begin with broad philosophical considerations, speculating about the place of group therapy in today's society. We move then to a history of small groups and of group therapy. From that foundation we explicate a theoretical basis, a road map the clinician can use in traversing the complicated terrain of a therapy group. After the theoretical section, we move to quite pragmatic material. We have sprinkled the book liberally with clinical examples in an attempt to bring the material alive. It is our goal that a mental health professional who reads this book can, with appropriate supervision, be a therapeutic agent as a group therapist.

For literary purposes we have used primarily the masculine form. We hope this is not offensive to any readers.

Were we to mention by name all the people to whom we are indebted for their assistance in this work, the acknowledgment section would be far longer than the book itself. But we would be remiss if we did not give special thanks to some. First and foremost, we are grateful to our patients, our finest teachers. Second, we were moved by the willingness of our colleagues and friends to offer their expertise and time to help us refine this work. Anne Alonso, Ph.D., Martin Keller, M.D., Cecil Rice, Ph.D., Robert Kunkel, M.D., Edward Klein, Ph.D., Esther Stone, M.S.W., and Katherine Stone read and reread various versions of the present book, and their contributions are inevitably woven into the present text. Furthermore, this book would never have reached fruition had it not been for the diligent and compassionate assistance of our editor, Sarah Boardman, and of Collamore's production manager, Merle Schlesinger. Because the secretarial assistance that goes into the writing and rewriting of any manuscript should never go unrecognized, we wish to thank Natalie Reynolds for the willing and patient work she so admirably performed. Finally, we are grateful for the loving forebearance given us through this arduous process by our wives, Jane and Esther, and our children.

Preface to the Second Edition

Much has happened since *Psychodynamic Group Psychotherapy* first appeared — in the world and in our profession. Group therapy is now a standard part of most training programs in psychotherapy. Group therapy has flourished and is offered in most clinics in North America. Psychodynamic theory continues to grow and to be elaborated on and embellished.

At the same time, psychodynamic theory and the practice of long-term psychotherapy are under siege, primarily because of economic factors. Insurance companies, Health Maintainance Organizations, and Preferred Provider Organizations concerned with the escalating cost of mental health services, have begun sanctioning practices that threaten the viability of dynamic therapy. They seem not to understand that therapy that aims at character change and in-depth understanding is cost-effective in the long run (Massad, West, & Friedman, 1990). In a cost-conscious atmosphere, the insurer emphasizes symptom reduction and time-limited treatment. Further, the confidentiality upon which dynamic therapy rests is threatened as insurance companies demand more and more information about the actual material from therapy sessions (Rutan, 1992b, p. vi). There is a strong movement for these holders of the mental health purse strings to dictate what services will be reimbursed, and typically they do not enthusiastically reimburse for long-term psychotherapy.

It behooves dynamic therapists to react to this time of crisis by adapting without forgoing the fundamental principles of our theory. It *is* possible to use dynamic principles, which seek to help the patient gain understanding rather than merely symptom relief, in time-limited treatment. It is mandatory that psychodynamic theorists continue research into the effectiveness of our treatment, thus demonstrating to insurers that it makes sense for them to support it. Actually, group therapy, which offers an economical form of dynamic therapy, should be enhanced in today's society.

We were very pleased with the exceptional reception this book received upon its original printing. We have reviewed that text extensively and have brought it up to date (a process that involved some changes and growth in our ways of viewing groups) where necessary. We have also added considerable new material in areas critical to modern group psychotherapists, such as time-limited groups, groups for difficult patients, and the combining of psychopharmacology and group therapy. We hope readers find this book helpful in their roles as group therapists and teachers of group therapy.

Finally, we gratefully acknowledge the assistance we received from our friends and colleagues in preparing this second edition. While too many have contributed to allow an individual listing, we would be remiss if we did not mention the special contributions of Dr. Leonard Horwitz and Dr. Saul Scheidlinger, who painstakingly reviewed the entire manuscript. Their invaluable contributions are woven throughout the text.

Contents

PSYCHODYNAMIC GROUP PSYCHOTHERAPY
Second Edition

1

Groups in Today's Society

Human beings are group oriented. We begin in small groups, our families, and live and work in various groups. The formation of our personalities is predicated upon our experiences with the different groups in which we interact, and the opportunities for modification and change of our personalities are very much affected by the groups in which we are involved. As Harry Stack Sullivan (1953) maintained, it takes people to make people sick and it takes people to make people well again.

The premise of this book is that groups are uniquely important today because of the structure of modern society. Much has changed in our society even in the decade since the first edition of this book. Nations have been split into historical and ethnic bands or reunited with traditional boundaries. The importance of the national "group" is even more profound today than in the 1980s. Group therapy is a uniquely important therapeutic modality in our 20th-century world, where economic considerations too have reinforced its value.

To place this in historical perspective, let us examine some of the differences between Freud's Victorian age and our 20th-century culture and see how each age affects the lives of those who live within it. This comparison highlights the unique advantages of group therapy in dealing with the ills that beset modern society.

CULTURE AND MENTAL ILLNESS

Pathologies confronting modern clinicians seem to be different from the pathologies that confronted Freud and his colleagues. It might be argued that these are merely semantic differences, but we believe the differences are more substantive than that.

1

In Victorian times Freud (1914) analyzed the pathologies of the members of the society in which he lived, and through that examination he made revolutionary discoveries about the formation and complexion of personality. The pathology that most fascinated Freud was hysteria. This disorder became the lens through which he focused his conceptions of individual psychodynamics. In modern times classical hysteria is not the pathology around which theory is formed. Masterson (1976), for instance, noted that today's patients usually do not come to psychotherapy "with a specific discrete symptom picture, such as an obsession or a phobia, as was reported in Freud's time. Rather, their complaint is more general and vague—of getting too little satisfaction in their lives" (pp. 10–11). The cutting edge of modern psychoanalytic thought has to do with narcissistic and borderline conditions, character disorders in which the pathology is manifested in the disturbed quality of relationships with others.

These "new" pathologies have been accompanied by other post-Freudian developments in our understanding of psychopathology and our practice of psychotherapy. Giovacchini (1979) observed that as psychoanalysis began to treat character-disordered patients, this "shifted our focus from a predominantly id-oriented psychology to an ego psychology. . . . It highlighted the importance of early development. The subtleties and vicissitudes of early object relationships have assumed paramount importance" (p. 3).

The etiology of psychopathology is multidetermined. Elements of temperament, genetics, and biology go into the human experience, along with the intrapsychic and interpersonal forces that are the province of psychodynamic theories.

The search for a link between cultural factors and mental illness began as early as 1897, when Durkheim wondered about the connection between suicide and social conditions. In 1939 Faris and Dunham suggested a causal relationship between schizophrenia and the living conditions in Chicago slums. Leighton (1959), in his well-known Stirling County (Nova Scotia) study, discovered both an overall correlation between mental illness and social disarray and correlations between specific sociocultural settings and particular types of psychiatric disorder. Dohrenwend and Dohrenwend (1974) found that while schizophrenia seems to be present in all cultures, there is considerable discrepancy in the types of schizophrenia that dominate in different cultures. Likewise, Cohen (1961) demonstrated cultural factors in the etiology of depressive reactions. (Eisenthal, 1979, has summarized the studies just mentioned as part of a sampling of the literature on this subject.)

Thus, the notion of a connection between cultural factors and the formation and expression of mental disorder has already been examined in some depth by other authors. For our purposes, the fact that cultures and ages have their own characteristic and dominant pathologies is of particular relevance. In our modern world, for example, there is great evidence that individuals have difficulty obtaining and sustaining intimate interpersonal relationships, even though our culture emphasizes individual gratification. We shall pursue these ideas by comparing the cultures, focal pathologies, and psychodynamic formulations of Freud's day and our own.

VICTORIAN CULTURE

The Victorian era was stressful and comforting to people in specific ways. Victorian society offered many fewer choices than does 20th-century Western society. Although it was vastly more open than the societies that preceded it, its members were nonetheless born into roles largely defined by class, church, ethnicity, and gender. Because there was little opportunity to go beyond those roles, hopes and aspirations were sources of frustration. On the other hand, individuals were spared the burden of ambiguity and choice. Acceptable behavior was highly codified, typically by a strong church morality, with the result that sexual drives in particular were restricted. (The presence of a vigorous body of Victorian pornographic literature indicates that these drives were not thwarted altogether.)

In Victorian society individuals had a definite place, though not necessarily a place they chose or relished. Concomitantly, individuals had an identity that was clear. Relational patterns were set within the framework of the church, the neighborhood, the extended family, the nuclear family, and the world of work, all of which provided most people with natural sources of support and stability.

Individuals in Victorian times were presented with many fewer choices about how to live their lives and with whom to live them. There was less ambiguity and uncertainty. This is not to imply that there was an absence of frustration and pain. If few complained about being "bent out of shape," it was only because being shaped was so universal. It is reasonable to suggest that the restrictiveness of that society might lead to pathologies that express conflict between individuals' powerful innate impulses and the introjects of a restrictive society.

VICTORIAN PSYCHOPATHOLOGY:
HYSTERIA REVISITED

Freud's theories developed as he treated his patients, many of them neurotic hysterics. Students of Freudian theory are familiar with the case of Anna O, the young woman Breuer treated from December 1880 until June 1882. She suffered from classic hysteria, or "conversion reaction." While nursing her dying father she developed paralysis of three limbs, contractures and anesthesias, a nervous cough, and other symptoms. Breuer conducted his first analysis of Anna O using hypnosis throughout the treatment. In the course of the treatment it was discovered that Anna O had two quite distinct personalities. Further, during the treatment the patient developed toward Breuer what later became known as a transference love (Freud, 1937).

Freud and Breuer often discussed this case, and out of these discussions came many of Freud's original formulations about the existence of unconscious material and the structure of personality. Shortly after this Freud saw Emma von N, and in this case he had the opportunity to observe firsthand the strange behaviors present in hysteria.

Freud postulated four major premises about personality: First, all behavior is determined, not random. Second, there are unconscious urges, memories, wishes—a vast reservoir of information outside the individual's awareness. Third, human behavior is purposeful and geared toward the protection of the self (*der Ich*), with even the most bizarre symptoms serving such an adaptive/compensatory purpose. And, fourth, Freud eventually suggested that there are two basic drives within human personality, the libidinal (pleasure-seeking) and the aggressive, with personality formed in the thwarting and harnessing of these two drives. These four postulates are, of course, a most summary attempt to distill the essence of Freud's theories.

Do psychotherapists see patients like Anna O or Emma von N in our offices today? Probably, though certain aspects of behavior, such as conversion reactions, are much rarer now, and when they are seen they are more likely to be seen by our colleagues in neurology or internal medicine. Perhaps more telling is the likelihood that patients such as these would be diagnosed differently today, probably with a label like *borderline personality*. Why the difference in diagnosis and understanding of psychopathology?

Freud used the models implicit in his society, its technology, and the theories available to him; he attempted to view personality in terms of energy and structure. The Victorian era was a time of rapid and monumental change, as industrialization and mass production changed the fabric of society and created a new world order. The people of that era had the conviction that "structure" could harness the very forces of nature, and their conviction seemed borne out by their unprecedented productivity, wealth, population growth, and hegemony over peoples of a more "primitive" nature around the globe. It is little wonder that Freud began to hypothesize about the "parts" that make up personality.

The theory that resulted is to a great extent that of an order based on structure, an organization of parts. The dynamic theories developed to understand modern pathologies refer not so much to faulty parts as to dysfunctional relationships and dissatisfying ways of living. Modern dynamic conceptions of pathology are cast less in terms of mismatched or unmeshed parts than in terms of disrupted developmental processes. Ironically, the recent reliance on the revised edition of the *Diagnostic and Statistical Manual of Mental Disorders* (3rd. ed., rev.), or (DSM-III-R), and a stress on short-term psychotherapy has led to a renewed conceptualization of psychopathology as a cluster of symptoms, or faulty parts of individuals.

Whereas modern theorists chart the evolution of personality through social systems, Freud viewed the ego as essentially the product of intrapsychic conflict. Though individual personality was understood to be affected by interactions with significant others (especially the mother), it was nonetheless not seen as predominantly formed in those interactions. Rather, personality was understood to be the result of a thoroughly inward process. The ego was conceptualized as a rational, unemotional arbiter between the instinctual urges common to all people and the acceptable mores of the particular society in which they lived. The superego was "the alien *it* which tyrannizes the ego" (Binstock, 1979).

It is difficult to criticize Freud for this focus, given the genius required to hypothesize as much as he did about human development. Rather, we should simply understand that he did not have the time or opportunity to expand all his observations to their logical conclusions. That was left to later authors, who elaborated on Freud's observations about the impact of human interactions and developed theories about personality resulting from interpersonal interactions, a concept that is now a given in all modern psychodynamic theories. The apex of this trend is seen in object relations theory, where the need for human relationship is understood to be common to all people and fundamental to the forming of personality.

If it is true that personality is formed in, through, and by relationships, then a therapeutic modality that uses the interactions of networks of individuals should be especially capable of altering disturbed or disturbing personalities.

MODERN CULTURE

In modern culture the traditional sources of identity and continuity are gone or waning. It is as if the Victorian and the modern era are opposites on many important axes. Mainstays of the community and identity, such as the extended (or even nuclear) family, the neighborhood, the church, and the ethnic group, are all diminishing in stability and dependability. The rate of change is so enormous that generations begin to have their own cultures. Mass media penetrates the nuclear family while mass transportation explodes it, and those central places that once gave individuals a sense of themselves are changing dramatically.

There was a certain dependability about the future in Victorian times. If a goal could not be attained in an individual's lifetime, there was always the reasonable expectation that it might be attained in one's children's or one's grandchildren's lifetime. This is not the case today. With increased technology change is exponential, occurring at a faster rate than at any time in history. As if that were not enough, we live under the realization that mankind now, for the first time, has the capacity to destroy all life on this planet in a matter of months—or even moments. And there is little in human history to inspire confidence that we will be able to avoid using this awesome capacity. The value of working for and investing in the future seems thereby diminished. The press to "live for today" thus finds external validation.

Further, modern individuals are confronted with a bewildering array of critical choices new to this era (Toffler, 1970). We can choose our profession, our mate, our geographic location, our educational level, and even our gender. While it is true that each of these choices is relative and within limits, nonetheless they are real. With the presence of such a proliferation of choices, modern individuals must also accept new and more pervasive ambiguity and uncertainty. Each choice involves the quality and type of relationship each of us will have with others.

There has been a strong trend in modern society to value happiness *now* at the expense of deepened relationships and firm foundations (Lasch, 1979; Marin, 1975). "Doing your own thing" is no longer countercultural ethos. It has become part of the value system in all sectors and strata of society. The ready option today is to change the relationship rather than resolve the conflicts. This tendency has become both the cause and the effect of the dramatic instability of modern marriages and family life (at present the risk of a marriage ending in divorce in the United States is approaching one in two).

MODERN PSYCHOPATHOLOGY

The ability to enter into cooperative, loving, interdependent relationships with others is a sign of psychological maturity and health. It is particularly a sign of health in this age. Indeed, a rough but accurate indicator of mental health is the degree to which individuals allow themselves to know how important others are to them.

Given the changes that have occurred since Freud's time, it is quite understandable that the stereotypical pathologies of today involve the ability to effect, experience, and enjoy intimate and sustaining relationships. Whereas in Victorian times individuals had primarily to struggle with conflicts about wishes that society would not allow to be fulfilled or even experienced (notably, aggressive and sexual urges), modern individuals have much more permission to experience those wishes and even on occasion to act on them. The terrible advent of AIDS has significantly affected the ability to act sexually. There are many more things that modern individuals may try, but there are fewer and fewer things upon which we can rely. Specifically, people today have fewer "guaranteed" relationships and sources of identity. The neighborhood is usually transient, the church is less cohesive than in past times, and the extended family (and even the nuclear family) has developed porous boundaries.

Thus, the modern psychopathologies that receive the most attention in the professional press are the narcissistic and borderline conditions, both having to do with an impaired ability to engage in authentic relationships. Fairbairn (1952a) was among the first to state the view that it is the relationship with the object (another human being), and not the gratification of an impulse or drive, that is the fundamental fact of human development. Modern patients who enter the offices of psychotherapists do not disable physical "parts" of themselves as Freud's patients did, nearly so often as they disable their relationships (as Kernberg, 1976, would suggest) or find their capacity to relate to be inadequate (as Kohut, 1971, would maintain). The development of object relations theory and self psychology represent not only the further refinements of psychoanalytic theory but also a modification of that theory that is mandated by the differences between Freud's culture and our own.

GROUP THERAPY

Our understanding of the structure, functioning, and objectives of therapy groups is consistent with our description of modern society and the pathologies it fosters.

Freud's patients lived in a structured and mechanistic world. This both affected the ills that beset them and determined the focus and form of the cure that would work for them. The focus of the cure for Freud's hysterical patients was abreaction, catharsis, and access to their repressed wishes and memories; its form was one-to-one treatment, which served them very well. Patients did not lack social connectedness. The social element was, in a sense, all too present. In therapy what was needed was a sacred and private place within which to explore the feelings and wishes that society prohibited.

Typically, the situation is reversed today. Individualism is so dominant that social connections are not formed or, if formed, soon unravel. The requirements and goals of psychotherapy are thus necessarily different. Modern patients need authentic human relationships, the skills for building them, and the ability to make the compromises necessary to live intimately with other persons. Today's individuals need help not so much with the structure of their being as with the process of relating and acting. From this perspective the benefits of group therapy, of a therapeutic community geared to assist patients in exactly these areas of individual and cultural deficit, become clear.

Therapy groups are supportive yet, in a way, restrictive communities. They are restrictive in that there is a cultural expectation akin to that of the Victorian age. Individuals are brought together into groups and are expected to *work* at their relationships with others in the group. The easy out of changing relationships is highly discouraged in favor of resolving conflict. The resolution of conflict implies the understanding of unconscious forces that drive present behavior and perception. Put another way:

> Group therapy, by its very format, offers unique opportunities to experience and work on issues of intimacy and individuation. In such groups the community is represented in the treatment room. It is usually impossible for individuals to view themselves as existing alone and affecting no one when in a group therapy situation over any significant period of time. (Rutan & Alonso, 1979, p. 612)

2

History of Small Group Theory and Practice

Differences between the way individuals behave when alone and when in groups have interested observers for many years. LeBon and McDougall were among the first to write about the impact of groups on the behaviors of individuals. Freud, F. H. Allport, Sullivan, Lewin, and Rogers are just a few of the well-known authors who have written about group psychology.

It is important to examine the historic interest in the effect of groups upon individuals if we are to understand more fully the possible ways in which groups currently are thought to be curative.

GROUP THERAPY THEORY

Aristotle referred to man as a "social animal," and he considered man's affiliative needs to be a source of strength. Rigorous scientific exploration of the effects of the group upon individuals began as early as 1895 when Gustav LeBon, a French social psychologist, referred to the phenomenon of the "group mind." Like other early authors in this field, LeBon was concerned with very large groups. Having been impressed by the primitive nature of crowd behavior, he used the word *foule* (crowd) to denote the object of his study. LeBon hypothesized that a type of hypnotic power engulfs individuals and causes behavioral change once they become part of a crowd. Individuals lose their sense of responsibility, and a group mind assumes control.

LeBon's (1920) main thesis was that something different occurs to individuals when they are in groups. The result, in his estimation, was

9

a diminishing of human functioning. He described large crowds as regressive, primitive, and uncivilized: "By the mere fact that he forms part of an organized group, man descends several rungs in the ladder of civilization. Isolated he may be a cultivated individual; in a crowd, he is a barbarian—that is, a creature acting by instinct" (p. 36).

In accounting for this change LeBon identified three factors: First, he believed individuals in groups experience a sense of *increased strength,* even invincibility, by virtue of their group membership. Second, he spoke of the *contagion* that occurs in groups, describing it as akin to a hypnotic state induced by the group on its members. Finally, he felt *suggestibility* (for LeBon the most important factor) was greatly increased in groups.

> We see, then, that the disappearance of the conscious personality, the predominance of the unconscious personality, the turning by means of suggestion and contagion of feelings and ideas in an identical direction, the tendency to immediately transform the suggested ideas into acts; these we see are the principal characteristics of an individual forming part of a group. He is no longer himself, but has become an automaton, who has ceased to be guided by his will. (p. 35)

This is not an auspicious or optimistic appraisal of the potential benefits of groups for therapeutic purposes! But succeeding authors have increasingly postulated that the power of groups can be effectively turned to therapeutic use.

William McDougall (1920), an Englishman, published *The Group Mind* at the same time that LeBon published his work. As the title suggests, McDougall had come to the same conclusion as LeBon with the premise that something additive occurs when individuals find themselves in groups. However, McDougall contributed an important new notion: While agreeing that groups have the potential for degrading the level of civilized behavior of individuals, he also saw the potential of groups to enhance individual behavior. McDougall is perhaps the first theorist to see the potential of groups as a means of helping persons change their behavior for the better.

The key for turning the power of groups into a positive force, according to McDougall, is *organization.* Of unorganized groups he was no more optimistic than LeBon, thinking them "excessively emotional, impulsive, violent, fickle, inconsistent, irresolute, and extreme in action." However, he stated that his book would "show how organization of the group may, and generally does in large measure, counteract these degrading tendencies; and how the better kinds of organization render group life the great ennobling influence by aid of which alone man rises a little above the animals and may even aspire to fellowship with the angels" (p. 28). McDougall further stated that clear goals and purposes are essential to the effectiveness of a group: "There is . . . one condition that may raise the behavior of a temporary and unorganized crowd to a higher plane, namely, the presence of a clearly defined common purpose in the minds of all of its members"(p. 67).

Thus, two of the earliest authors on the impact of groups upon individuals identified several important phenomena: the power of groups to affect the behaviors of individuals; the presence of "contagion," or the capacity of groups to fill each of the members with affects; and the importance of organization, group agreements, and goals.

Sigmund Freud (1921) added a great deal more to our understanding of groups. He was intrigued by the effect of the group on the individual, and his study of group dynamics was a step in his further conceptualization of the superego, which had been thought of as the ego ideal. As he considered what constituted a group, in contrast to a collection of people, Freud posited that group formation necessitates having a sense of purpose (a goal) and the emergence of clear leadership. Using the theory available to him at the time, Freud suggested that groups form when members develop libidinal ties to the leader and to one another.

The nature of the ties of the members to one another and to the leader differ. Freud speculated that group members identify with one another as a result of their libidinal ties to the leader. He used the example of an army to illustrate his hypothesis: "It is obvious that a soldier takes his superior, that is in fact, the leader of the army, as his ideal, while he identifies himself with his equal and derives from this community of their egos the obligation of giving mutual help and for sharing possessions which comradeship implies" (p. 56). Inherent in this formulation of identification between members is a regression and dedifferentiation of each individual, who is no longer seen as having individuality except to meet a common goal. This phenomenon helps explain some of the attraction as well as some of the fears experienced in entering group life.

A second dynamic emerging from Freud's formulations concerns the process by which an individual relinquishes his ego ideal and accepts instead the group leader's goals and ideals. Freud compared the members' relationships to the leader with being in love, a situation in which the loved one is overvalued and idealized. He suggested that "when we are in love a considerable amount of narcissistic libido over-flows onto the object. It is even obvious in many forms of love-choice that the object serves as a substitute for some unattained ego-ideal of our own" (p. 66). This dynamic linked individual psychology to processes operating in groups and offered an explanation of the behaviors observed by LeBon and McDougall. (Freud did not directly refer to the operations of small groups. Rather, his observations concerned large groups such as armies and nations. Fritz Redl, 1963, was much clearer in relating Freud's work to group psychotherapy.)

Freud pointed the way toward resolution of the regressive phenomena occurring in groups in his frequently quoted reference to empathy: "A path leads from identification by way of imitation to empathy, that is to the comprehension of the mechanism by means of which we are enabled to take up any attitude at all towards another mental life" (p. 66). This pathway suggests that individuals, following the initial regression associated with group formation, can reverse the process by learning to temporarily identify emotionally with others. This process, empathy, enables a reidentification of each individual to occur and, for the purpose of group therapy, enables individuals to learn about their own emotional life and the emotional life of others.

The closest Freud came to conducting an actual therapy group was probably the famous Wednesday Evening Society, which met in the first decade of this century. This group of analysts met regularly and discussed the theoretical concepts of psychoanalysis, using examples from their work with patients. Early analysts such as Adler, Andreas-Salomé, Federn, Graf, Reik, Nunberg, Sagner, and Wittels attended regularly. The group was initially an educational group; however, the founder of the group, Wilhelm Stekel, had been a patient of Freud's, and thus the legacy of using Freud for therapeutic purposes was built into the fabric of these sessions. The members regularly engaged in mutual personal sharing, with Freud remaining in the role of group leader. Ultimately, as documented in the minutes of the Vienna Psychoanalytic Society, the meetings became exceedingly affective and passionate. The group ceased meeting when the conflict between Adler and Freud reached its crescendo.

GROUP THERAPY PRACTICE

While scholars were theorizing about how groups affect individuals, practitioners were already experimenting with the use of small groups as therapeutic agents.

Joseph Pratt (1969), an internist in general medicine at Massachusetts General Hospital in Boston, is widely credited with being the founder of group psychotherapy. In July 1905 he established a group of 15 of his tuberculosis patients. Pratt's groups were not group therapy as we know it today; the format of the meetings was primarily a lecture presentation. Pratt's groups are cited as a beginning point for group therapy for two reasons: First, they represent the initial known attempt at having patients discuss and learn about their common problem in a small group setting, and, second, they involved a contract that each member had to enter into before being allowed to join the group. Each participant had to agree to give up working and to live essentially out of doors as part of the treatment. Pratt reported very positive results from this new type of treatment.

Other early pioneers who experimented with the effectiveness of small groups for therapeutic purposes included Edward Lazell, the first to see psychiatric (largely schizophrenic) patients in groups (at St. Elizabeths Hospital in Washington, D.C., in 1919); Trigant Burrow, who saw neurotic patients in groups in 1920; Alfred Adler, whose theories about man as entirely a social creature led him to use groups with patients as early as 1921; Julius Metzl, a pioneer in group techniques for alcoholics, who began using groups in 1927; Cody Marsh, who presided over lecture-type groups in New York City in 1930; Rudolf Dreikurs, who in 1930 conducted the first private therapy groups; J. L. Moreno, who used groups in psychodrama in the 1930s; and Sam Slavson, an engineer by profession, who began seeing disturbed children in "activity group" therapy in the 1930s.

It is evident that small group psychology bears a strongly American flavor. Not only was America receptive to the use of groups, but the rise of fascism in Europe at this time meant that many eminent Viennese psychologists immigrated to America, bringing with them their interest in small groups. Julius Metzl, who was doing innovative work with alcoholics, and Rudolf Dreikurs, who was experimenting with small groups for psychotherapy, represent but two of these Viennese psychologists.[1]

HISTORY OF SENSITIVITY GROUPS

The sensitivity group movement, developing roughly parallel in time with the development of group therapy, is another wellspring of theory and experimentation about the potential uses of small groups for purposes of human growth and education. Kurt Lewin was the man most responsible for using small groups in situations where alleviation of psychopathology was not the goal.

In order to place Lewin's contributions in context, one must understand the scientific tenor of the time. This was an era in which scientists were seriously questioning the reductionistic model of scientific investigation. As smaller and smaller units of matter were discovered,

[1]See Cartwright and Zander (1960, pp. 9–30) for a more complete discussion of these adverse conditions.

it was postulated that the universe might not be nearly so well ordered as had been previously assumed. A specific example is found in the theory of light: Newton's time-honored corpuscular theory of light had originally won favor over a wave theory proposed by Huygens because it seemed to explain more of the characteristics of light. However, in succeeding years scientists discovered increasing evidence in support of *both* theories. Finally, Planck, recognizing a *field* of forces, offered a resolution in his formulation of quantum theory, which conceptualized light not as either waves or corpuscular units but in terms of both.

Lewin, along with Freud and others, applied the concept of a field of forces to personality development. Just as we have recognized that it is too restrictive to posit simple one-to-one relationships in most instances in the physical sciences, so too must we recognize, as Lewin did, that in personality development we must consider whole fields of influence that touch upon each person. Perhaps the most important forces in each person's field are other persons. Given his interest in the field of forces in personality development, it was natural that Lewin would become interested in the interaction of people in small group situations. Primarily a researcher and theorist, Lewin experimented with groups as a means of enhancing decision-making power and was interested in ways of increasing group effectiveness and group morale. After the war Lewin continued his work at the Massachusetts Institute of Technology, Research Center for Group Dynamics, the first agency specifically designed to study the dynamics of small groups. In 1947, the year Lewin died, three of his students—Kenneth Benne, Leland Branford, and Ronald Lippett—initiated a series of workshops in Bethel, Maine, that culminated in the formation of the National Training Laboratories (NTL), the first of the sensitivity group, or T-group, organization (NTL referred to their groups as T-groups or training groups).

Another school of small group practitioners was being developed concurrently by Carl Rogers at the University of Chicago. This project began as a means of training counselors for the Veterans' Administration shortly after the war. A major difference between Rogers' and Lewin's groups was in their goals: "The Chicago groups were oriented primarily toward personal growth and the development and improvement of interpersonal communication and relationships, rather than having these as secondary aims. They also had more of an experiential and therapeutic orientation than the groups originating in Bethel" (Rogers, 1970, p. 4).

Thus, the sensitivity group movement can be identified as a separate entity by the 1940s with at least two distinct traditions: the tradition that uses the small group as a forum for improving individual and task effectiveness and traces its roots back to Kurt Lewin and the tradition that uses the small group primarily as an emotional education for individual growth and traces its roots to Carl Rogers.

MODERN THEORIES OF GROUP THERAPY

In the beginning group therapy was conducted on a trial-and-error basis, with practitioners trying to meld the individualized theories of psychotherapy, notably Freud's, with the observations of LeBon, McDougall, Lewin, and others on how groups function. However, a satisfactory integration was not forthcoming, and theorists varied in their emphasis; some focused on the individual while others examined group-wide phenomena. Imbedded in the theories was the proposition that multiple interpersonal transactions could illuminate the individual's inner conflicts or expose group-wide processes. Although we still have not achieved a unitary theory, therapists have come to use a combination of group dynamic, interpersonal, and intrapsychic psychodynamic theories as the foundation of group psychotherapy practice.

Group-as-a-Whole Approaches

Bion: The Group as a Whole

The contributions of Wilfred Bion, whose name has become almost synonymous with one theoretical view of groups, stem from work done during the 1940s, the decade encompassing World War II and a time of extensive attention to small groups by many great thinkers. Although Bion's experiences conducting groups composed of colleagues interested in learning about group processes and patients in psychotherapy groups involved only a short portion of his productive career, his influence has nonetheless been enormous.

Bion conceptualized every group as having two levels. At the overt level groups have a task and a purpose, and the group works toward that end. The leader is not the only one with skills; he leads only as long as he can serve the purpose of the group. The members are discrete individuals who contribute to the task and operate at the level of secondary process. Bion referred to this as a *work group*. In Bion's (1960) view, "the work group is constantly perturbed by influences which come from other mental phenomena" (p. 129). These phenomena are the basic assumptions, which represent a second level of group functioning. However, "the work group is very powerful, and it is noteworthy that it survives with a vitality that would suggest that fears that the group will be swamped by the emotional states proper to the basic assumptions are quite out of proportion" (p. 98). While the overt level of group operation is always present, Bion's theory has primarily to do with the other level of group functioning, the *basic assumption group.* Bion posited that in addition to their attention to the designated tasks all groups operate on fundamental unconscious assumptions, as if members are meeting in order to fulfill emotional needs and/or avoid dreaded relationships. Bion hypothesized three basic assumption groups.

1. In the *dependency group,* behavior is *as if* the members could gain security and protection from one individual, the leader, who is omnipotent and omniscient. Although this fantasy is unrealizable, the members act *as if* they really can create a situation that will conform to their wishes.

2. In the *fight–flight group,* behavior is *as if* the members could gain security and preserve the group through battle or escape. Action is essential and individual needs may be sacrificed in order to preserve the group. This is a group that may "fight" the ideas of self-examination; the group may flee the therapeutic task by engaging in trivial talk. Members may demonstrate other overt flight behaviors such as tardiness, absence, or even premature dropping out of the group.

3. The *pairing group* operates *as if* it were to produce a messiah. The discussion often appears intimate or sexual and is future-oriented. Two people create something in the future; the hope is that what is produced will save the group from intense feelings in the present.

These are the basic assumption groups Bion observed, but he indicated that there may be others.

Bion utilized two additional concepts to account for group interaction. One concept is *valency,* which refers to an individual's primary tendency to enter into group life with one of the aforementioned basic assumptions. Individuals differ in their valency to the three basic assumptions, with some entering into a dependency basic assumption and others entering into the fight–flight or the pairing assumption. However, the concept implies the instantaneous and involuntary nature of each individual's tendency. A second concept follows from the application of Melanie Klein's idea of *projective identification.* Bion, who was analyzed by Klein, makes use of this concept in his understanding and interpretation of a member's unacceptable wishes or impulses being disowned and poured into other members of the group or the leader, where an individual projects the disowned and unacceptable aspects of self into another who contains those projections and is influence by them.

Bion visualized group life as alternating between basic assumption group and work group status. He did not posit a developmental model in which basic assumptions led to maturation; his model emphasized the members' relationships to the leader and to the group at archaic levels, but it did not address interpersonal relationships. Brown (1992) suggests that group dynamics are not fully explainable from only authority relationships and that "unmodified basic assumptions result in groups from avoidance of genuine personal encounter, so that difficult feelings in relationships are disavowed" (p. 216).

The therapeutic goal for Bion was to enable people to learn about their earliest problems with authority, to free them from their historic bonds through an understanding of their natural valences and basic assumptions, and ultimately to enable them to enter into more satisfactory peer relationships. This theoretical orientation results in a particular style of leader intervention, a style that has the flavor of noninvolvement punctuated by mystic pronouncements. In the Bion tradition the leader sits on the group boundary and attempts to make interpretations aimed primarily at helping the group members examine the manifestations of the basic assumptions under which they are functioning. Probably no group therapist functions exclusively in this mode, but Bion's emphasis on understanding the unconscious aspects of group life has had a major effect on therapists utilizing group-as-a-whole concepts. Furthermore, Bion's work illustrates the group processes that are at work in all groups. Some group therapists opt not to focus on these processes, but they exist and are at work nonetheless.

Ezriel: Psychoanalytic Group Therapy

Henry Ezriel (1973) became interested in groups through his membership in Bion's first group. Soon, however, he found that Bion's theories, which were based upon Melanie Klein's work, were not to his liking, and he formed his own theory based upon the work of Guntrip. Ezriel began with the hypothesis, derived from object relations theory, that individuals seek to reinforce repression and avoid contact with frightening unconscious fantasies. The reinforcement is accomplished through the development of object relationships that help deny the unconscious fantasies; such relationships are labeled the *required relationship*. In this view such relationships or transferences take place in many situations and are not part of a developmental process, as in the formation of a classical transference neurosis. The required relationship is precisely that; it is required in order to bypass the *avoided relationship*, entry into which would result in a calamity (the *calamitous relationship*). These three object relationships constitute the tripartite model associated with Ezriel's work.

A common group tension, which is unconscious, emerges as patients try to express the three relationships. Since no two patients have identical intrapsychic conflicts, each tries to express something different and to impose his own pattern on the group. Tension at a latent level then develops among the members. As the process evolves in the here and now of the meeting, the therapist demonstrates the common group tension and each individual's contribution to it. Essential to this approach is the idea of *communicating by proxy,* by which Ezriel meant that a patient may not say anything but may unconsciously or silently identify with another patient.

Ezriel stated that no interpretation is complete without elucidation of all three relationships for the group as a whole and, in addition, as thorough an interpretation as possible for each individual. (Ezriel preferred a group size of five patients). For example, if members are involved in a highly intellectualized discussion about there being insufficient emotional sharing in the group, Ezriel might suggest that the group is talking about there being too much analysis and not enough feelings (the required relationship) in order not to directly criticize the therapist, who represents the analytic point of view (the avoided relationship) because they fear that he will not feed them or care for them (the calamitous relationship). Ezriel would then elucidate how each member's personal conflicts were woven into the discussion.

For Ezriel, all interpretations are rooted in the here and now, and therapists restrict their activity solely to interpretations. Indeed, he/she may remain silent until he/she is able to clarify the common (unconscious) group tension and the individual's contribution to it. A successful interpretation frees individuals so that they can more successfully face the avoided relationship. Then memories and associations from the past will spontaneously emerge. However, Ezriel also believed that avoidance of the past may be used as a defense, since revelations of past conflicts might expose an avoided relationship in the present.

In this purist approach, Ezriel has no contact with patients outside the group meeting and limits himself entirely to interpretive comments. Other interventions are conceptualized as gratifying the required relationship, lowering anxiety, and undermining the work of the group. The therapist is central in this approach, and peer transference is viewed as a displacement from the therapist (rivalry among group members is required because to struggle with the therapist could be calamitous). Interpretations are made to the group as a whole, at the level of the common group tension, and to each individual member. Overall, this method attempts to integrate object relations theory with group-as-a-whole concepts.

While Ezriel has many fewer followers than Bion in contemporary group therapy, he remains important as one of the first in the group-as-a-whole tradition to pay attention to the individual members as well as to the group itself.

Foulkes: Group Analysis

Group analysis is the name applied to the therapeutic approach of S. H. Foulkes (1948), an English analyst who finished his analytic training in Vienna in the 1920s and wrote his text on group analysis in 1948. Foulkes was heavily influenced by classical Gestalt psychology, maintaining that the group is more than the sum of its parts and that no individual can be studied successfully in isolation, since individuals exist only in networks that are their social group. The original social structure is the family, from which the individual derives his personality and identity. The neurotic person, according to Foulkes, is isolated from the family network and is unable to communicate his distress accurately. This isolation from the family network is described as a process of the person's changing from a nodal point in a network to becoming a focal point. Utilizing the classical Gestalt notion of figure-ground, Foulkes maintained that individual pathology would appear as the *figure* in the midst of the group's *ground*. For Foulkes, the individual and the group both required the therapist's (the conductor's) attention.

"What distinguishes group analysis from other approaches is its unique integration of psychoanalytic concepts within an open-systems Gestalt framework that underpins both its theory and practice" (Pines & Hutchinson, 1993). For all the group analysts, the notion of the *matrix* is central. This refers to an awareness of the place where communications and relationships take place, "a common shared ground which ultimately determines the meaning and significance of all events and upon which all communication and interpretations, verbal and non verbal, rest" (Foulkes, 1964, p. 292). The concept of *resonance* describes reverberation of a theme among the members, who react at different levels of consciousness and regression according to their needs, developmental level, and regressive state. *Mirroring* is the aspect of the self that is reflected in others. Through identification and projective mechanisms members become aware of unknown (unconscious) parts of themselves (Zinkin, 1983). At times, with difficult patients, a therapeutic impasse or potentially destructive group process emerges when members are unable to own the split-off and projected parts of themselves.

The therapist has the task of widening and deepening communication. This may take into account differing psychological levels that "range from the more conscious objective 'everyday' relationships to increasingly subjective and unconscious fantasy relationships, from more to less clearly differentiated and individual relationships" (Brown & Pedder, 1979, p. 129). The therapist is actively engaged in the group and is not an austere observing authority placed on the group boundary. Both group and individual dynamics are taken into account, and interventions to individuals will reverberate through the matrix and affect all present. The group analytic therapist models communication in addition to assisting members through interpretation, with the goal of increasing communication. The members are actively involved in the analysis of events occurring within the group. Group analysis, as Foulkes (1975) has stated, is "psychotherapy by the group, of the group including its conductor" (p. 3).

The group provides opportunities to discover similarities and differences between members through a comparison of oneself and others (the mirror). At times the individual is speaking for the group, and at other times the individual's needs are represented by the group. Taking into account the members' differing communication levels, the therapist recognizes that group interpretations may not be accurate for each individual.

Group analytic teachings have been a major force in group work in Europe. The Institute of Group Analysis, which began in London, has developed a network of training centers in a number of major European cities as well as in Australia and in Israel.

Whitaker and Lieberman: The Group Focal Conflict

The group focal conflict approach is an integration of the work of Thomas French (1952) and group dynamic theory. First described by Whitman and Stock (1958) and elaborated in a monograph by Whitaker and Lieberman (1964), the central notion suggests that all or almost all of the verbalizations and behaviors of patients in a session can be understood as efforts to solve an intragroup conflict. By definition, the focal conflict is closest to the surface (i.e., preconscious) and will account for the observable data. The theory further posits that as conflicts are integrated, deeper material becomes exposed for interpretation, enabling patients to learn about themselves.

In this approach it is postulated that a wish (the disturbing impulse) becomes generated in the group but cannot be directly exposed for fear of some negative consequence (the reactive motive) and is therefore expressed in a compromise fashion (the solution). Focal conflicts may be elaborated into themes, which may then be expressed during a series of sessions, or certain solutions in themselves may stimulate further conflicts. After conflicts are actively clarified and worked through, the group may enter a conflict-free period during which more personal material can be examined, responded to, and worked on without stirring unmanageable anxiety or resistance.

An individual patient may or may not respond to any particular conflict; however, in this theory, as in others, the notion is advanced that silence is not lack of interest but is often a cover for significant emotional participation (resonance). Therefore, the therapist may make appropriate groupwide interpretations, which are believed to affect each member, including the member who seemed not to be participating in the discussion.

Notions derived from group dynamics include those of the group culture, which are used in this context to describe how the group deals with the focal conflicts, namely, by either enabling or restricting solutions. The enabling solution allows the group greater safety so that conflicts can be worked through at great depths. If conditions become unsafe for an individual, he may attempt to alter the group culture through habitual defensive maneuvers, thereby setting in motion another focal conflict. An enabling group culture provides the patient an arena in which it is possible to understand and relinquish habitual maladaptive patterns.

In utilizing the group focal conflict model therapists are in emotional touch with the group but stand apart from it so that they can interpret it; they observe the group process and attempt to interpret restrictive group solutions. The theoretical framework (which is quite similar to the tripartite object-relations-based model proposed by Ezriel) leads to attempts by the therapist to interpret the disturbing motive (the wish), the reactive motive (the fear), and the solution.

Successful interpretations alter the group solution and increase the safety of the group culture, which in turn will benefit the individuals within the group. The therapist's strategies are directed at the focal conflict and may include translating an individual problem into one that applies to the whole group. An intervention to one member may address the group conflict (Whitaker, 1989, p. 248). However, Whitaker and Lieberman (1964) caution that the therapist needs to be aware of the potential effects, both negative and positive, of such interpretations. Their main point of view is that all therapists' interventions have an impact on the group process. Awareness of the response to interpretations enables the therapist to follow the group's struggles toward new and, hopefully, enabling solutions to focal conflicts.

Interpersonal Theories

Irvin Yalom (1985) elucidates his theory of interpersonal learning as it occurs in group therapy in *The Theory and Practice of Group Psychotherapy.* Yalom trained in the Sullivanian tradition, and many of his notions derive from that interpersonal orientation. He believes that the major therapeutic thrust for change occurs in the group interaction as it takes place in the here and now. He does not preclude discussion of outside ideas or events, but the main arena for learning is the therapy group. With proper structuring this evolves into a social micro-cosm, a miniaturized representation of each patient's social universe.

Through repeated experiences in the group setting, patients learn about their maladaptive interpersonal transactions and their percep-tual (parataxic) distortions that elicit negative or undesirable responses from others. The mechanisms involved in helping patients learn are feed-back from others (consensual validation) and self-observation. During this process patients learn that their fears may be groundless in the present and that their anxieties arise from perceptual distortions. As patients learn about their behavior patterns in the group, they become more able to observe comparable behaviors both inside and outside the group, thereby increasing their ability to manage themselves suc-cessfully. The ultimate responsibility for change rests with the patient. Increased insight alone will not guarantee change.

Interpersonal learning takes place at several levels, according to Yalom. As in other theories the therapist is viewed as representing paren-tal figures, and interactions with group members represent both authori-ty and sibling relationships. Transference and insight are considered aspects of interpersonal learning, but they are considered of less ther-apeutic value than the "corrective emotional experience" of authentic human interactions that occurs in the group. Transference is understood, in the Sullivanian tradition, primarily as an interpersonal perceptual distortion, and the work of the group involves working through these distortions. Insight is categorized as learning at four different levels: (1) how one is seen by others, (2) what one is doing in relation to others, (3) why one might be doing what is being done, and (4) genetic insights.

For most patients Yalom feels that the first three levels of insight are sufficient for change. He suggests that intellectual understanding (insight) is a critical element for change, but he does not feel that this must extend into the patient's past in order to be useful (depth of in-terpretation and insight are not correlated with potency).

The therapist's role in this model is that of a real person whose tasks include the creation of an appropriate group culture where inter-personal behaviors can be examined. The group therapist, by attend-ing to the development of group cohesiveness and appropriate norms, shapes a social system. Because Yalom believes that the greater the group cohesion, the more likely will be the influence of interpersonal feed-back, he emphasizes cohesion. Rothke (1986) specifies the characteris-tics of useful feedback: It is clear, has a high degree of immediacy, focuses on the sender of the message, is of an affective nature, involves risky self-disclosure, deals with the sender–receiver relationship, and is minimally evaluative (p. 228).

Particularly in the early sessions, therapists must be attentive to tardiness, absences, subgrouping, extragroup socializing, and scapegoating. Their task is primarily as gatekeeper, and they shape the norms of the group through their use of authority and by presentation of a rationale for their work. At various stages in the group's existence the therapist utilizes different techniques. The therapist models the group's behavior by offering feedback, by clarifying the concept of responsibility, by disconfirming fantasied disastrous consequences, by reinforcing generalizability of learning, and by encouraging risk taking. The therapist also attempts to demystify his or her power and reinforces the members' capacities to help one another (Leszcz, 1992). Yalom does not exclude group dynamics and group-as-a-whole phenomena, but he relegates them to a secondary position and focuses primarily on the interpersonal interactions and transactions within the group setting.

Intrapsychic Approaches

This approach to group therapy emphasizes the principles of intrapsychic conflict and translates the psychoanalytic model into the group therapy situation. The paradigm is that of an individual within the group, that is, psychoanalysis in a group setting. Group dynamics in their pure state are seen as resistances and interferences with the basic therapeutic task. This orientation was central to the work of Sam Slavson (1950), and Alexander Wolf and Emmanuel Schwartz (1965) have given a scholarly exposition of this position. Theoretically, the group provides a situation where regression takes place; this allows for elucidation of the transferences and resistances that then become available for interpretation. Regression may take place in libidinal, object relations, or cognitive lines of development. Libidinal regression to oral-dependent or anal-controlling power phases is very common. Emergence of preoedipal patterns of object relations is manifest in fears of fusion and loss of self. Defenses consistent with early object relations include splitting, projective identification (see Chapters 11 and 12 for further elaboration), projection, and denial (Rice, 1992). Cognitive processes may regress from secondary to primary forms. However, it is uncommon for psychotic mechanisms, such as hallucinations, delusions, or loss of time–space orientation, to appear (Ashback & Schermer, 1987, p. 46). Scheidlinger (1968) distinguishes between *group-formative* regressions, which are responses to the group interactive patterns (i.e., the members' manifestations of dependency as they orient themselves to a new group) and the transferential expressions of the individuals' earlier developmental modes of functioning.

The presence of other members enhances the possibilities for exposing a variety of relationships, thereby broadening the context in which the patient's intrapsychic problems can be examined. The group provides unique opportunities for the development of parental (vertical) and sibling (horizontal) transferences. Peers represent the possibility not only of sibling but also of parental transferences. Initially, peer displacements may be easier to analyze than the more commonly identified therapist parental transferences. Furthermore, the presence of peers means more affective stimuli to elicit associations, memories, and affect.

There is controversy as to the depth of the regression and transference that can occur in group psychoanalytic therapy. Therapists at one end of the continuum maintain that the group setting provides a special matrix in supporting the individual and creating a safe environment, which along with all the stimuli of the other members enables an in-depth regression. At the other end, clinicians maintain that the presence of others and the need to share time is a significant limitation to the depth of the regression and, consequently, to the extent of therapeutic benefit. Either possibility may account for the differences in transference and resistance observed in group and in dyadic therapy. However, the basic premises remain, namely, that significant transferences develop and that through interpretation of these transferences neurotic conflicts and character styles can be analyzed.

Exploration of genetic material is seen as crucial in helping patients develop thorough self-understanding. According to Wolf and Schwartz (1965), the group analyst is not "concerned so much with the collective effort as he is with the emerging wholesome individual ego. He is not preoccupied with how the mystique of the group feels, an irrational projection, but with how the individual within the group thinks, feels, fantasizes, dreams and behaves" (p. 246). Thus, for these authors, the therapist in group psychoanalysis helps patients explore the latent motivation behind their current interaction; the here and now is suffused with the there and then, and the interpersonal is translated into the intrapsychic.

The group psychoanalyst interprets the nature of the unconscious processes among patients and between therapist and patient. The patients learn to understand the latent meaning of their interactions and make interpretations among themselves, thereby acting as auxiliary therapists. The therapist does not allow any single member to become the sole focus of the analytic action but shifts attention from one member to another. The analyst searches for transferential material or defensive operations he or she believes to be appropriate to work on at a certain time, exercising judgment in these individual choices and paying less regard to the reactions of others. As Wolf and Schwartz (1965) state, "If he didn't, he would fail to function effectively as an analyst" (p. 269).

Most contemporary psychoanalytic group therapists do not adhere exclusively to this individual-within-the group model but utilize their awareness of group dynamics to help explore issues that may be relevant to more than one individual.

General System Theory

In the past decade many practitioners and theorists have found an incompleteness in psychodynamic theory and have explored a broader theoretical basis for understanding human behavior. This has led to the application of general system theory (GST) to group psychotherapy. The work of von Bertalanffy (1966) serves as the foundation upon which to build a new theory for the practice of group psychotherapy. This theory provides a model for examining the interrelationships among the intrapsychic, interpersonal, group-as-a-whole, and social aspects of the treatment group.

A number of important assumptions make GST an attractive conceptual model. For example, GST maintains that though a wide diversity of form and behavior is exhibited by the various systems, fundamentally they all possess a common underlying structure, *isomorphy*. Additionally, there are similarities in organizing processes, which are conceived of as self-organizing and are labeled *living structures* (J. Durkin, 1981, p. 28). Further, GST holds that transformation or change takes place across boundaries that each system or subsystem can autonomously control.

GST is a growth or change theory, not a conflict or deficit theory. In GST, transactions are seen as occurring across boundaries, whose nature is a critical concern for GST (Rice, 1969). It is at the boundary level that attention should be paid, whether it be between group members, between group member and leader, or even between the boundaries separating aspects of an individual. Boundaries must be permeable enough to take in and give out what is necessary and yet impermeable enough to offer protection and separation. The opening of boundaries (e.g., to allow a transfer of information or emotion) is essential for the system (individual or group or any structure) to survive. Gaining the capacity to open and close boundaries appropriately is an important goal for members of groups. Thus, group therapists focus their attention on various levels of boundaries, depending upon which boundary is the focus at any given moment in the life of the group.

The therapist in GST is seen as a boundary regulator (though not the exclusive regulator; a group member could take on this role as well) and a boundary observer (Astrachan, 1970). Therapists monitor boundaries and make interventions that are appropriate to their diagnoses concerning the permeability or impermeability of boundaries.

Clearly, from this perspective the precise level at which therapists opt to intervene is related to their conceptualization along the lines described by the other psychodynamic theories. But GST provides a unifying approach that does not require a major shift of conceptual levels when moving from intrapsychic to group levels of inquiry and observation.

One of the problems tackled by GST theorists is that of energy exchange. The transmission of information and emotion across boundaries implies a shift of energy. Systems, in order to remain alive, must counter entropy, the process by which systems gradually become disorganized. *Negentropy,* the inherent self-organizing activity of systems, counters entropy and is fueled by energy shifting across boundaries. Although this aspect of the theory is incomplete, it suggests an avenue for exploring the flow of emotions that occurs in group situations.

Agazarian (1992) has applied systems thinking to clinical work with groups. She has emphasized the hierarchical nature of the system within which the group is embedded (the group as a whole, the subgroups, and the individual) and within that framework she conceptualizes the subgroup as the basic unit to be examined. For Agazarian, the major task is to increase communication across boundaries. She actively works to establish subgroups that will contain the splits inherent in individuals. "Communication within and across the boundaries of the subgroup is the therapeutic focus; *how* the group communicates is always more important than *what* it is communicating about" (Agazarian, 1989, p. 176). Subgroups form naturally as an expression of the "inherent opposition to differences" (p. 191). Within homogeneous subgroups the therapist attempts to demonstrate that members can be alike and still be different. If differences are disruptive, the clinician demonstrates the members' covert likeness. These strategies open the boundaries for increased communication and understanding of resistances to learning about the walled-off aspects within the self.

RECENT INTEGRATIVE ADVANCES

Originally, group therapy was founded on established psychodynamic theories. However, those theories were based on dyadic practice. A great deal of attention has been given to the task of finding an authentic integration of individual and group therapy theories.

Group Psychodynamic Formulations

Efforts at integrating group and individual processes and theories are exemplified in the work of Helen Durkin (1964) and Henrietta Glatzer (1953). These authors focused on the transferences and resistances in group psychotherapy, utilizing the interactions that emerge to help clarify those phenomena. They took individual psychoanalytic theory and made initial inroads in establishing a meaningful integration with group psychodynamics. According to these authors, in addition to transferences to individuals, transferences to group phenomena exist as well. An example of the latter would be a situation where one patient is the focus of attention, which stimulates rivalrous feelings in other members. Analysis of the transference or the resistance to this sibling transference becomes the focus of the group's inquiry.

An additional integrative model has been proposed by Lowell Cooper and James Gustafson (1979a, 1981, 1992) in a series of publications describing "unconscious planning in small groups." Elaborating the control mastery theory of Weiss and Sampson (1986), Gustafson and Cooper propose a general theory integrating individual member behavior and group dynamics. They posit that individuals enter into groups with unconscious and conscious expectations of what will be dangerous and what will be protective. Patients execute a series of tests (their unconscious or preconscious plan) to determine if they will be traumatized in the present as they have been in the past. If conditions of safety are met, they will risk exposing previously withheld information. In this process members align themselves with subgroups that will provide safety. Gustafson and Cooper suggest that three major plans are utilized: (1) *transferring,* in which the therapist is treated as a parent figure, the test being to determine if the clinician will behave differently from the traumatizing parent; (2) *turning passive to active,* the test being to determine if the therapist, or another member, will have a more constructive solution to defending against historic pain than the patient initially had (thus growth takes place through identification); and (3) *remembering,* the test being to see if connections from the past can be integrated into the patient's experience of internal continuity.

Inevitably, clashes take place between subgroups when there are conflicting plans. The therapist must then steer between the two plans, recognizing the validity of both as necessarily arising from the individual members' historic past. For example, one member (representing a subgroup) might need to idealize the therapist to test the degree of protection available before risking an autonomous behavior whereas another subgroup might need to maintain their independence (and will test to determine if that is acceptable) before exposing their wishes for caring from a parental figure.

The model is a growth model; according to the authors, it can be applied to drive, object relations, or self-psychological theories. Gustafson and Cooper believe that Bion's theories are a special instance of conflicts, for instance, between basic assumptions or between a basic assumption and a work group.

Hierarchical Integration

Integrative efforts also have been approached from the perspective of the group as a whole. Kernberg (1975), who was heavily influenced by Bion's concepts about object relations, suggested that group-as-a-whole interventions address one developmental level of psychopathology—that of preoedipal development. In contrast, more individual transferences (and resistances) are at a more advanced level of object relations development, representing dyadic (envy) and triangular (oedipal) conflicts. Thus, Kernberg posited that the group therapist may choose the intervention most appropriate to the group and individual levels of functioning.

A technical integration has been suggested by Horwitz (1977b). Trained in a group-as-a-whole tradition, Horwitz modified his initial position and suggested that the group therapist conceptually must maintain a hierarchy of group-as-a-whole, interpersonal, and intrapsychic formulations. With this in mind the therapist assesses the group members' abilities to examine their functioning within a group. Horwitz suggested that in most instances group members are emotionally able to understand comments about themselves before understanding comments relating to their relationships to the groupwide issues. This approach represents a technical advance because it highlights the need for collaboration and alliance between the group therapist and each individual group member. The more traditional group-as-a-whole approach does not sufficiently value or utilize the importance of the therapeutic alliance.

CONCLUSION

In general, group-as-a-whole theorists have highlighted authority (parental) relationships in contrast to the interpersonal theorists, who have paid closer attention to peer (sibling) transactions. Relationships with both authorities and peers are obviously very important considerations in psychotherapy, and most patients referred to group psychotherapy have difficulty in each sphere. Therefore, an integrative conceptualization is necessary for the psychodynamic group therapist.

The social structure of the group and the impact of social forces must be kept in mind at all times. Just as in the world at large, individuals in groups exist within social systems, complete with leaders, followers, and colleagues. Furthermore, not only do the social forces affect and impact upon each individual in the group, but each individual in the group affects the group as a whole. Thus, the group therapist has the considerable task of keeping complex interacting forces in mind. Sometimes the group-as-a-whole factors are the most significant, as, for example, when a new member enters the group; whenever the group's basic boundaries are changed or endangered, the entire group reacts, and individuals are best helped by careful attention to the group-as-a-whole process. At other times the group-as-a-whole processes may fade into the background, though they never disappear. We must always remember that the job of the group therapist, despite the powerful influence of the group dynamics, is to treat *individuals* who are seeking help, not groups. We choose to utilize the forces within the social systems in order to maximally assist our individual patients. The uniqueness of each individual should not be lost in our eagerness to understand the workings of the group. The purpose of this book is to help the group therapist understand and harness the forces at work in a therapy group in order to move effectively across boundaries from group-as-a-whole to interpersonal to intrapsychic foci, thereby taking advantage of the therapeutic power residing in therapy groups.

There will continue to be innovative shifts in emphasis as long as our understanding about human beings continues to broaden. Three primary considerations emerge from examining the diversity of approaches subsumed under psychodynamic group psychotherapy: First, there is an emphasis on the individual's internal life (the *intrapsychic*). This component examines the patient's character formation, typical defenses, problem-solving techniques, internal object relations, and so on. The second component is the *interpersonal,* information about which is acquired from analyzing relational styles and deducing what internalized conflicts are being replayed in the interpersonal field. This component includes inquiry about individual role, style, and externalization of the internal role through projection and projective identification.[2] These are elements subsumed under Sullivan's term "parataxic distortions." Finally, the *sociopsychological* component is the broad context in which the group occurs, including but not limited to the social structure of the group. In this component the group-as-a-whole dynamics are explored, including group norms, values, assumptions, and restrictions.

[2]Projection is a one-person mechanism wherein an individual projects the unwanted, unacceptable aspects of self onto another. The other person may be completely unaware this has occurred. Projective identification, on the other hand, is a two-person mechanism wherein the unwanted aspects of self are projected onto another, who in turn accepts those projections and is influenced by them.

3

Group Development
and Group Dynamics

Even a neophyte group therapist observing two groups, one having been in existence for three or four sessions and another for several years, would quickly be able to determine which is the older, more mature group. What development has occurred that accounts for this change? Understanding the broad outlines of predictable group evolution, complete with the tasks involved in the various stages of that evolution, provides an anchor for the therapist. Just as a knowledgeable individual therapist can gain a deeper understanding of his patients' ideas and associations by having an appreciation for the developmental levels and the associated tasks for individuals as they grow, so too are group therapists helped by an understanding of the usual stages of group development. Like individuals, groups do not move forward in a linear fashion: they are subject to forward and backward movement. Furthermore, these fluctuations do not take place automatically or by any set timetable.

Group development is a product of the individual members and their interactions among themselves and with the therapist. Nonetheless, accurate assessment of the developmental level can aid the therapist in attempts to notice shifts in groupwide functioning. For example, more primitive patients may make major therapeutic gains while working on the early issues of joining and belonging to a group. These patients derive the most therapeutic benefit when the group members are examining aspects of building trust and belonging. Patients who have conflicts at a more advanced developmental level often make less therapeutic gain at early levels of group development. If a group is composed entirely of patients with preoedipal problems, that group will likely remain at early levels of development for a prolonged period, which would be quite beneficial to such patients. If healthier patients remain stuck in an early stage of group development for a prolonged period, this would indicate either a case of misdiagnosis or significant problems of transference or countertransference.

As discussed in Chapter 2, some therapists emphasize group development and focus on little else. The stages of development, however, are best used as indicators to help the therapist more fully understand what is going on in the group. One stage is not inherently more valuable than another. A common misconception among therapists is that in order to have a "good" group, it is imperative that the group attain and maintain the most advanced developmental level. For many patients this would be asking the impossible. Rather, there should be a reasonable fit between the level of group development and the dynamic issues salient for the members.

Most of what we know about group development emerged from studies of time-limited, closed-membership groups (Tuckman, 1965). Generalization of these ideas to ongoing, open-membership psychotherapy groups has often been done indiscriminately. There is overlap, but the two situations are not identical. For instance, a psychotherapy group has only one actual beginning. Yet, with each addition of one or more new members there is a modified new beginning, usually accompanied by reemergence of themes and modes of relating similar to those at the time of the initial sessions. Moreover, events inside or outside an ongoing group may set off a recrudescence of the power struggles that characterized the second phase of development. The repetition of various developmental phases provides an opportunity to rework previously traversed ground, sometimes in greater depth and with increased insight, and therefore has considerable therapeutic potential. Keep in mind that these are schematic presentations; only the careful study of processes in each particular group, as well as in the individuals involved, will provide the basis for meaningful therapeutic change.

Not everyone endorses the concept of development within groups. Slavson (1957) attempted to expunge group processes from psychotherapeutic groups; he focused purely on interpersonal interactive processes. Slavson's position represents an effort to transpose classical dyadic psychoanalytic concepts (transference and resistance) into group psychotherapy settings. By linking group interaction closely to dyadic therapy, Slavson and others (Wolf & Schwartz, 1962) stressed the continuity of psychodynamic/psychoanalytic concepts. This historic bridge made group therapy acceptable, if not attractive, to the mainstream of the American psychotherapeutic community.

Gradually the tradition of linking individual psychodynamics to group psychotherapy included the transposition of individual developmental stages to groups. Group development came to be seen as replicating oral, anal, and phallic stages (Gibbard & Hartman, 1973; Saravay, 1975). Using such traditional analytic metaphors does not do justice to the complex phenomena observable in groups; an expanded perspective that encompasses the more complex data of individual and group interactions is necessary. Within the group matrix are a variety of relationships—among the members, between the members and the leader, and between the members and the group as a whole. These patterns develop in a rather characteristic fashion.

One of the tasks for members is to determine what will make their efforts in the group most useful. When a new group forms, these tasks are unknown, and the members, through trial and error, discover which tasks, roles, and norms will create a safe environment and also serve to accomplish their goals. Learning is reflected in shifts in how the members relate and examine themselves and in the nature of their relationships to each other and to the leader.

Thus far, no schema describing group development has been able to do justice to the complexity of internal fantasies and behavioral transactions that occur when a small group of individuals organize and begin to work together, but it has been observed that two elements are always present in successful groups: accomplishing the goal and simultaneously attending to the emotional needs of the members. Bion's model of group functioning separates these elements and describes their alteration. The *basic assumption* group is one in which the members are responding primarily to their emotional needs; in contrast, the *work group* is rational and functions to achieve goals. This model is more descriptive than developmental. In group psychotherapy, where the goal is improved emotional functioning of the members, the overlap between the two tasks is extensive. Nonetheless, the components can be separated, and it serves a heuristic purpose to do so.

An individual's attainment of goals and fulfillment of emotional needs are central considerations in group psychotherapy and can be seen to occur in each of the four phases of group development: the group formation phase, the reactive phase, the mature phase, and the termination phase. It is important for therapists to remember that the ultimate goals of therapy, improved intrapsychic functioning and self-learning, can occur during any of these four phases.

THE GROUP FORMATION PHASE

There has been a plethora of contributions to an understanding of group formation. Yalom labeled this first phase "orientation, hesitant participation, and search for meaning." Hill and Grunner (1973), Fried (1954, 1971), and Schutz (1958) have stressed the issue of inclusion. Some of those espousing a psychoanalytic framework (e.g., Benis & Shepard, 1956) emphasize the dependency aspects in this initial phase. Savaray (1975) likened this early phase to that seen in the childhood progression of oral drives. Day (1981) emphasized both the patients' dependency needs and their inevitable competition with one another during this initial phase. Slater (1966) suggested that the main concern of members of a new group is the fear of being controlled or engulfed by the group; thus, he viewed the deification of the leader as the normative and characteristic response. Common to all the contributors is the notion that a series of expected processes routinely takes place in a new group, processes involved in the tasks of joining and forming a group.

The major task facing patients entering into group therapy is forming a group. In the case of a newly formed group this is obvious, but it is equally true when a new individual joins an ongoing group. When any new member joins, a new group must be formed. Belonging implies that a level of agreement has been reached, not always consciously, regarding common goals, ways of relating, and ways of resolving problems. A member must loosen personal boundaries in order to emotionally enter this larger collective labeled "the group." And this task must be accomplished in the face of stranger anxiety.

Every member approaches this task with his own personal history, developmental needs, and conflicts. Still, there are some common experiences in our culture. Growing up has provided each person with prior experiences in small groups, beginning with the family and then continuing with schools and a host of religious, business, or social institutions.

In group therapy, particularly the relatively unstructured situation in dynamic group psychotherapy, clues regarding how to proceed are minimal. Members have to orient themselves through trial and error to see what will work, and they go about those tasks in a variety of ways. The ambiguity of the situation stimulates regression. Each member tends to regress to a personally important developmental stage, and his or her response in the group may represent either a successfully or an unsuccessfully completed task. The situationally induced regression is clinically useful to the therapist in gaining an understanding of a member's manner of managing anxiety.

While it is expected that patients will regress when they join a group, it should not be expected that all patients will respond to this regression identically. For some this is a time for gaining insight into the nature of their relationships to their parents, since many patients respond to joining primarily in terms of feelings of dependency, helplessness, and confusion. Those patients often replicate important aspects of their relationships to their parents and demonstrate important transferential reactions to the therapist. Others regress to developmental stages of fear, self-dissolution, annihilation, or intense desire for merger and engulfment, along with the consequent response of fight–flight behaviors. Still others might turn away from the therapist and approach peers in their efforts to determine the best way to proceed. These patients are often labeled counterdependent by theoreticians who emphasize the regression to dependency upon the leader.

It is hard to join a group "wrong" since whatever happens becomes a part of the group history. Whatever a new member does in an attempt to join is clinically relevant because it represents an opportunity for learning. No patient generates totally new behavior just for this situation.

Whatever the level of regression, a tension soon develops, stimulated by the members' respective needs and defenses. This tension sets in motion the important process of belonging to an organized group having a common task. During group formation, conscious and unconscious responses are activated in the members. As a result, subliminal agreements are reached that help members contain their fears and anxieties. These agreements become the group norms and standards.

Typically, new members look to the therapist to determine how they should proceed, what they should talk about, what behavior is "good" group behavior. Common questions are addressed (though not always overtly): What information is relevant? Are past events significant or do we just focus on what happens in the meeting? How do outside relationships fit in with what is happening here? How far can we take these relationships after the therapy hour ends? Am I expected to share all my secrets with these people? These and many other questions generally produce interaction among members, stimulating a variety of opinions and conflicts and stirring affects. How these affects are managed becomes embedded in the group norms and provides valuable therapeutic information. Members may not be ready to face angry encounters and therefore may establish the norm "Let's be friendly and not angry." One individual may aid in maintaining the norm by joking whenever angry feelings are likely to erupt; another might shift the topic of discussion. That these patterned distractions by members are allowed is an indication that a group norm is operating.

Patients not only ask questions, but they also tell about themselves and their experiences. Under the pressure of getting to know one another and the anxiety about how to proceed, patients usually tell their "story," including informing the group about why they have come and what they hope to gain. This may take the form of a "go around" with one member acting as the conductor. Patients experience intense pressure to conform, and seldom will they refuse to tell something about themselves. They might tell about anxiety-laden or frustrating situations they have encountered or are encountering. These stories also should be heard as unconscious metaphors for the individual's experience of being in the meeting itself. The therapist, acting to help establish the most therapeutic environment, may choose to translate the metaphors into the here and now of the meeting, with the goal of establishing a norm of examining the in-group transactions and affects. Since this implies more openness and directness, the norm becomes fully established only as it is experientially validated, that is, as members gain real help by examining their in-group interactions.

The emotional position of the members in a newly formed group, or of a new member joining an ongoing group, is analogous to that of meeting strangers. Rarely are first encounters anxiety-free, but when the task at hand includes sharing the most intimate details (and secrets!) of one's life, the stakes are very high. All the usual concerns about trust and safety, quite appropriately, are central in the minds of the participants. Gustafson and Cooper (1979) have pointed out that members enter a group planning a series of tests. These tests, containing both conscious and unconscious elements, revolve around the individual's anxiety: Will he or she again be traumatized by a group, as happened in early childhood or with significant others in the past? Added to this formulation is the important idea that patients are not only testing but are actively trying to master and resolve earlier conflicts around trust and safety.

Patients reveal themselves both verbally and nonverbally. Many therapists emphasize the members' need to tell their story, but an exclusive focus on verbalization misses significant information about a person that emerges in the manner in which he or she interacts. Members relive their difficulties and demonstrate their maladaptive styles. They reenact rather than recollect. The reenactments often are outside the individual's awareness, but their presence provides an avenue to gaining self-understanding.

The very processes that set regression in motion also contain the seeds for solutions. The anxiety and apprehension regarding the formation phase also represent the first commonly shared experience of the group. Everyone (including the therapist) approaches the unknown with his or her own internal fantasies and mechanisms of defense and mastery. This situation is particularly true before the first meeting of a new group. Since there is no reality for this group as yet, there can only be fantasies. The sharing of anxieties represents the first in-group experience of being involved and less isolated; it represents a beginning step for experientially based group cohesion. The sharing of these anxieties occurs even when an individual joins an ongoing group because the veteran members observe and perceive the new member's anxiety and are reminded of their own initial anxieties upon entering the group. And they also have their own anxieties about meeting a stranger. As those anxieties are shared, a common beginning point is again forged.

The overriding characteristic of the formative phase is the members' unique responses to the emotional and work aspects of group formation. Within expectable variations, members try to orient themselves to the task of learning the ground rules for making group therapy work. The theme then revolves around gaining information, either by asking the leader or inquiring amongst peers to see if there is an expert in the group. When such information is not readily forthcoming—it never is—self-protective mechanisms and reactions to frustration are manifest. The frustration and ambiguity inherent in the task exert a regressive pull upon the members. The emotions stimulated by this situation then dovetail as all the members struggle to form a group that feels safe enough for them to do their work. In the following clinical vignette, a group member unconsciously uses metaphor to convey his concerns about the therapy:

> A group that had been meeting for only a few weeks began one meeting with a period of silence. The silence was broken by one member telling about a recent vacation in which he was learning to ski along with other novices. He had found it a frightening experience, both because of the novelty of the sport for him and also because of the various stories he had heard about skiers breaking bones. Moreover, he was quick to point out, the instructor had given them too difficult a slope to begin with and in general had done such a poor job that many of the class had quit.

This vignette highlights the anxiety of the new group enterprise, adding the specific fear of being injured. The blame for this traumatic experience is placed directly on the instructor's (therapist's) shoulders for picking too difficult and dangerous a task and for not instructing the group properly in advance. An implicit threat to quit is present. One can imagine a new group getting caught up with such a story and giving such advice as "Change instructors" or "Choose a less steep hill." Indeed, advice giving is a characteristic of early group formation. Yet another response from the group might be for the other members to begin associating to similarly harrowing experiences in their own lives or to comparable times of insufficient instruction or assistance. If the members are particularly insightful, they might see the metaphorical aspects of the story and begin discussing their fears in the group and their concern with the amount of preparation they are or are not getting from their therapist.

Different group therapists might handle this early group vignette quite differently, depending upon their theoretical orientation. A therapist who wants the norm to be that the member will examine *only* the in-group interactions might point out that the member has taken the focus outside the room. For this therapist the member's story is a resistance, and he or she would exert pressure for members not to talk about events outside the group itself.

A psychodynamic therapist, on the other hand, might welcome such a sharing as a metaphor for the patient's feelings within the group itself, complete with references to the perceived danger of the new venture and questions about the skill of the leader. By linking the story to possible groupwide feelings, the therapist helps set the norm of curiosity about potential deeper meanings of communications, placing out-of-group and in-group events in juxtaposition, with each offering possible elaboration and insight into the other. Yet other therapists, still within a psychodynamic frame of reference, might interpret the member's story in a similar manner but decide to make no comment at all. That approach serves to enhance the members' dependence upon one another for input and sharing. If the discussion is positive and the members seem to enjoy the interchange, they may feel more positively about the group, thereby enhancing cohesion. By keeping the overt input of the therapist to a minimum, the opportunities for the patients to make assumptions about the therapist's point of view on the basis of their own history and basic assumptions are enhanced.

The therapist's role in the formative stage, as in all phases of group development, is to help establish useful norms so that the members feel safe enough to be spontaneous in their participation. Then his or her role is to help the members learn from their feelings, behaviors, reactions, and memories so that they may resolve their interpersonal and intrapsychic difficulties.

An important task that patients need to accomplish is the development of a sense of basic trust in both themselves and in others. Slater (1966) observes that groups go through cycles in which members exhibit their conflicts at progressively deeper levels. Trust at each level must be established before threatening information is revealed. Some individuals with early developmental conflicts may verbalize their distrust and appear to have made gains managing their feelings only to have another's absence expose a deeper level of the same anxieties. The problem may be expressed verbally, but more frequently it appears behaviorally. The therapeutic opportunities afforded by these experiences inherent in the working-through process are detailed in Chapter 4.

The therapist and group members all contribute to the movement from one phase to the next. The resolution of conflicts over joining is never complete, and a variety of stimuli or stresses may reactivate conflicts over belonging. Nevertheless, transition to the second phase becomes manifest when issues of trust diminish and reactions to belonging are prominent.

THE REACTIVE PHASE

In the formative phase the focus is on joining and finding commonalities; in the second phase of group development members are preoccupied with their reactions to belonging to the group. In this reactive phase the individuality of the members becomes more apparent and important. Some authors (e.g., Gustafson & Cooper, 1979) have suggested that rebellion is characteristic of this phase. Because Schutz (1958) noted that individuals seem to share the common purpose of maintaining control, he labeled this phase one of power. Authors (e.g., Savaray, 1975) emphasizing the similarity between group and individual development refer to the anal quality of the transactions during this phase; that is, transactions are alternately characterized by withholding and outbursts. Tuckman (1965) succinctly labeled this the "storming" phase.

Descriptively, this phase is characterized by emotional outbursts and unevenness of commitment to the group. The norms that arose in the initial phase are now tested and modified. The group agreements will be tested. This is a time when members often arrive late or not at all, threaten to quit or actually do so, or become tardy in payment of their bills. Emotionality is rampant, making it difficult for members to think clearly and rationally; obvious distortions in perception occur, and members experience transactions within the group as controlling, demanding, or otherwise injurious. Anger and sadness, two of the affects most accepted in our culture, are expressed and shared.

The tasks of this phase revolve around moving from a sense of "we-ness" to a sense of belongingness that includes "I-ness." As with the growing child, members often react as if they are saying, "Me do it!" Yet, just as with the child, this should never be interpreted as a wish to no longer belong to the family. Members are freeing themselves from the enthrallment with the therapist and the group. The honeymoon has ended. Early norms are now experienced as rigid and inflexible. Members try to exert their individual mark upon the group by testing how far they can bend, break, or more constructively alter the norms. Other individuals are not seen as having their own needs or wishes but are viewed as exerting control and power. It is during this phase that many patients experience their presenting problems most powerfully within the sessions. This is often a painful reality for the patients, and we frequently hear comments such as "This group is no different from my family!" or "Why should I stay here? I have as much trouble talking in here as I do in the world outside!" It is important that therapists help patients understand that the change in attitudes about membership during this phase is very helpful for their therapy, since therapy groups are much more effective when individuals are actually experiencing their problems within the group itself.

It is common in this phase for one or more members to abruptly threaten to quit, vigorously complaining either about the therapist or the group for not meeting their expectations. Typical complaints are "This group won't solve my problems!" or "These people are not at all like me." Sometimes the therapist is labeled incompetent, uninvolved, or uninterested. These members are not only expressing their own concerns but are also speaking groupwide fears. The threat to quit may represent an expression of the control and helplessness affects of this phase. The disaffected member accuses the others of discussing trivial or irrelevant issues, and the threat to drop out is an effort to control and change the direction of the meeting. Such protests may also represent a test to determine how safe it is to express such feelings.

The reemergence within the therapy of early internalized styles of object relationships enables individuals to learn a great deal regarding their developmental problems and tasks. There can be very important congruences between individual development and group development, and the growth potential stimulated in this rebellion/differentiation phase is very important in helping individuals resolve comparable problems in their individual development.

Fried (1970) distinguished among various types of anger shown in groups. One type is the anger shown in response to disappointment and hurt. The other, very salient to this developmental phase, is the equivalent of normal assertiveness. Patients' historic patterns of handling angry feelings, whether originating within themselves or coming from others, are characteristically exposed during this phase.

Not all patients experience or demonstrate overt anger, rebelliousness, or assertiveness. For some the emotional response is withdrawal, passivity, and compliance. Many patients do not have direct access to more active forms of aggression and use passive aggression instead. For these individuals crucial developmental tasks may be accomplished during this phase as they learn to balance anger and withdrawal with assertiveness and compromise. Such affect-laden tasks are neither quietly nor permanently achieved, but as groups move back and forth through this phase the individuals within them are provided repeated opportunities for mastering their particular developmental tasks.

Powerful group processes impact upon individuals in this phase.

The rebellion or hostility may be concentrated exclusively in one or two "difficult" individuals, and the remaining members seem peaceful and even scornful of the troublesome ones. Often the difficult member is the spokesperson for others who have similar affects, felt by others, and the therapist must never assume that quieter members do not share the affects verbalized by the more overtly troublesome member. Indeed, the hostility may be increased or aggravated in the rebellious member as the others unconsciously project their feelings into him and disown the feelings themselves. This is the commonly observed process of projective identification. A converse situation arises when the anger is not universally shared. In order to maintain the appearance of togetherness, thereby protecting themselves against retaliation or rejection, angry members try to recruit others to their point of view. Powerful forces for conformity are unleashed under these conditions. Although this is also a time of conflict among members, some of their fighting may be a displacement of anger felt toward the leader, because in our society hostility and assertiveness are more condoned when directed toward peers than toward authorities.

Not every group has a volatile "storming" period, just as not all 2-year-olds are "terrible 2's." Theories of development offer guidelines based upon common behaviors seen in many groups. But groups go about the tasks involved in development according to the unique mix of individuals, not according to a set of unvarying steps. If a group is not experiencing the storming phase overtly, its therapist would be mistaken to persist in viewing this as a sign of grave dysfunction.

Nonetheless, most groups do seem to move from a stage of giving information, advice, or opinions to a stage of exploring emotional reactions within the meeting. They seem to move from a stage in which the members are preoccupied with belonging, of developing we-ness, to one in which they are preoccupied with themselves as individuals and compete to have their needs met. In the emotional transactions that occur in this period, members bond to one another in much more authentic ways than were possible before. This is vitally important if groups are to gain maturity, where the curative factors are predominantly within the membership and not the leader.

In the following clinical vignette we see how seemingly minor details can spark volatile interactions between group members during the reactive phase of group development:

A group of eight members had been meeting for an extended period. They had made progress in their capacity to experience a feeling of belongingness and inclusion, but they had remained stuck in that comfortable stage for many months. The underlying themes of competitiveness between members and concern about the power of the therapist began to emerge initially through a seemingly innocent argument about whether or not a window should be opened! Some members wanted the window open while others did not; and all seemed quite concerned with the therapist's opinion in the matter since they feared his power and did not want to offend or anger him by their actions. In the middle of this debate, as fate would have it, the therapist canceled several meetings in order to fulfill various professional obligations. The therapist, concerned about the number of sessions missed, suggested that the group meet for a double session to replace one of the missed sessions (see Chapter 10 for a discussion of a variety of responses to leader absences). This offer was experienced by the group as an effort at control and domination by the therapist. "You just need our money, Doc!" was the way one irate individual put it. The initial intense rejection of the idea of a double session was modified because the group was quite cohesive and members found it pleasant and helpful to meet. Moreover, the members were trying their best to understand their feelings and reactions rather than simply acting on them.

In the discussion prior to the proposed double meeting, one member abruptly announced that this was to be his last meeting. "My insurance has been discontinued for some time, and I've been thinking about stopping treatment," he said by way of explanation. In reality, he held a relatively high-paying job, lived alone and within his means, and could easily have managed the financial obligations. The remaining members were enraged, but they could neither help him explore the meaning of this sudden flight nor deter him from actually terminating. One of the primary interpretations the group offered this member was the notion that his sudden desire to leave was directly in response to his feelings about the power and control of the leader.

The theme of power and control was also evident in another way just prior to the double session. The members joked about the extended session, and they explored the need for an intermission, for bringing in food, and for allowing time to feed parking meters (despite the fact that the group met at night, when the meters did not require feeding). There was also sufficient feeling of belongingness and togetherness among the remaining members to stimulate curiosity regarding their worries about what might happen in the longer session.

The remaining seven members all appeared on time for the 3-hour session. The meeting was characterized by considerable fear of overinvolvement, which dominated the first 90 minutes (the usual length of the group). Within 5 minutes of the halfway point, one man ostentatiously juggled his coins and left the room to buy a cola. Upon his return two men in succession left the room, announcing they were going to the bathroom. When all the men were back in the room, the group discussed

these events, and the exploration clearly showed both conscious and unconscious feelings of rebellion by the men who left. As one man said,
"I sit through business meetings and sporting events that last three hours
or more without having to go to the bathroom." Moreover, the group began to recognize that there were subtle encouragements by the women.
One woman, for example, said, "I saw him get those coins, and I hoped
he would get up and leave."

In this instance a change in format provided an opportunity to
bring simmering rebelliousness into the open. In the context of the
emerging conflicts, this rebellion was not a protest against the loss of
a maternal object (the therapist) but, rather, an opportunity to test one's
own power to control one's fate. The members' fear of the strength and
power of the therapist, along with their wish to take him on, was
manifest in their responses to the double session. The terminated member's rebellion was clearly echoed in the less self-defeating rebellions
of the remaining members.

Understanding the members' behaviors in the context of a phase
of group development diminishes the risk of viewing the responses solely
as evidence of individual psychopathology, an approach that could result
in scapegoating. It would not be difficult to imagine the group in the
clinical example focusing their anger at the member who abruptly terminated or blaming one of the men who left the room during the meeting
for being disruptive, but if the therapist had also viewed these behaviors
as examples of psychopathology, he/she would have missed the opportunity to help members learn from the broader context.

For the less experienced therapist, this storming phase often brings
about a crisis of confidence. The harmonious group that had been such
a joy has suddenly become an uncomfortable, affect-laden group that
occasionally calls the leader's credentials into question. It is important
to remember that the release of these affects represents a sign of progress,
not failure, for the group and the group therapist.

THE MATURE PHASE

The mature group is a working entity. In the schema used here, this
phase represents the apex of group effectiveness. Since a number of
authors have contributed to our understanding of this developmental
stage, we will first review selected formulations.

Review of Literature

In the group-as-a-whole tradition, Bion (1960) refers to the mature stage
as the *work group*. Some of the characteristics of a work group are goal-

directedness, an ability of the individuals to cooperate in an activity, and the ability to relate to reality. For Whitaker and Lieberman (1964), group maturity is attained when no focal conflict is evident and group members work on their problems in a concerted fashion. This is rare and appears to coincide with a group subculture that "provides the patient with a special form of safety which guarantees that certain damaging or disastrous results will not occur when he relinquishes the personal habitual solutions heretofore regarded as essential to his existence. Under these special conditions of safety, the patient may take steps to test the necessity of maintaining his old maladaptive solutions" (p. 166). Tuckman (1965) labels this the *performing stage.*

J. Durkin (1981) has attempted to describe optimal group maturity in the terminology of general system theory. He views the mature group as having a balance between open and closed boundaries. Boundaries that are too open do not protect the individual sufficiently, and boundaries that are too closed stop the necessary exchanges of information and feeling. Durkin suggests that maturity coincides with the establishment of semipermeable boundaries that allow new information to be processed appropriately. H. Durkin (1981) maintains that this strictly systems point of view is incomplete without adding a psychodynamic understanding of the individual. In an earlier work contrasting life as it is viewed by psychoanalysis and ordinary living, she suggested that the former almost completely cancels reality and focuses on transference whereas the latter obscures transference in the reality interchange (Durkin, 1964). Group therapy falls in the middle, where reality is present but diminished and transference is present but available for examination. Mature groups for both Durkins are those in which free interaction is made possible by a permissive and safe atmosphere, this free interaction being the basis for the development of multiple defenses and transferences that are then analyzed and understood.

Gustafson et al. (1981) have drawn another parallel between group and individual development. Utilizing Mahler's (Mahler, Pine, & Bergman, 1975) stages of separation and individuation, these authors suggest that a mature group is like the practicing toddler: Members periodically return to the leader for reassurance and support, but they can continue practicing on their own and do so with increasing effectiveness. With their attention to cooperation and clashing of interests, Gustafson et al. maintain that members' abilities to tolerate differing points of view and conflicting feelings is a sign of a maturing group.

Day (1981) has introduced the concept of the group working within an envelope, by which he means that a symbolic membrane has developed. This state is characterized by the members' mutual appreciation of one another and trust for one another. Consequently, members gain the flexibility to understand themselves more completely in relation to the other members and the leader; they become able to process, rather than merely experience, transferential relationships.

Garland (1982) defines a working group as one in which the members have become less interested in the problems they came to the group to solve and more interested in the group interactions that were initially viewed as *not* a problem—the nonproblem. This essentially means that the norm of focusing on the here-and-now interaction has been firmly established as part of the group subculture. Within such an environment patients are able to expand their views of their respective problems to include elements of their lives that they did not know were problems but that are in fact essential in understanding the initial problem.

Indications of a Mature Group

With this general review, we can more closely examine some of the indicators of a working group environment:

1. Mature working groups emphasize the intragroup responses and interactions as the primary source of learning and cure. A sense of history develops so that current episodes are linked to prior events and members become sensitized to repetitive patterns in themselves and other group members.

2. Despite the primacy of in-group interactions, flexibility develops that allows discussion of relevant outside events in the members' lives. Groups develop the capacity to distinguish between outside events brought into the discussion as resistances and outside events discussed as part of the therapeutic quest. Where possible, members seek to bring such outside material into the group in order to clarify issues. For example, an individual who complains about his interactions with a significant person in his life might be helped to understand his contributions to these interactions if members are able to link the outside problem with their in-group awareness of the individual's behavior.

3. In mature groups the members develop a more collegial relationship with the therapist. The therapist is viewed as an authority and expert, but he is demystified and not imbued with magical powers. In other words, a therapeutic alliance has been established that allows for a more realistic appraisal of the leader as well as a more complete conviction that he or she is an ally in the therapeutic venture. While transference reactions are still cooperative, members are able to help one another gain objectivity on distorted perceptions of the leader and each other.

4. Members have developed confidence in their ability to tolerate

anxiety and to examine problems themselves. They no longer look solely to the therapist as the primary source of caring, concern, guidance, and understanding. They have learned that no permanent harm will result from intense affective interactions, and they do not consistently interfere with heated exchanges. The members are more able to trust that it is helpful to share spontaneously the affective responses they experience during the meetings without undue regard for politeness, rationality, or embarrassment. At times individuals remain unable to tolerate specific affects, but such instances are used as opportunities for self-understanding. Members have developed an ability to distinguish between expressions of feelings and destructive attacks.

5. Through repeated experiences members gain a deep understanding and appreciation for one another's strengths and weaknesses. Compassion and tolerance are founded upon the knowledge that unconscious factors operate for everyone and often adversely affect interpersonal relationships. Members in mature groups have also learned that the most abrasive aspects of behavior are often defenses designed to protect against pain, not indications of inherent malice in the individuals in question. Members have an appreciation of the unconscious, even if they do not understand its sources, and they attempt to understand the behavior of their fellow members as well as their own. Similarly, the therapist's strengths and weaknesses can be appreciated or accepted without overwhelmingly intense or prolonged affective swings.

6. Finally, members have learned that transactions inevitably involve two distinct components: the interpersonal and the intrapsychic. They know that behavior is not always what it appears to be and that there are personal meanings that might produce particular behaviors. They further appreciate that identical behaviors might have very different meanings for different individuals. Members strive in a consistent manner to respond to behaviors from two perspectives, from that of the recipient of behaviors (external observer) and from that of one who understands empathically the more personal meanings of the behaviors (internal observer).

THE TERMINATION PHASE

Termination, which represent the final phase of group development, is of such significance that it will be discussed in detail in Chapter 12. In time-limited groups, the final meetings of the group are completely devoted to the ending of the group. Even in such groups where the members seem not to speak about the ending of the group, dynamically we must assume that all group content is related to the imminent ending.

In ongoing psychodynamic groups, the termination phase occurs whenever an individual member decides to terminate membership in the group.

The affects associated with the sense of graduation and saying good-bye to the group are seldom easily managed either by the departing or the remaining individuals (including the therapist). Terminations are emotionally painful and joyous, but never simple.

One vital aspect to the development of group maturity is the *successful* termination of a member. In the early months members struggle with their fears that this treatment might not be truly therapeutic. Indeed, the first terminations usually are therapeutic failures, that is, patients who flee the group prematurely. It is often quite a long time before any patient successfully completes the work he or she set out to achieve and leaves with a sense of well-being and accomplishment. It is not unusual for members to refer to such a patient for many years, using that memory as an antidote to doubts and worries about the effectiveness of the group. Mature groups almost invariably have at least one termination that is perceived as successful by the great majority of the members.

New members also become symbols of successful or unsuccessful treatment because they fill seats formerly occupied by individuals who have terminated. Groups develop oral legacies, whereby history is remembered for a long time. The ways in which various members leave take on powerful meanings for groups. During a period when a number of members leave happy and fulfilled, the sense of confidence and maturity is raised greatly. Perceptions of new members are obscured by the shadows of the members who left before their arrival: A new member who happens to fill a seat occupied by a member who left prematurely is greeted differently from someone who fills the seat of an honored member who left with work completed. Both situations have their problems. Examination of the impact of termination on feelings about the replacement member or about the group as a whole provides one more opportunity for members to differentiate reality from the affective response and is an exercise that contributes considerably to group maturity.

THE EFFECTS OF GROUP DEVELOPMENT

Similar events may be handled differently at different stages of development. In order for the therapist to maximize learning, it is important to understand the differences in how groups respond to similar events at different developmental stages. For example, throughout the life of a group, individuals will from time to time break the agreement regarding prompt attendance to all meetings. Such breaches are inevitable, but members use those breaches for learning in quite different ways, depending upon the stage of group development.

In the formative stages lateness is often ignored or only cursorily addressed. Commonly, reality reasons are offered to explain the tardiness, and these reasons are quickly accepted by the others. Thus, a late member might casually announce "The bus was late" or "My boss kept me in a meeting" or even "I misplaced my car keys." Such explanations, accompanied by a sincere apology, are usually satisfactory to the others, and the attention of the group moves on to some other subject. These responses are multidetermined. At one level members do not know how to explore or appreciate such behavior. Sometimes members offer advice about how to avoid such situations in the future, but there is little permission in the group to express feelings about such situations. If a member has an intense affective reaction, such as anger, it is usually kept under wraps out of an even more pressing need for acceptance. Furthermore, members at this stage seem to view the lack of condemnation or attack from the therapist as a sign that they too should offer no strong response to the tardy member. They are still looking to the therapist for direction about how to behave. Finally, there is a powerful but subtle unconscious pressure *not* to comment upon breaches in the group boundary since at this stage of development members may feel a need to employ the same behaviors. It is as if no one wants to bolt the door too securely lest they be forced to stay in the group and experience intense emotions.

As members develop a sense of belongingness, and thereby move to a different stage of development, there is usually increasing pressure to arrive on time, as well as to honor the other agreements. Lateness in the reactive phase occurs at the expense of potential censure from one's peers, and it may represent either a displaced expression of dissatisfaction with the developing group norms or a more direct expression of rebelliousness and assertiveness. Whereas lateness in the forming stage may represent some response to anxiety about joining, such as a fear of being engulfed or becoming dependent, lateness now represents a move toward individualizing, toward fighting for fulfillment of one's own goals at the expense of the others. Often the rebelliousness begins as an attack on the leader, and this can include overt or covert collusion with the other members. Patients in this mode may pay no more attention to the lateness than do patients in the earliest stage of development, but in this case the affective tone is quite different. Whereas in the initial stage the nonattention is out of naïveté or unwillingness to try to understand a defense that others might want to employ, now the affective responses to the perceived or actual tyranny of the group are understandable. A member's breach of the group agreements frequently produces strong emotions, which then are directed either toward the offending member or toward the leader. At the same time, recognition is dawning that underlying or even unconscious motives for a breach exist. For example, no longer is the excuse "I misplaced my keys!" accepted without question as an explanation for lateness. Following the lead of the therapist, members, who by now have had occasion to see the fruit such inquiries have borne in the past, begin to explore lateness for hidden meanings. They are freer to communicate emotions, not just thoughts, and they have begun to internalize the therapist's use of curiosity about behavior as a means of learning important information about themselves and their colleagues.

In mature groups the members have begun to examine the meaning of breaches of the group's agreements, both for others and for themselves. For example, coming late or not at all is understood as a potentially powerful communication. The members may still be enraged by the fact that an individual arrives late or occasionally does not come to the group at all but have begun to accept that not all individuals are the same and that absolute conformity is neither just nor fair. Thus, members can use such interactions to study both their own external and internal responses and, concurrently, the inner meanings for the delinquent member. Finally, members begin to explore the possibility that such behavior on the part of one individual member is in fact a group event. It is commonly observed that lateness and absenteeism tend to increase as a therapist's vacation approaches, and these breaches of the group's agreement about attendance are in fact a groupwide commentary about the therapist's impending absence.

Many variations on this theme occur, but common to mature groups is the capacity to establish a norm of viewing behavior as communication and therefore as one more pathway to knowledge. Understanding the multiple determinants of behavior, including recognition of processes impacting on the entire group and exploration of the reactions various individuals have to the behavior, becomes a powerful therapeutic tool when the members are attuned to exploring these arenas.

GROUP DYNAMICS:
CULTURE, NORMS, AND ROLES

Group Culture and Norms

In the course of group development, particular ways of handling conflicts or affects become ingrained in the interactional patterns. A group develops a particular kind of culture, which helps define what individuals can and cannot do, as well as how they express themselves and deal with a variety of affects.

For example, two beginning-phase groups may attend to the issues of joining in quite different ways. The members in one group may look to the therapist for solutions to the problems of joining whereas members in the other talk primarily to one another and ignore the therapist. These represent two differing group cultures; members are negotiating the same tasks of joining and forming a group but are doing so in different ways. The study of a group culture helps define how the members relate to one another, to the therapist, and to the group as a whole. It is a way of viewing the organization of the group. Each group develops norms (both conscious and unconscious) regarding appropriate behavior. These norms begin with the expectations of the members and the therapist.

The therapist serves as a regulator of the group boundaries and tries to help define what is in and what is outside the interests of the group (Astrachan, 1970); consequently, the therapist is a powerful contributor to group culture. For a leader who focuses on the here and now and the affects raised in the therapy room, a description of a childhood event would be a distraction; soon members of his group would no longer relate childhood events. For a therapist who values the metaphorical value of a childhood story, such a memory might throw light on the group's dynamics in the immediate setting; this therapist might delight in hearing such a story from childhood and would thereby reinforce the likelihood that other members would share comparable stories from their past. For a therapist who values the place of genetic exploration, this might represent an important piece of personal work for the patient. Since the therapist is a potent initiator of group norms, the reinforcement of members' behavior through the therapist's expressions of interest or through his failure to interfere during an interaction serves to establish appropriate ways of interacting within the group. There are therapists who emphasize transferences to the leader, thereby helping individuals learn of their inner fantasies, and therapists who focus on peer transactions, which highlight the learning of social skills and the giving and receiving of feedback but diminish exploration of the unconscious (E. Klein & Astrachan, 1971). Groups led by therapists from these different theoretical positions might be equally effective, but they would carry on their work quite differently.

The therapist is not solely responsible for normative behavior and the subsequent group culture. The individuals who constitute the group are constantly changing the norms and altering the ways in which they are expressed, although usually these are not major changes because, once established, norms are rather difficult to alter. In a study of T-groups, Lieberman, Yalom, and Miles (1973) found that the expectations members brought with them were a powerful set of constraints that were unlikely to be reversed in the actual state of affairs and that, in determining eventual outcome, the individual's impact on the group's norms is as potent as the leader's.[1] Recognition of norms and the resultant group culture provides another perspective for the therapist to use in beginning to explore the individuals within the setting as well as in understanding differences in group development.

As the group culture develops, there are forces operating that pull members together or lead to dispersal. The attractiveness and sense of belonging to a particular culture has been labeled *group cohesion* (Day, 1981). The ability of a group to influence behavior—and, indeed, for members to identify with its values and goals—is in part a product of its attractiveness. Unfortunately, group cohesion has been thought of as a static phenomenon whereas, in truth, it is dynamic and changing. What might make a group attractive in a beginning developmental stage (e.g., sharing stories of outside experiences) would be seen as a distraction for a mature phase group and would create a shift in the sense of cohesiveness if it proved difficult to modify. Implicit in the notion of cohesion is a basic trust that members will not be willfully injurious and that efforts will be made to understand members' inner worlds and their interactions. This formulation is similar to the holding environment described by Winnicott (see Garland, 1982). Members' capacity to recognize individual differences and idiosyncrasies increases the attractiveness of a group. Patients learn to hear what others are feeling and experiencing even if it differs from their own perceptions. Put simply, a group experience has the potential to prompt a member to ask, "Where else can I go and have emotionally meaningful exchanges in an atmosphere where I can trust and be trusted?"

Individual Roles

In business an owner hires others and assigns tasks for them. These may be specialized functions such as factory worker, salesperson, advertising executive, and so on. In the beginning the only clear function (role) in a therapy group is that of therapist. As groups develop, specialized functions emerge that serve to manage the emotional and work tasks. As in business, some individuals have particular talents to fill specific roles that successfully interact with the group culture and norms.

---

[1]Since this was a study of groups whose duration was limited to 30 hours, the opportunity to alter the norms through analysis of groupwide and individual resistances was diminished.

Others are "assigned" roles that fail to fulfill their own personal needs but may serve the group (Astrachan, 1970). When the concept of role is used to describe behaviors in a therapy group, it is important to distinguish between specialized functions within the group itself and characteristic patterns of behavior of a particular individual. The fact that groups often typecast their participants, utilizing personal roles to fill certain group functions, simply confuses the matter further.

Examined from the perspective of the whole group, roles may be thought of as serving emotional and task functions. Some roles seem to facilitate the group effort to work on problems by encouraging exploration of affect or important topics. Others serve to maintain a restrictive culture and norms (Benne & Sheats, 1948). A host of specific titles may be assigned to the roles, but basically a groupwide function is being addressed. For instance, roles that help select or focus on group tasks, that function to clarify issues of importance to the members, might be termed the information seeker, the coordinator, the historian, and the elaborator. Another set of roles, those that maintain or build the group's culture, includes the gatekeeper, the standard setter, and the compromiser.

Of considerable importance are roles that serve to regulate affects (Arsenian, Semrad, & Shapiro, 1962). Some feelings need to be elaborated and explored whereas others need to be diffused and modulated in order to maintain the group's functioning. In this context the encourager, the joker, the silence breaker, and the soother function to monitor the level of affect.

It is important to understand that groups require roles both to help contain feelings and to further work. Groups might utilize a particular individual in a specific role to perform these functions or several individuals using different roles. For instance, in a situation where intense emotion is present, the group members may regulate the intensity through joking, direct soothing, or diverting. It is the function that is important, rather than the individual or even the specific mode.

Members enter a group with their own specific repertoire of roles, which they have used in other life situations. Only rarely are roles generated by group processes. One of the purposes of gaining personal historical information is to help the therapist and patient become aware of these stereotypic patterns. However, it is not unusual for an individual to take on a role with past determinants unknown to either patient or therapist. When this happens, the opportunity for therapeutic gain is great, since unconscious conflicts are observable in current behavior.

To illustrate the overlapping between group and individual behaviors, we can look at common early group behaviors. There is often a "host" or "hostess" (and sometimes more than one) who will initiate the introductions and fill up silences. This function may become "assigned" to one person, who will routinely handle affects surrounding newness, beginnings, or silences, or it may be divided among several individuals. Individuals who routinely accept the host and hostess role may be demonstrating a lifelong pattern of bearing the emotional burden of their family, an exhibitionistic need to be the center of attention no matter what the psychic cost, or a need to be the favorite child in the family. Whatever the origin of the role, it is generally quite facilitative to the group.

Often there are members who are essentially mute in the initial meetings, and this silence also is not a new behavior generated specifically for this difficult situation. Individuals bring out habitual responses of silence to cope with this new stress. It may represent a passive-aggressive position, commanding attention through the power of passivity; it may be the youngest sibling once again playing out the role of waiting until last to be fed; it may represent a chronic altruism, an assumption that the needs of others must come first; or, of course, it could be the manifestation of terror in this interpersonal arena.

Another subset of roles includes those that are unique to an individual's character (Benne & Sheats, 1948). These roles satisfy individual needs and are fundamentally irrelevant to the group development, but they may become a dominant force operating within the group. Individuals taking on these roles are viewed negatively, and there is often a strong wish to extrude them from the group. These roles include the monopolizer, the help-rejecting complainer, the naive one, the supplicant, and the playboy. The therapeutic management of some of these roles will be discussed later in this book.

Of course, not every behavioral pattern or role is equally helpful or harmful to individuals. The therapist needs to discriminate between the useful and adaptive roles and the destructive and constraining roles. The same role can be both healthy and, if pushed to an extreme, pathological. Moreover, the group therapist needs to alternate continually between the group and the individual developmental perspectives (see Chapter 8). A role that may be productive for the group may be constricting for the individual, and vice versa. A balance must be struck regarding which aspect to explore and in what order so as to maximize the therapeutic effectiveness of the group for all members.

SUMMARY

The concept of group development is valuable in orienting therapists to a number of processes common to group psychotherapy. Familiarity with the phases of development helps anchor therapists in their work and provides a road map to help them understand what is occurring within their groups. A great deal of valuable therapeutic work can be accomplished in each phase. Indeed each phase offers unique opportunities. Further, since groups are dynamic organisms composed of living beings, the phases are not rigid and steadfast; they are best considered guidelines, not laws. As groups grow and are confronted with crisis and change, the phases will be revisited regularly.

As development takes place, each group forms its particular culture and norms; these have a major impact on how the group goes about fulfilling its goal of helping the members solve their problems. The therapist has considerable importance in the evolution of the culture, but the members also contribute greatly. Roles are linked to the group's requirements for building and maintaining its culture as well as to individuals' past habitual methods of handling stress and anxiety. Both aspects of role require consideration and frequently can be observed as overlapping within the group.

The developmental stages we have delineated refer specifically to open-ended psychodynamic groups. Time-limited groups go through the same stages, though the stages are compressed. Furthermore, the reality of a forced ending creates a special emphasis on termination issues. Indeed, most time-limited groups begin making references to the end of the group in the first meeting. Furthermore, from the halfway point in the group until the end, the entire process of the group can usually be understood as a response (usually unconscious) to the approaching end of the group.

4

Curative Mechanisms and Processes in Group Psychotherapy

Ａll theories of psychotherapy have explicit and implicit convictions about how best to help people grow. Psychoanalytic theory belongs to the philosophical tradition that holds that "the truth shall make you free" (John 8:32). That is, people grow as they gain information and understanding. Freud recognized that a great body of information is unconscious and that emotional knowledge (and therefore freedom) requires making the unconscious conscious. The fact that psychoanalytic theory belongs to an educational philosophy has many implications in an era in which mental illness is increasingly defined in medical, symptom-relieving ways. Whereas the *Diagnostic and Statistic Manual of Mental Disorders* (3rd ed., rev.), the DSM-III-R, conceptualizes psychopathology as separate from the personhood of the individual (e.g., a patient "has depression"), psychoanalytic theory is more holistic (e.g., the patient "is depressed"). According to psychoanalytic theory, pathology represents an adaptive response to inner pain, a response that originated in the past and that is counterproductive today.

Through a variety of windows into the world of the unconscious, including transference, we may deduce a great deal about the conflicted aspects of our patients' lives and histories that have led to their counterproductive patterns. Other windows are free association, slips of the tongue, body language, character styles, dreams, repetition compulsions, and resistances. It is posited that patients will regress in the therapeutic process to a level where they have not mastered a developmental task or have become fixated because of intrapsychic conflict (Rutan, 1992a).

In classic psychoanalysis the patient's regression is fostered by the dependent position on the couch, the absence of visible stimuli from the analyst, and the use of free association. In group psychotherapy, regression is stimulated in part by stranger anxiety and group process. Change is effected by assisting patients in gaining emotional understanding of their reactions inside and outside the therapy situation and by examining the basic assumptions that support their characteristic perceptions and behaviors. For psychoanalytic group therapists, observing patients actively involved in interpersonal matrixes represents a unique opportunity for gaining insight into the patients' unconscious worlds.

Modern modifications of classical Freudian theory stress the interpersonal aspects of personality formation and the etiology of psychopathology. The object relations theorists (e.g., Fairbairn, Winnicott, Guntrip), hypothesize that the need to be in a relationship is the primary drive that forms personality. Stressing the importance of authentic and healthy human relationships as therapeutic factors, object relations therapists pay special attention to the quality of patients' relationship styles. In group therapy the presence of a network of human relationships, rather than the single relationship to the analyst, provides a forum for examination of the relationship style of each patient.

Ego psychologists (e.g., A. Freud, Hartmann, E. Kris, Loewenstein, and Blanck and Blanck) further underlined the importance of relationships in rebuilding fragmented and flawed egos. In this theory health is defined by the quality of defenses employed by the individual. Groups offer ideal settings for therapists and patients to explore the types of defenses patients use to protect themselves from interpersonal pain.

Self psychologists (Kohut and his followers) stress the importance of viewing others as distinct and separate individuals. In this tradition therapy groups offer marvelous opportunities for analyzing the degree to which others are selfobjects or separate entities for each group member.

In the interpersonal tradition of Harry Stack Sullivan, Yalom (1985) has developed the following list of twelve "curative factors" that operate in group psychotherapy:

1. Instillation of hope
2. Universality
3. Imparting of information
4. Altruism
5. Corrective recapitulation of the primary family group

6. Development of socializing techniques
7. Imitative behavior
8. Interpersonal learning, input (feedback)
9. Interpersonal learning, output
10. Group cohesiveness
11. Catharsis
12. Existential factors

MacKenzie (1987), reviewing 23 studies employing variations of Yalom's curative (therapeutic) factors as measures by which members assessed their own groups, noted that although the studies were not readily comparable and had design shortcomings, four of Yalom's factors consistently received the highest ratings by the surveyed group members; in descending order of importance these were as follows: catharsis, interpersonal input, insight, and group cohesiveness. At the lower end of the patients' ratings, starting with the least important factor, were identification, family reenactments, and guidance. MacKenzie observed that these latter categories represent theoretical constructs and appear to be "categories which suffer from poor item construction" (p. 28). For populations of more impaired individuals (i.e., those attending day treatment centers), universality and the installation of hope appear to have greater importance in effecting improved functioning (Butler & Fuhriman, 1980).

Within each of these psychodynamic frameworks important commonalities appear. All presuppose a warm but neutral and fairly unobtrusive therapist who strives to create a safe supportive and therapeutic relationship. Supportive elements are intrinsic in all dynamic therapies; those contributing to support in group psychotherapy will be discussed in the following paragraphs.

The therapist's stance, along with the anxiety created by the group setting (Ganzarain, 1991), promotes regression in the individual members. This allows their pathologies to emerge in the interpersonal transactions and the inner fantasies about the relationships within the group. The regressive recreation of the patient's inner world in the group setting may simulate the family of origin and/or it may resemble the patient's current interpersonal world. The stereotypical fantasies and responses are the transferences from which members may gain an understanding of their repetitive responses. These responses (either behavioral or in fantasy) may have been necessary for self-protection in childhood or at other periods in the patient's life but are counterproductive in the present. Yalom (1985, p. 45) considers transferences to be a component of the patients' disturbed interpersonal transactions. However, we would add that transference is an omnipresent part of the human condition and is particularly obvious in the fantasied recapitulation of the primary family group.

Followers of each of the aforementioned theoretical variations emphasize the importance of emotionally charged interchanges taking place within a safe environment (Kauff, 1993). Through these exchanges individuals gain the opportunity to understand and alter their inner responses and previously unexamined hypotheses about life and interpersonal relationships.

THE SUPPORTIVE ENVIRONMENT

It is not unusual for a patient to request a "support group," which is somehow considered different from a psychotherapy group. This is an unfortunate misunderstanding of the nature of support and of psychotherapy groups. Analytic technique focuses on interpretation of the transference as the mutative treatment element. This means that less attention has been paid to the supportive elements intrinsic to all dynamic therapies. Historically, supportive interventions have at times been thought to be too gratifying of infantile needs and, consequently, detrimental to the patient's motivation for change.

The accumulation of treatment experiences with developmentally less mature individuals has broadened the application of analytic theory and technique to this population. In order to hear and make use of an interpretation, these more primitive patients need to feel a sense of safety, which includes the respect, interest, and optimal responsivity of the therapist. The strict analytic posture, which probably only existed in rare instances, did not provide—to use Kohut's (1978, p. 481) felicitous expression—sufficient "psychological oxygen" in the atmosphere for patients to grow. Research at the Tavistock Clinic (Malan, Balfour, Hood, & Shooter, 1976), where the therapist attempted to limit all interventions to interpretations, supports this notion with the finding that the main beneficiaries were patients with prior treatment who could withstand the austerity of the approach.

Pine (1985), comparing the treatment setting with children's developmental needs, stated: "Children develop under conditions of optimal strain, optimal demand, optimal frustration. Too much strain gets in their way, leading to anxiety or anger or frustration or helplessness at levels that are not constructive and too much to deal with; but too little strain, too much gratification, also stands in the way of development" (p. 166). Dichotomous theorizing that pits support against exploration is no longer viable in as much as supportive interventions are now recognized to be present in all forms of psychotherapy.

These experiences have led us to recognize what should have been obvious all along: All patients do better if they experience the therapy setting as fundamentally supportive, no matter what theoretical orientation is being used. In group psychotherapy the complex relationships are embedded in the concept of cohesion, an early definition of which was "the attractiveness of a group for its members" (Frank, 1957, p. 54). This pithy definition does not do justice to the concept, since group cohesion includes member to member, member to therapist, and member to group-as-a-whole elements.

In a review of the concept of group cohesion, Evans and Jarvis (1980) differentiated between members' attraction to the group, which is the usual manner in which cohesion is measured in research studies, and group cohesion. Attraction to the group was conceived of as members' feelings about the group, which may lead to being a "good" group member and remaining in the group. Cohesion was understood to denote qualities of "closeness among members of the group, similarity in perception of events, and perhaps bonding together in response to the outside world" (p. 366). Thus, according to Evans and Jarvis, cohesion refers more to group properties whereas attraction more closely addresses the individual's goals in remaining a group member. We will incorporate this useful distinction in our discussion of group cohesion.

Cohesion is a dynamic, not a static, concept. What might make a group attractive at one stage of development might be antithetical to cohesion at a different point in treatment. For instance, an individual entering a group wants to be accepted and liked in spite of whatever defenses he may erect. Thus, the therapist must be aware that confrontations or hostility, which would evoke a sense of emotional danger, might be perceived by a new member (or a new group) as a sign that this is not an attractive—that is, "safe"—group. At a later stage, when members are more prepared to manage conflict and to learn from affect-laden interactions, a group atmosphere that would limit free expression may well be experienced as saccharine and constricting. As Yalom (1985) observed: "Cohesiveness is not, for example, synonymous with inter-member acceptance and understanding, but is interdependent with these factors" (p. 50).

According to MacKenzie (1990), group factors that contribute to the sense of support and cohesion are the instillation of hope ("Others have had similar problems and have conquered them"), acceptance ("People here will listen, try to understand me and not respond to me merely from their own perspective"), universality ("I am not alone with these problems"), and altruism ("I can be helpful to others"). Patients may also feel that the group provides an opportunity for meaningful contact with others at an emotional level; within this context they can explore their own ways of making empathic contact. This latter element is particularly meaningful for certain isolated members who have erected character defenses that have interfered with their belief that they can truly understand another person's emotional life.

The therapist plays an initial role in providing support, which eventuates in cohesion. As we will discuss in Chapter 7, the group agreements serve to establish a boundary between the treatment room and the outside world. A respectful examination of boundary infractions, such as tardiness or absences, is experienced as supportive since ignoring such violations may convey to the members that neither the therapist nor the group is ultimately dependable. Of course, the therapist's manner of addressing these and other attempts to alter the group boundary carries multiple complex meanings that eventually have to be understood for the patients' benefit.

Many therapeutic interventions, such as linking group members' feelings or ideas, connecting present feelings to history, inquiring what others feel (this implies to all members that the therapist is able to listen and care about such matters), are supportive. The demeanor the clinician conveys through eye contact, posture, and mannerisms carries messages that can be interpreted by the patients as supportive. Many ordinary courtesies initially serve to promote respect, a sense of safety, and a desire to belong. In object relations terms the group is the "holding environment." Through his or her verbal or nonverbal behavior the therapist provides an initial model for support. Subsequently, members and the group as a whole contribute their share to the support and cohesion. Certainly, the interpersonal setting of a group is not conducive to a stone-faced, inhuman therapeutic stance.

TRANSFERENCE

The role of unconscious drives, wishes, affects, and defenses in interpersonal transactions and their specific function in the formation of transference neurosis have held center stage in analytic psychotherapy. The psychoanalytic situation was thought to be the optimal setting in which patients would reexperience their past relatively free from external stimuli and from the impact of the person of the analyst. Within the analytic relationship a relatively specific reenactment of the central (pathological) conflict was expected to emerge, and interpretation of the transference was believed to be mutative (Strachey, 1934).

Freud (1905), almost from his earliest theorizing, appreciated the omnipresence of transferences: "Psychoanalytic treatment does not *create* transferences, it merely brings them to light like so many other hidden psychical factors" (p. 117).

The early group therapy theoreticians transposed the dyadic situation into the group and with it the therapist's efforts to maintain a blank screen attitude, which was thought to elicit a transference neurosis. In the extreme, this resulted in what Leo Stone (1961) referred to as the "cadaver model" of the therapist. In this framework, peers were representative of siblings or objects of displacement from the authority of the therapist (Wolf & Schwartz, 1962). The argument was considered valid for individuals who grew up with siblings and, as well, for the single child, who would inevitably have fantasies about brothers and sisters. In this model it is thought that the impact of the therapist is minimal and that the therapy setting itself allows the transferences to emerge.

A more contemporary model emphasizes the contribution of patients' perceptions of the analyst and the treatment situation and takes into account their reciprocal interactions. This approach searches for and focuses on the here-and-now transactions (Cooper, 1987; Greenberg & Mitchell, 1983). The interactional patterns in groups provide opportunities to explore differing aspects of transferences; that is, the transactions with the therapist, these among the members, and each member's image of the group as a whole (W. Stone, 1988).

Group-as-a-whole theorists have focused on the parental nature of the transference (Bion, 1960; Durkin, 1964; Scheidlinger, 1974). Because the theory of individual development had been transposed to stages of group development, patients' responses to the therapist were formulated as transferences at the oral, anal, and oedipal instinctual levels (Saravay, 1978). The image of the group as a whole also became a transference object and has been described metaphorically in terms of the bad and good maternal object (Durkin, 1964; Scheidlinger, 1974; Agazarian, 1992).

The enduring patterns of wishes, affects, and interactional patterns are approximations of the transference neurosis in psychoanalysis. A great many group interactions can be understood as fragments of transference responses: "If the therapist regards the intercommunications as free associations and searches out their latent intent, he will have no difficulty in identifying transferences in the group" (Durkin, 1964, p. 147).

This expanded perspective places transferences along a continuum in which the person of the analyst, the peers, or the image of the group as a whole can be objects of transferential feelings. Transference manifestations include the individual's habitual reaction patterns, which overlap with character formation; for example, a person's manner of entering a group, of greeting another, of managing separations, or of nonverbally communicating (i.e., how they hold their body) can be explored both as character and as transference.

Supportive elements (including cohesion) and transferences have been separated in this discussion in order to provide some clarity. However, in practice many internal obstacles to the development of a cohesive group (transference resistances or character traits) to the development of a cohesive group require exploration. Much of the early learning that individuals gain in their group is the result of the examination and modification or dissolution of those obstacles; for some this may be the central element in all their therapeutic gains.

Ultimately, it is the maladaptive habitual responses, assumptions, and interactions that are objects of study and modification. The salient psychological mechanisms for change are discussed in the following paragraphs. The therapeutic processes of change, confrontation, clarification, interpretation, and working through (Greenson, 1967, 1983), are considered in the final section of this chapter.

THE MECHANISMS OF CHANGE

The mechanisms of change refer to the psychological mechanisms involved in change. People grow and change in groups through three major psychological mechanisms: imitation, identification and internalization (Kelman, 1963).

Imitation

In therapy groups individuals have the opportunity to observe many interactions, styles of relating, and problem-solving techniques. Much of the early learning in groups is imitative. Patients who have difficulty tolerating and sharing strong emotions can first observe as other members interact intensely. As they learn that members are not harmed but, rather, are typically drawn closer by such exchanges, such patients see some hope for change and, as a consequence, begin to share feelings by imitating those who are more successful in that task. Though primarily used early in group membership, imitation remains one of the ways in which members gain new behavioral options throughout their treatment. The patient's experience of success following imitative behavior makes the group more attractive for him, enhances his wish to belong, and increases group cohesiveness. This furthers identifications among the members. Imitation is by no means limited to group therapy, but group therapy, by virtue of the multiple interactions and relationships, expands the opportunities for change through imitative learning.

Identification

Identification has been defined in a variety of ways. We are using it here, following the description by Loewald (1973), to mean an unconscious process in which the subject takes on parts or aspects of the object. By taking on aspects of another, the individual changes by altering perceptions or affects. Identification may be used in the service of growth or resistance, and each instance must be understood separately.

Freud (1921) initially postulated that group formation takes place as group members identify with one another via their shared affection for the leader. Without these bonds there is no group. Peer identification also takes place as the members tell about their life experiences as well as their reactions to current events, both within and outside the group. These identifications may be consciously expressed as feelings of attraction, belonging, and attachment to the members and the group. These are the building blocks from which group cohesiveness develops. Similarly, universalization, the development of the sense that one is not alone in his or her feelings, furthers group attraction and identifications among members. A circular process begins that enhances these powerful influences members have upon one another. In turn, the resultant identifications alter fundamental ways in which the members perceive and respond. The incremental building of identifications forms the base for lasting change.

Unconscious identification can be observed readily in group interactions. For example, unconscious identification can be seen in nonverbal behavior when two or more patients simultaneously shift body positions during a discussion about another member, resulting in several members unconsciously adopting the same body position. This usually reflects a similar affect or perception by these individuals regarding the individual or topic under discussion.

It is not uncommon for these identifications to become conscious during the group. Members will point out that individuals have changed in how they respond or interact, that they seem to view situations differently now than in the past. Although these observations may startle individuals who have been unaware of the changes, upon reflection they often easily agree that their inner response is different, less conflicted, and more flexible.

Sometimes patients will note that they are taking positions on subjects that feel foreign to their accustomed stances. They are puzzled by their behaviors and their inner states. Such identifications usually are temporary unless the sources can be analyzed and integrated by the individual. One such source can be identification with the therapist. Sometimes this identification takes on concrete forms, such as dress ing in clothing and a style similar to the therapist's, or purchasing an automobile like the therapist's; male patients have even been known to grow a mustache in identification with a mustached therapist! Patients often surprise one another with the observation, "You sound just like the doc!" or, "You're playing doctor again!" Particularly important are the hoped-for patient identifications with the therapist and the therapeutic attitudes of tolerance of feelings, introspection, and willingness to understand as well as react.

The processes of imitation and identification are two of the major mechanisms by which change takes place. Much change can be accomplished on the basis of these mechanisms alone. They form the underpinnings for group attraction and cohesion. Through these mechanisms much of the information necessary for understanding the complex connections between the unconscious and the conscious, the past and the present, is made available. For example, imitation and identification may explain the changes that occur in those patients who grow and change although they sit rather silently in their groups.

Internalization

Internalization is the most advanced and durable mechanism of change. Internalized change is not the result of something taken in from the outside; rather, it is due to a shift in the psychic structure of the individual so that his experiences, both conscious and unconscious, are shifted to a more mature level of functioning.

Internalization produces greater flexibility in handling both internal and interactive states and is the result of working through conflicts or building new psychic structures to handle previously disruptive anxiety. The therapist can facilitate healthy internalization by detailed examination and reexamination of emotion-laden interactions. Through confrontation, clarification, interpretation, and working through, individuals integrate knowledge gained in the here and now transactions with their sources and prior assumptions. This results in an increased integration of affects and object relationships as well as in diminished inner conflict. The outcome can be observed in the therapy setting where a patient might indicate a new way of behaving to recurrent stimuli. For example, a patient who had entered therapy suffering from paranoid ideation was eventually able to state, "This year when you announced your vacation, I again felt that you were not going to meet this group because you needed to get away from me in particular. I fantasized you were going to continue to meet all your other groups. It's the same old fantasy I've had in previous years. But this year it's just a fantasy, and it doesn't even have much emotional power for me. It's the price I've paid all these years for being the only child in my family to be put up for adoption."

Summary

We have separated the mechanisms of imitation, identification, and internalization for heuristic purposes; in practice these mechanisms are not completely distinct. Furthermore, they must take place in the context of appropriate support and group cohesion in order to be effective. Change can occur so subtly that it is often observable only after it has taken place.

The manner in which members come to value dreams might be used as an illustration of how these mechanisms occur. When a member first reports a dream, there is usually some interest shown by the others. The therapist too, by his verbal and nonverbal communications, indicates his interest. It is not unusual for some members to begin reporting dreams by way of imitation of others who have done the same. They do so to please the therapist. Furthermore, other members initially imitate the therapist's investigatory style of trying to understand the dreams. At the level of identification, the members may find that they have a new attitude about dreams. They may experience a sense of excitement and stimulation when a dream is being reported, and they may develop a sense of curiosity not only about the dreamer's associations to the dream but about everyone's associations. These are not entirely conscious responses; rather, they arise as identifications with the therapist's interactions with the members. At the level of internalization, members may find themselves experiencing a fundamental shift in their thinking about dreams and dreaming. Dreams are now seen as useful ways of learning about the self or of uncovering hidden aspects of group interactions. The use of the dream for exhibitionistic needs or as a shield diminishes, and the members believe that dreams are valuable tools for learning. In other words, the patients internalize the therapist's value system regarding dreams.

THE THERAPEUTIC PROCESSES

Therapeutic process refers to "how" the therapeutic mechanisms are facilitated in the treatment context. The foregoing descriptions are made more complete by linking them to the processes by which they occur in therapy groups. Following the working model of Greenson (1967), we believe that the processes that induce and promote imitation, identification, and internalization are confrontation, clarification, interpretation, and working through. The result of these processes is increased insight and understanding, eventuating in change.

Confrontation

Foulkes (1961) spoke of groups as "halls of mirrors." This phrase aptly connotes the potential effectiveness with which groups can confront individuals with aspects of themselves they previously were unable to see. A particular advantage to this treatment modality arises from the opportunity for the multiple interactions that soon directly expose patterns of behavior. In dyadic treatment the therapist has to rely upon reports from the outside world or utilize the interactions in the two-person field.

Pines (1981) has described one of the dynamics that precedes confrontation. He maintained that as an individual becomes a functioning member of the group, his neurotic inner problems become evident as a communications block. Such blocks, or blind spots, may be raised to a level of self-awareness through confrontation.

Confrontations in this context are efforts to point out to the patient his behavior, his emotional state, or his problems. They primarily address external aspects of behavior and as such are observations or responses to interactions or comments on the affects aroused in the confronter. Confrontations do not address inner motivations or unconscious assumptions. A comment such as "You are always interrupting others!" is a confrontation whereas "You are always seeking attention!" is not. The latter is an attribution of meaning and as such is an interpretation. Often (particularly, early in group experience) when patients make comments to one another that assume or attribute meaning and motivation, they are met with denial or anger. Confrontation is an attempt to indicate to a patient that a problem exists; it is not an effort to gain or impart understanding per se. Recognition of the problem is necessary before there can be agreement about what work needs to be done.

In dyadic therapy the therapist is the confronter and therefore judges the pace at which confrontation should occur. Group therapy provides more complex and varied opportunities for confrontation because there are a great many potential confronters in a group. Indeed, to the degree that the members heed the agreement to share their emotional reactions to one another honestly, there is continual confrontation and feedback. Because confrontation is considered such an integral part of group psychotherapy, a great deal of effort is spent in making the group safe for confrontation and in making sure the confrontations are useful. This is especially true because many patients enter group psychotherapy with explicit requests to have feedback about their behavior. Though consciously wishing for such information, patients discover that they also have considerable resistance to learning about themselves. Confrontations may be constructive, destructive, or a mixture. It is important to create a supportive atmosphere that enables members to give and receive important information through helpful confrontations.

Many members are quite limited in their ability to give feedback. Others can give feedback in only the most benign situations and become anxious and frozen the moment intense affects are mobilized. The therapeutic task is not only to train someone to overcome these fears but to understand the dynamic underpinnings. The attainment of the ability to give nonjudgmental feedback or confrontation signals an advance in ego functioning. Indeed, members often cite their newfound ability to confront as a major step in their therapeutic growth and one of the special advantages of group therapy.

Learning to confront successfully includes acquisition of a sense of timing, the capacity to form an alliance, and empathy. Although these elements may not be consciously integrated, their absence can be readily discerned. Timing rests in part on an appreciation of another's inner state and on a judgment as to whether the information can be productively assimilated at the time. The state of the alliance also influences the usefulness of a confrontation. It is not unusual for accurate feedback to go unheard because of conflict. In such circumstances the comment "I don't trust you, so why should I listen to you?" might be heard. Therapists have long been aware that negative transferences block learning. This is particularly so in dyadic treatment. One of the major advantages of groups is the opportunity to learn about oneself from peers, with whom less intense negative transferences may develop. Finally, for members to momentarily put themselves in another's shoes and learn about the other's inner world is essential not only for understanding the other's emotional state but also for being able to anticipate the effect on him or her of receiving the information (Stone & Whitman, 1980).

Many, if not most, confrontations carry with them an implicit request to stop doing whatever is being done. This is particularly the case when there is intense emotion in the group. For example, a member might blurt out something about another group member that has not been spoken of before, perhaps something like "You always attack us!" or "You continually put down women!" The message is clear though not explicit: "Stop doing that!" A hostile attack may be revealed by the use of such extreme expressions as "always" and "continually." Their use most certainly will evoke defensiveness in the confronted patient. This situation rarely results in increased curiosity; usually it results in a struggle between the confronter and the confronted. Such a struggle may be productive for all concerned, but it is different from the growth-promoting confrontation. Of course, therapists are not above making confrontations bearing the covert message "Stop doing that!"; in these cases a struggle results between the therapist and the confronted patient.

How information is conveyed to the individual being confronted thus becomes a matter of central concern when it is done insensitively or in anger. However, most patients are capable of finding ways of confronting one another in ways that are helpful and therapeutic.

The group agreements are a significant source of therapeutic leverage and provide an opportunity to confront members with their self-defeating behaviors. Patients agree to a variety of constraints in order to maximize their therapy. The agreements are not adhered to at all times, nor would that be expected. Rather, patients learn to be *responsible* for their agreements to the group, as distinct from always absolutely abiding by them. The therapist should be aware that life is filled with layers of conflicting contractual agreements and that how individuals choose their priorities is very important. As patients choose to keep or break their agreements, they have many opportunities to be confronted about their characteristic styles and values. On many occasions entire groups will collude to avoid confronting a specific patient over a breach of the agreement; in this case the group as a whole may be confronted and through that strategy the members may gain new self-awareness.

Some authors have suggested confrontational techniques concerning patient's uses and abuses of the agreements. Borriello (1979), for example, has elaborated a radical technique of confrontation with regard to breaches of the agreements that he believes is crucial in working with patients suffering from severe acting-out character disorders. Following any violation, he directly tells his group that the rationale of the "contract" (his term) is to help patients break self-destructive patterns and that members do themselves a disservice by continuing their therapy while being unwilling to do what is required to change. Ormont (1967) addressed a subtler violation of the contract. He differentiated between expressions of feelings and personal attacks, viewing the latter to be acting out and therefore antitherapeutic. Fortunately, even unsuccessful or erroneous confrontations, when properly handled, can provide an opportunity to study interpersonal modes of relating.

Most confrontations take place among members or between therapists and members. However, one form of confrontation in groups is distinct. Looking into the hall of mirrors, patients might observe others involving themselves in unproductive and pathological behavior and begin to be curious about the extent to which they too engage in identical or similar behaviors. This is a form of self-confrontation. In a therapy group no confrontation is given in isolation. Every member of the group hears and is affected, even though the confrontation may have been directed primarily at another member. Thus, interventions must take into account more than an appreciation of the openness of a particular individual to hear them; they must include an awareness that the other members will have their own responses.

Clarification

"Clarification refers to those activities that aim at placing the psychic phenomenon being analyzed in sharp focus. The significant details have to be dug out and carefully separated from extraneous matter" (Greenson, 1967). The group provides special opportunities for clarification to take place. The richness of experiences in the group itself enables patients to see repeating patterns. Members are a well of information about one another's behavior. It is a common experience for members, after a confrontation, to remember similar interactions or behaviors that occurred in previous meetings. Often incidents dating back months or years in the group are recalled in vivid detail; in other instances members will recall important pieces of history that were previously shared and will relate them to the current confrontation. Clarification serves to organize and highlight such data. Much affect-laden material, previously split off and disconnected, can now be brought to bear on a specific and related issue. It is the weight of these episodes being repeated over and over in the group that stimulates individuals to question themselves. This increased curiosity represents an important aspect of the change process.

Clarification essentially results in patients gaining new understanding about the "when" and "where" of a particular action, feeling, or interaction. The "why" awaits interpretation. Nonetheless, it is very therapeutic and freeing for individuals to begin to notice repetitive patterns to their behaviors or feelings. Clarification often flows from those interactions among group members and from those interactions between members and nonmembers that are revealed to the group. The process then deepens as the clarification evokes new (though connected) feelings and responses. In addition, more than mere recollection is occurring since in the immediacy of the recall in the group new interactions are happening. If maladaptive patterns are continuing, they will emerge in the interaction.

In contrast to individual psychotherapy, the main thrust of the clarification in groups takes place in a public arena. While some of the clarification in individual therapy necessarily occurs in the examination of outside events that are reported in the therapy, most clarifications emerge from the relationship between patient and therapist. In group therapy outside events are also utilized, but usually the in-group relationships are sufficient to provide the necessary clarification. This expanded data base is used by both patient and therapist in examining perceptions, feelings, and behaviors. When patient's complain about the behaviors of a spouse, for example, it is usually possible to understand the patients' contributions to the marital dilemma from an examination of their interactions with group members of the opposite sex.

It has been maintained in some quarters that the intensity and extent of transference is limited in group psychotherapy since groups focus more on the here-and-now interactions, but transference *is* a here-and-now experience. It is the eruption of previously acquired distortions into the present. Groups offer an even wider set of opportunities for the exploration of such distortions. From our perspective the development of a cohesive transference response in groups is at least as intense as in individual therapy and indeed may even be amplified by the experience of multiple peer transferences.

Interpretation

An interpretation is distinct from a clarification in two important ways: First, an interpretation is aimed at the unconscious, whereas a clarification is directed to the conscious or preconscious of our patients. Second, clarification broadens the data base by citing similar examples and sharpening the focus on a particular behavioral constellation. Interpretation is designed to make unconscious phenomena conscious, that is, to attach meaning to an event or feeling. It attempts to help the patient gain an understanding of the hidden motivations and conflicts contributing to pathological behavior.

In dyadic psychotherapy, interpretations are classically interpretations of transferences, resistances, and defenses. In group therapy, interpretations of interpersonal *style,* with resultant implications about underlying character and defenses, are also available.

Two major components are intertwined in a successful interpretation: the emotional and the cognitive. Further, no interpretation will be effective unless the timing in which it is offered is correct. By definition, interpretations help patients become aware of something they have been unaware of previously. This is most effective if there is an optimal emotional element involved. Interpretations can be too intellectual, or they can be delivered in the midst of an emotional storm. There is little likelihood that interpretations at either extreme will be effective.

Ideally, the patient is first given the opportunity to truly experience the affect—the here-and-now interaction of the group enables therapists to make interpretations at points where they have considerable emotional relevance and impact. Interpretations can be offered a long time after the affect was most heated, with the time lag providing sufficient distance for the individual to integrate what is being examined, the "strike while the iron is cold" approach (Pine, 1985, p. 153). When there is too much affect, the interpretation cannot be integrated. Unfortunately, there are many occasions when interpretations are offered solely (though unconsciously) to protect the therapist or the group members from the intensity of affect. In such cases the therapist prematurely offers "understanding" and thereby shuts down the affect.

Interpretations, by definition, examine unconscious conflicts and wishes, as well as the subsequent defensive responses or adaptational shifts. Optimally, interpretations should go even further by including some speculation as to causality. This does not necessarily include a genetic reconstruction, but linkages with individual development are not excluded.

Group leaders are confronted with a myriad of variables in attempting to frame an interpretation that will be most useful to the individual and the group. They must decide, for example, where to focus their interpretation: Should it be on specific individuals, the interactions between individuals or the group as a whole? On the interactions between individuals, between specific individuals and the leader, or between a subgroup of members and the leader? On in-group phenomena or on fantasies about the outside world? Each focus is an apt target for interpretation, and the art of being a group therapist is to know when to use which. As Foulkes (1973) elegantly states:

> We can focus on the group-as-a-whole or on any one individual or individuals in their specific interaction. As that happens in meaningful form, any point of view and the different meanings dovetail. It is not the case that one viewpoint is right and the other wrong. It is rather as if we took photographs from various positions. One picture may be better for certain purposes and others less good, but all of them show what is true from the position from which they were taken. However, the total process must always have been defined from the total field. (p. 153)

In the paragraphs that follow we will elaborate guidelines to help group therapists decide when, how, what, and where to make interpretations.

Group-as-a-Whole Interpretations

The followers of Bion have demonstrated that there are always group-as-a-whole processes at work in groups. To dismiss interpretations at that level is to overlook a source of great learning for our patients. An examination of the process provides insight for the members by helping them understand their involvement in and contribution to group-wide phenomena. There are two types of group-as-a-whole interpretation: those focused on the group's reaction to the leader and those focused on the group itself.

Leader-Related Interpretations. Beginning with the formulations of Freud, emphasis on transference to the therapist has been one of the cornerstones on which psychodynamic psychotherapy is based. Therapists are very important people to their groups by virtue of the powerful position they occupy. Group-as-a-whole therapists have always made good use of leader-related transference interpretations. Indeed, therapists who assume the role of the relatively silent, nonintrusive psychoanalyst encourage feelings to be directed toward themselves by the very nature of that role. The task of interpretation is to bring these responses into the members' awareness. Nonetheless, as important as leader-related transferences are, there are limitations to the effectiveness of focusing exclusively on them. Such an exclusive focus unnecessarily diminishes the multiplicity of peer transferences and relationships that are uniquely the province of group psychotherapy.

Group-Related Interpretations. In addition to transferences to therapists, it is possible for individuals to have specific transferences to the idea of the whole group. Patients may experience the group itself as engulfing, destructive, warm, protective, or secure. H. Durkin (1964) and Scheidlinger (1974), for example, suggested that on occasion the transference to the therapist (irrespective of gender) is paternal whereas the transference to the group is maternal. Kernberg (1975) expanded that notion, suggesting that patients with preoedipal pathology are particularly prone to the development of whole-group transferences and he maintains that whole-group interpretations are important in helping such patients gain insight and understanding.

Whole-group phenomena are most evident at fairly predictable developmental points and during crises. Whenever a boundary is breached, as when a new member enters, the entire group responds. The precise reaction for each individual varies, of course, but the group has to integrate the newcomer. After all, as soon as a new member enters, it is from that point on a different group. It may be assumed that each individual member is coping with, or avoiding, the groupwide task of assimilating or rejecting the new member.

Group-wide phenomena are operating all the time. Affect-laden interactions stir responses in each member, who in turn respond in some way. Nothing happens that does not impact on the whole field. A member's prolonged silence may have as strong an impact as the revelation of a poignant or dramatic event.

Leader-directed and group-directed interpretations are too often viewed as competing, mutually exclusive foci. In fact, they are very complementary. Group-directed interpretations tend to help individuals examine issues of universality and commonality and, from that involvement in a common cause, to learn of their uniqueness. Roller (1989) has observed the paradox, "You can discover individuality in a group setting" (p. 96). Leader-related interpretations tend to focus upon individual differences and from that to a deeper understanding of the fact that beneath the differences is a similar yearning for love and affiliation in all people. (While it may seem contradictory to speak of group-as-a-whole interpretations leading to insight about individuals, in fact the goal of all interpretations is to help the individual members. By understanding one's unique reactions to group-as-a-whole phenomena each group member has the opportunity for self-understanding.)

Incorrect or poorly delivered interpretations in any mode may be injurious. When group-as-a-whole therapists err, it tends to be in the direction of offering interpretations in an oracular, mystical fashion, fostering regression and dependency. Furthermore, any group-as-a-whole interpretation in some way homogenizes the members and runs the risk of being experienced as rejecting or hurtful or narcissistically injurious by individuals. The individual may feel hurt, diminished, or just plain ignored. Malan et al. (1976) have documented the clinical ineffectiveness of a therapist's exclusive adherence to interpretation of group-as-a-whole, leader-related transferences.

Even the most rigorous group-as-a-whole clinicians are sensitive to the feelings of individual members. It is quite possible to blend a group-as-a-whole focus, which underlines the importance of group process and transference to the leader, with interpersonally based foci, which take into account more of the uniqueness of individual members. One successful solution is to make individual interpretations around a common group conflict and then, when sufficient work has been done, make a group-as-a-whole interpretations to demonstrate certain commonalities or a primary theme (Horwitz, 1977b).

Individual Interpretations

Interpretations in group therapy are often made to individuals. Therapists should not lose sight of the fact that groups do not come for therapy; rather, it is individuals who come for help, and therapists choose to offer those individuals assistance in a group setting.

One strategy available to the therapist is to make an interpretation of individual behavior preparatory to making a whole-group interpretation. There may be a specific advantage to this approach because it provides members with an opportunity to examine for themselves where they might fit into a particular groupwide conflict.

A second strategy for making an individual interpretation does not have reference to groupwide intervention. Such interpretations are primarily aimed at helping the individual member gain self-understanding. Usually such individual interpretations are most successful when they elaborate specific individual reactions to, contributions to, and resonances with the group themes going on at the time. Thus, for example, the entry of a new member sets up a number of reactions within a group. The therapist may point out the groupwide response and then indicate each member's unique contribution to it.

Not all interactions are a primary product of group transactions. Some represent a specific pathological configuration that emerges in the group. One such example arises when one member dominates and controls meetings. The therapist then has the complex task helping the other individuals understand their reactions and contributions to the process as well as assisting the monopolizer in understanding the sources of the monopolization.

Some patterned individual behavior becomes especially apparent in a group. Interpretations of those behaviors are particularly powerful when they include specific reference to the group process and the emotional sequencing that occurred.

CLINICAL EXAMPLE

Sally, a severely borderline woman, rarely spoke in group. When she did, she usually gave a religiously oriented "speech" about the sins of the world. After many months the therapist noticed that Sally varied her behavior in one repetitive manner. Whenever another woman missed a meeting, and especially when a woman terminated the group, Sally became much more agitated and yet much easier to understand. When the therapist accumulated sufficient evidence of this behavior, he pointed out the behavior while also offering an interpretation. He said, "Sally, it seems that whenever a woman is not in her usual seat in this room, you feel just as you did when your mother was hospitalized." The comment was offered in a spirit of mutual curiosity, not as a dictum presented from "on high." The members immediately confirmed that they too had noticed that Sally's behavior was notably different in those specific instances. This was a beginning point in helping Sally gain increased insight into the effects on her adult personality of her psychotic mother's having been permanently psychiatrically hospitalized when Sally was 3 years old.

The fact that many people are present adds an important dimension to interpretations directed toward any particular individual. On the positive side, as other persons hear interpretations directed toward a specific member, they gain a deeper understanding of that person, which they may subsequently apply in their dealings with him or her. Other members may also find specific interpretations relevant for themselves, even though the interpretation was directed to another. It is not uncommon for members to have an "ah ha!" experience while sitting back and observing interactions between the therapist and other members. Finally, members' observations of various resistances in others to hearing interpretations is often useful in helping them understand the various ways they themselves resist hearing new information.

There are also drawbacks entailed in an individual's overhearing interpretations directed toward others. The most obvious and difficult problem is that some patients are ready before others to hear an in-depth interpretation. The therapist is thus confronted with a dilemma: to withhold information and understanding from a member who is ready to hear and use it or to protect another patient who might be overwhelmed by the interpretation even though the interpretation is not directed to that member. In such instances it is better to offer the interpretation. In cases where it is clear that another patient will find such an insight painful and alarming, the therapist can offer empathic understanding that this comment will likely be difficult for him or her to hear even though it is directed to another. For example, as a therapist prepared to interpret erotic transference from one female patient, he first said to a newer member with a history of brutal incestuous experiences with a stepfather, "I am aware that it may be difficult for you to hear what I am about to say to Joan, but it represents an opportunity for both of you to learn more about yourselves." A rule of thumb in such matters is to side with growth and not with pathology. Thus, to withhold the interpretation from the patient who is growing in order to protect the more fragile patient usually does no good for either member.

What to Interpret

Interpretation is an art and is not conducive to learning by rote. Often the therapist feels rather than knows what is the proper target of an interpretation, since at any meeting there are probably several options for offering insight. In the early days of psychodynamic group therapy, the exclusive mechanism for change was considered to be the interpretation of transference and resistance, the mechanism used in traditional analysis. As experience in the workings of groups increased, therapists began to understand that communications are responded to by all members and that their responses can serve as a reliable guide for making interpretations. Those explications of the group process or of individual responses that will enable patients to more fully understand what they are unconsciously or preconsciously communicating are usually the most successful interpretations. The therapist continues to help the patients see that various dysfunctional behaviors are in fact *solutions* to earlier, often unconscious or repressed, problems.

An example of the process the therapist must go through in determining when and if to offer an interpretation is the following:

> A relatively new group of recovering alcoholics was uncertain about how they might consider the emotional components of their drinking problems. One member began the meeting with a remark about feeling upset and anxious before going to church. Another continued, remembering that she had been upset by bad dreams and wondering whether she could do anything to stop them. Yet a third wondered if the second member was speaking about dreams or delirium tremens. And all this was followed by a discussion of the physical problems associated with alcoholism, most notably blackouts.

The therapist for the group in this clinical example was confronted with a dilemma. Should she offer an interpretation that would clarify the unconscious or preconscious communications in the group? She could, for instance, point out that the members seemed to have some anxiety about coming to the group (church) and that the anxiety seemed to relate to their concerns about whether psychological or emotional (e.g., bad dreams) issues might be addressed. Indeed, she could point out that in response to those topics the group shifted the focus to biology (bad dreams or delirium tremens?), which led to a discussion of the physiological state of nonawareness (blackouts). By documenting the path of the group's associations, the therapist could offer an interpretation of the covert communications hidden beneath the overt content and could thereby help the group gain insight into what were the "real" concerns in the room. However, such interpretations require a state of therapeutic alliance and motivation, a state not yet attained by the group. Interpretations offered prematurely serve only to stiffen the resistance and the commitment to not knowing.

In this immature group the therapist chose not to offer an interpretation of the defenses. She understood her dilemma as, on the one hand, her desire to demonstrate her knowledge and her capacity as leader and, on the other, her recognition of the group's current inability to tolerate the affective components of their problems. The choice was made to provide a model for identification rather than an interpretation. Thus, the therapist quietly turned to the patient who had been disturbed by her dreams and asked that she relate them to the group.

In this instance the therapist determined that the group would be best served by *demonstrating* that she and the group could tolerate emotions, rather than by interpreting the fears about that. Had there been greater group maturity, with demonstrated capacity to tolerate powerful affect and a history of strong therapeutic alliances, the therapist would have offered the interpretation. It likely would not have been an error to offer the interpretation even at this early date. This would have allowed the therapist the opportunity to observe the groupwide response and to test her hypothesis regarding the capacity of members to tolerate strong affect. The modeling response, however, represented a low-risk opportunity for the group to mature and postponed the risk of displaying vulnerability to a later date.

This example not only indicates the complexities of a therapist's decision about when and if to make an intervention, but it also demonstrates the variety of useful responses available to the therapist. There is rarely one correct response. The therapist in this example could instead have offered a model for identification by turning to the woman who was anxious before going to church and asking for more details about her anxiety. This would have served just as well as the revelation of the dream material. Or a confrontation aimed at focusing the affect could have been included, with the therapist saying something like, "Perhaps people are wondering just how much feeling can be shared in here?"

The rationale for making one choice rather than another is aided by the therapist's capacity to predict the outcome of the intervention. Interventions that lead to an elaboration of the material discussed, associations to new ideas, or exploration of affects are generally effective. Closing of the topic, repetitious descriptions of similar events, or constriction of affects are indicators of an unproductive therapist intervention. In the example, the therapist predicted that interpretation of unconscious material at this time would be met with resistance and instead chose to utilize the authority of her leadership to function as a model for identification. The primary goal at this time was to help set an important group norm; namely, "Feelings can be expressed and explored in this group."

Recent advances in technique following the concepts of psychology of the self (Kohut, 1971, 1977; Stone & Stevenson, 1991; Stone & Whitman, 1977; Stone & Whitman, 1980) have given new richness to our understanding of the functioning of interpretation. In the self psychology tradition, interpretations are focused on the phenomenon of narcissistic injury. Group therapy provides fertile ground for under-standing narcissistic injuries since members frequently feel ignored, left out, insulted, or misunderstood. When interpretations by the therapist are directed to other individuals or to the group as a whole, some mem-bers feel injured, as if they have received major blows to their self-esteem. In groups many sequences are activated that result from natural, everyday varieties of narcissistic injury. Interpretations may be aimed at demon-strating to the members the process of their interactions, pointing out the precise sequence of behaviors as it emerged in the session. This is done so that the injured members can examine the sequence to learn more about their vulnerabilities and their responses to injury. For some individuals the interpretation can provide genuine insight and increased capacity to contain their feelings of hurt. With increased ability to main-tain their balance they are more able to see others as separate people with needs and wishes of their own. The result is increased reality testing. Moreover, such an interpretation might help some members by mak-ing them aware of certain sadistic elements in their personalities, ele-ments that might have contributed to the injury felt by other members, as well as by other important people in their lives.

Peer Interpretations

Most patients enter groups not knowing how to make interpretations. In this regard we do not refer to artificial attempts to understand other members as a defensive maneuver to fend off self-exploration. The mechanisms of imitation, identification, and internalization may be in-strumental in helping members gain increased interpretive skills, as they observe and are influenced by the therapist and by members with strong skills in this area. The ability to make interpretations may represent an expansion of self-awareness or may precede it.

Peer interpretations have unique power in groups in that patients often have less resistance to learning about themselves from their peers than they do from authorities. For certain counterdependent patients, peer interpretations seem to be the *only* interpretations that are accept-able early in treatment. The fact that peer interpretations have special influence makes it important for the therapist to be willing to suffer the narcissistic threat of allowing someone else to offer an insight that he or she has known for weeks. The therapist will not get credit from the group for having helped, even though he or she actively deferred offering the insight in the hope that a peer would provide it. Of such occasions, Foulkes and Anthony (1965) have said, "There are times when the therapist must sit on his wisdom, must tolerate defective knowledge and wait for the group to arrive at solutions" (p. 153).

This is not to suggest that peer interpretations are routinely superior to those of the therapist. In fact, peer transferences within the group can considerably complicate the interpretations given and received. From a technical standpoint peer interpretations are often ill-timed, too superficial, too deep, or just plain wrong. In sum, they carry the same risks as those of the therapist. Such mistakes on the part of patients, of course, are not tragic because they become grist for the therapeutic mill, setting in motion new interactions and opportunities for learning.

Working Through

For most patients psychotherapy requires an extended period of treatment to produce substantial and enduring change. Freud introduced the concept of working through in 1914, when attempting to answer the question "What accounts for the fact that psychoanalysis takes so long?" (Brenner, 1988, p. 94). (It should be remembered that this was at a time when an analysis of one year was considered lengthy.)

Working through is the final essential element in enabling patients to change. Confrontation, clarification, and interpretation help the patient to become aware of conscious and unconscious elements that create difficulties. Through these processes patients become familiar with the many facets of their fundamental psychological patterns and become aware of the habitual resistances to seeing or integrating solutions to those problems. However, these elements alone are insufficient to bring about deep and lasting change. In working through, the emphasis is on increasing patients' capacities to examine themselves, to understand conflicts and areas of vulnerability, and to interpret their own behavior and on helping them develop more varied and flexible defensive systems that are capable of protecting them from undue anxieties while allowing them more authentic intimacy with others and access to their own personal potentials.

There is considerable diversity regarding what constitutes working through (Brenner, 1988). Is it something the patient does or something the clinician does? However one conceptualizes working through, it is a slow and incompletely understood process.

The working-through process consumes the major portion of time in psychodynamic psychotherapy. Pathological behavior, thoughts, feelings, and reactions appear and are worked on and understood only to reappear later in slightly different form. It often seems that in the process of working through we are essentially saying to our patients, "There it is again; there it is yet one more time!" The repeated opportunities for patients in groups to examine the many facets of their problems are a major contributor to change.

It is one of the therapist's creative tasks to examine the multiple facets of a problem and to find a way of presenting them to the patient or the group that will not be boring or repetitious. Sometimes obvious repetitions cannot be seen or heard until they are presented with a slight variation in meaning or phraseology. This does not mean that the initial understanding was incorrect but that individuals pick up and respond to interpretations or confrontations in their own idiosyncratic ways. Therapists must try to reach the individual on his or her own level and must not ask that their own words or precise manner of phrasing be accepted as the final word. As more data are added, new material is also uncovered that adds to the richness of understanding and further helps the individual gain self-knowledge.

Therapy groups offer special advantages, along with some potential shortcomings in facilitating the working-through process. In this setting, the group itself is an arena in which patients demonstrate their pathologies in great richness and subtlety. The opportunity to expose and explore many variations on a common theme results from these multiple relationships. The process is facilitated and inhibited by the presence of others. Sometimes feedback about behavior and character style can be received more easily from group colleagues than from the authority-figure therapist, and group members often pick up subtleties of behavior that the therapist misses. Further, members may use the group to try out new ways of coping or managing conflict and anxiety. Groups provide instant feedback on the success or failure of such new behaviors, at least in terms of their interpersonal consequences.

On the other hand, working through can be inhibited by the presence of others who vie for time. Sometimes the feedback and interpretations offered by group members is incorrect or a consequence of their own pathology, and this can complicate the working-through process. On occasion it may appear that a member's capacity to fully experience a transference reaction is inhibited by the consensual validation of the other members. Glatzer (1989) questions whether or not "the presence of fellow members makes therapeutic regression in analytic group psychotherapy different because of the quicker check with reality" (p. 293). She implies that working through even the most difficult issues is possible in group therapy. Though therapy groups are not the same as real life, they involve experiences that are more generalizable than those in dyadic therapy.

In psychodynamic therapy it is the study of the resistance, and the elaboration of the defenses that is the point of the inquiry. Whatever latent conflict or emotion is hidden away will come to the surface of its own accord when the defensive structure is understood, appreciated, and made more flexible and appropriate. It is the working-through process that allows the patient to become accepting of his defensive structure and to recognize that once it served a valid function in history, even if it has become too burdensome in the present.

Membership in a therapy group exposes predictable patterns of interaction, and this in turn facilitates working through. Ongoing therapy groups provide repeated experiences with newcomers, departures, trust, autonomy, competitiveness, exposure and shame, and sexuality. Each reexperiencing of these issues and events offers a new opportunity to gain new understanding, attempt new behavior, and to work through chronic character styles. The relationships with the therapist and among the members as they learn to know, accept, and respect each other's subjective experiences are bound to be a part of the working-through process (E. Wolf, 1988, p. 153).

An example of working through as an analysis of resistance is the handling of acting out. Acting out, which could take place either in or out of the treatment setting, has been a topic of much concern for group therapists because the psychotherapy situation is rife with opportunities for patients to "do" rather than to "feel." Psychodynamic group therapists, however, understand that such action is more than acting, that it is also communication. Ackerman (1949) pointed out that acting out need not be an impeding factor; rather, patients have the opportunity to act out or demonstrate their transference reactions through their relationships with other members. In fact, acting out is used not only to avoid feelings or understanding but is also a covert means of communicating about and gratifying the impulse in question.

Exploration of acting-out behavior can be utilized as a vital element in helping patients understand the breadth and intensity of their feelings.

CLINICAL EXAMPLE

Ruth had experienced early losses in her life. In the group she talked extensively about loneliness and emptiness whenever a member left the group or even when one was absent for a meeting. As the transferences intensified, Ruth began to cope with her distress by establishing a liaison with another member outside the group meetings, a relationship that helped her experience continuity. She also began to miss sessions herself prior to and following any interruptions in weekly meetings. These actions were initially unconscious, then well rationalized. Gradually, Ruth, with the help of repeated interpretations, came to understand these behaviors as attempts to manage the deeper, painful feelings surrounding separations both inside and outside the treatment setting. At that point she began to experience great pain and despair, which was followed by a period of growth.

Friedman (1988) describes the working-through process as follows: "When, because of personal involvement with his psychoanalyst, a patient is inclined to accept the analyst's view of his mind, then he begins to look for problems relevant to analysis, starts to see questions and answers of an analytic sort, and practices them in many examples (called working through)" (p. 239). When her group therapist first began linking Ruth's behavior to her feelings about loss she was nonaccepting; she could neither see nor experience any connection. Over time, however, she began to accept the therapist's view, and this helped her make internal connections between her affect and the various behaviors that followed.

In contrast to individual therapy, where much more time might be spent in examining and understanding the patient's transferences, current life, and history, the group situation provides a breadth of experiences in the here and now. Working through is characterized not merely by having the same old memories reworked and reworked or by having the same problem examined over and over; rather, group patients have ample opportunity to see and live out many manifestations of their current distortions and pathologies. Working through takes place as the patient connects in-group insights with real world experiences and historical data (see example of Sarah in Chapter 7).

SUMMARY

In this chapter we have examined the elements that are essential in the process of helping patients change through psychotherapy. Fundamental to effective group psychotherapy is the conviction on the part of the members that focusing on the intragroup events represents a major opportunity to learn about themselves. The therapist's position is that of both an expert and an emotional participant. The therapist alternates between the stance of a separately functioning individual who observes the process and the individuals to that of one who has an emotional engagement within the group and whose own affects are available for observation. The data collected from these vantage points are used to reflect to individuals that which might not otherwise be apparent to them. The therapist is also an object for the transference fantasies of the members. Within the safety of a supportive, cohesive group, bounded by the mutual agreements and protected by the presence of the leader, members are free to interact spontaneously, express strong emotions, talk about aspects of their lives felt to be shameful or terrifying, and step back and observe the effects of such sharing. Gradually they come to understand that patterns of interpersonal relating often represent consequences of intrapsychic conflict. Alonso and Swiller (1993) have summarized the following as the curative factors in group therapy: (1) vital enactment of the characterological dilemmas of the members, (2) exposure and resolution of shameful secrets, (3) support around the universality of the members' wishes, fears, and distress, and (4) reintegration of split-off aspects of the self.

We conceptualize individual change as taking place via the mechanisms of imitation, identification, and internalization. The multiple opportunities for relating and observing that groups offer facilitate these changes.

Through the processes of confrontation, clarification, interpretation, and working through, members gain insight and self-understanding. These processes lead to shifts in the intrapsychic structures and capacities to manage stress and anxiety. Groups provide unique and potent opportunities for each of these mechanisms and processes to work effectively.

5

Patient Selection

In planning a psychodynamic group, the therapist needs criteria to determine which patients are best suited for this type of treatment. Clear inclusion criteria can also be helpful in communicating with other therapists who might refer patients. Unfortunately, there is a dearth of data to provide specific guidelines; the clinician must therefore rely on accumulated experience focusing mainly on unsuitability for group psychotherapy rather than on positive indicators.

An obvious, but often overlooked, element in the selection process is the prospective member's willingness to join a group. A significant proportion of patients who initially are referred to a group never join one. In a study comparing short-term individual and group treatments, Budman et al. (1988) reported a significant difference in rejection rates between group and individual therapy. In the study individuals were referred to group or individual treatment through random assignment. Of 76 patients assigned to groups, 26 (34%) failed to join a group. The reasons given included outright rejection of group treatment, time conflicts, moving out of the area, and loss of insurance due to job change. In contrast, of 51 patients assigned to individual treatment, only 3 (6%) defected from the study. In another study R. Klein and Carroll (1986) retrospectively examined 716 referrals to an outpatient group treatment component of a large university hospital clinic. Astonishingly, 41% never entered a group. For the majority of these individuals, the reasons given were unkept or canceled appointments (deemed inappropriate by the staff), lack of interest in further treatment, and lack of interest in group treatment in particular. In the same study, approximately 8% of all patients who had agreed to enter a group failed to come to the initial meeting and never attended. These studies, which were in clinic and HMO settings, may not reflect the experience of the private practitioner, but they do highlight the discrepancy between the number of individuals referred for group treatment and the number who actually enter such treatment.

These studies indicate the importance of careful screening and careful preparation of patients for group therapy. Clearly, many patients contemplate the initial phases of treatment in a group with more fear and anxiety than they feel toward the presumably safer and more contained dyadic setting. Furthermore, since most individuals seeking therapy come with a preconceived notion that they will receive individual therapy, a referral to group therapy must be thoughtfully worked through with them.

In the pioneering period the one positive indicator for group therapy was relative poverty. Just as cost was a primary criterion in recommending group therapy then, so too in today's economy is cost once again a factor in making group an attractive therapeutic alternative. Ironically, the relatively low cost of group therapy has contributed over the years to its image as a second-rate treatment.

In the past many patient populations were seen as poor risks for group therapy. Today categorical exclusion is a waning phenomenon. Most exclusionary recommendations in the group therapy literature can be countered by other publications in the same literature that contradict such recommendations. This is particularly true for the homosexual population (Frost, 1990; Stein, 1963; W. Stone, Schengber, & Seifried, 1966) and is increasingly apparent for persons with borderline and narcissistic character disorders (see Kanas, Deri, Ketter, & Fein, 1990; Roth, 1979; W. Stone & Whitman, 1977; Wong, 1979). For therapists the dispositional question is not so much "Should group be considered for this patient?" but "Are there mitigating factors *against* considering group therapy for this patient?" (Rutan & Alonso, 1979, p. 612)

POOR-RISK PATIENTS

Certain exclusion criteria are valid in our experience and are also supported in the literature. The most frequently stated reason for exclusion is that the patient is in an acute crisis. This can be a developmental crisis (such as marriage, divorce, retirement), a situational crisis (death of a loved one, physical illness), or a crisis of pathology (eruption of a psychotic process or extraordinary anxiety). These patients require a great deal of attention, and they do not have the time or interest to meet and develop relationships with a number of strangers in a therapy group. By the same token, the group has little incentive to devote great amounts of time to the crisis of a stranger. Naturally, patients who are already group members and who undergo a crisis find their groups to be extraordinarily healing resources during these troubling times.

Other populations are routinely excluded from heterogeneous psychodynamic groups. These include individuals with insufficient impulse control (so that the physical safety of other members cannot be guaranteed), chronically psychotic patients, patients with organic brain syndromes, and sociopathic patients. Taken as a whole, these patients share a common trait. None can establish the minimal object relatedness that is required for a therapy group to work effectively. They are often the patients whom individual therapists find so difficult to treat that they refer them to groups.

Patients who would normally be considered unsuitable for a group might be effectively treated in homogeneous groups. For example, Comstock and McDermott (1975) found that homogeneous groups for individuals who recently attempted suicide held the most hope of any treatment modality for helping these patients. Similarly, groups of sexual offenders or alcoholics (Bratter, 1981), who are homogeneous as to symptom but quite different in underlying psychodynamic configurations, can be very effective in diminishing pathologic symptoms. It is not uncommon for these patients to require individual therapy to assist them in integrating the data generated in their groups. (The practice of combining individual and group therapy is discussed in Chapter 13.)

Further research concerning patient selection has focused on identifying high-risk patients, who tend to drop out prematurely. If such patients can be identified, then steps must be taken to protect them and the groups. The most cited study is that of Yalom (1966) who developed a list of nine categories that characterized early departers: (1) external factors, (2) group deviancy, (3) problems of intimacy, (4) fear of emotional contagion, (5) inability to share the doctor, (6) complications of concurrent individual and group therapy, (7) early provocateurs, (8) inadequate orientation to group therapy, (9) complications arising from subgrouping.

Reexamination of Yalom's data suggests an alternative way of categorizing his information. As Yalom suggests, the categories do not clearly separate individuals, which makes it difficult to use the various categories. Using the tripartite perspective of (1) intrapsychic defense mechanisms, (2) interpersonal relatedness, and (3) group-related factors allows for a reassessment of the material.

The data on dropouts should also be considered from the perspective of the treatment process, since dropping out generally occurs as a result of the patient's interaction with other group members, the therapist, or emerging group norms. For instance, a patient who is fearful of intimacy might present with externalization, denial, or somatization; depending on the perspective of the observer, the same patient could be seen as deviant, an early provocateur, having fears of emotional contagion, or having difficulty sharing the doctor. Further, the individual characterological styles of patients interact with group processes. Some groups, for example, can tolerate silent, withdrawn members for long periods, whereas others may welcome an individual who is provocative, outspoken, and occasionally acts out.

The group agreements (see Chapter 7) highlight certain additional exclusionary criteria. Patients who cannot realistically be expected to abide by their agreements, owing to either pathology or life circumstances (as, for example, the professional athlete who cannot commit to a regular, weekly meeting because of his team's travel schedule) should not be included in group therapy. A problem also arises with individuals who may have planned an extended period away prior to their entry into the group, for example, the school teacher who will be away for 2 months in the summer or an individual who anticipates elective surgery and an extended convalescent period. Sometimes group leaders desirous of filling their groups will allow such members to join. Inevitably, however, these "special cases" prove difficult for all concerned. If at all possible the entry of such patients should be deferred until a more continuous commitment can be made.

In summary, we have identified four subgroups in the poor risk category: (1) patients in crisis as a result of either an adult developmental stress or an outbreak of uncontrolled psychopathology; (2) patients who have significant difficulty with impulse control, usually due to organicity or sociopathy, and who might best be treated in a homogeneous group; (3) patients with characterological defenses of major magnitude that severely diminish interpersonal relatedness. These defenses become a problem when a conflict develops between these character styles and group norms. However, we do need to underline the fact that we refer to *major* problems with interpersonal relatedness. Obviously many severely disturbed individuals are best treated in groups. (4) Patients who are unable or unwilling to accept the group agreements. Our caveat regarding these criteria is a recognition that we have not reached a stage of sophistication enabling us to predict a specific individual's success or failure in therapy. As a result, we opt for an optimistic appraisal regarding the usefulness of groups for even those patients with major difficulties in interpersonal relatedness, and we are likely to put them in our groups. The interaction between character styles and group composition can either enable or frustrate these individuals' participation.

PATIENTS FOR WHOM GROUP
IS THE TREATMENT OF CHOICE

Stein (1963) approached the problem of selection primarily from a psychodynamic perspective. He suggested that group treatment would be appropriate for patients who exhibited intense, sticky transferences in individual treatment; those with superego problems, particularly patients with overly strict superegos; patients with obsessive–compulsive features and guilt; and those who need ego support and reality testing through identification with others. As a corollary to the problem of intense transference, Stein noted that other members served as displacement objects, enabling an individual to work on problems without the disruptive intensity of an individual transference. Examined thirty years later, Stein's criteria are suggestive of patients diagnosed as having preoedipal psychopathology. Perhaps this schema served to direct the therapist to a position of understanding rather than categorizing, thus enabling the clinician to include more comfortably, these patients into group treatment.

Guttmacher and Birk (1971) expanded Stein's list by emphasizing the therapeutic advantages of the here-and-now axis of group therapy. This axis can be used as a selection criterion by focusing on those patients who can learn from confrontation. Patients who fulfill this criterion do not view themselves as responsible for the conflicts they experience; their pathology is ego-syntonic. Groups offer repeated opportunity for such patients to get feedback about the effect of their behaviors on others; moreover, because of the group experience, such behaviors gradually become ego-dystonic and thus more amenable to change. The increased interaction and the development of multiple transferences is not necessarily equivalent to the dilution and diminution of transference reactions (see Ethan, 1978). Guttmacher and Birk, for instance, emphasize that the frustration evoked by having to share the therapist can expose intense and important conflicts around envy and rivalry.

Kadis, Krasner, Winick, and Foulkes (1963) proposed a slightly different schema for selecting patients, also on the basis of dynamic considerations. They suggested that patients be assessed across four dimensions: (1) ability to tolerate anxiety, including the potential for disruptive anxiety upon entering a group; (2) identification and empathy with others, including the background and similarity of experiences that would allow them to sit with others; (3) ego strength, including vulnerability to interpersonal stress and the potential to tolerate attacks, criticism, or closeness; (4) interlocking of patients' defense systems. The first three criteria are designed to predict the kinds of responses a patient might exhibit upon entering treatment. The fourth dimension is specifically a group-related criterion and is used to predict whether or not patients' characteristic defenses will work well together or clash with those of other members.

Zimmerman (1976) also considered group-related dimensions in the selection process. He emphasized the ability of prospective patients to maintain a sense of self in the face of group processes that might be experienced as sucking them into an undifferentiated mass. Patients who might be vulnerable to that pull are described as adhering inflexibly to social, professional, political, or moral positions; they may appear arrogant, pedantic, and extremely prideful (characteristics reminiscent of the deviant whom Yalom, 1966, pinpointed as a possible early group dropout). In pregroup interviews, Zimmerman evaluated an applicant's ability to change roles, for example, to move from listener to speaker to empathizer and so on. He also raised questions about the patient's ability to maintain confidentiality and secrets, and he suggested that persons in politically or socially prominent roles, or their relatives, be excluded.[1]

In contrast to the dynamic classifications are the behavioral/phenomenological approaches, which consider as appropriate for group membership those patients who have problems with intimacy or who lead lonely, isolated, dreary lives, that is, patients who avoid social situations or have a paucity of intimate personal relationships. Conversely, patients who are overdependent or overdemanding are recommended for group therapy in order to dilute these behaviors (Neumann & Geoni, 1974). Classifications such as these tend to emphasize problems in effective interpersonal functioning that fall at both ends of a continuum (Grunebaum & Kates, 1977): At one end are the withdrawn, socially inept, uninvolved individuals, at the other end the demanding, self-centered, and controlling ones. In this view groups are expected to act as equalizers by activating those who are withdrawn and socializing the more narcissistic, self-centered, or acting-out individuals.

Recommendations regarding the inclusion of patients with somatic complaints seem to follow the trends we have already noted. Some therapists believe these are precisely the patients who can learn about themselves and their inner world. Others believe somatization is a poor prognostic sign since such patients will not have the psychological mindedness necessary to utilize psychoanalytic group psychotherapy most effectively.

Interest has been growing regarding patients with alexithymia, a term coined by Sifneos (1972) to describe individuals who have no words

[1]Cultural differences could account for this suggestion, since Zimmerman reported on work conducted in Brazil. Grotjahn (1975), in a contrary opinion, described successful integration of famous people in his groups.

for feelings. Initially, this deficit was thought to be characteristic of patients with psychosomatic illnesses. But difficulty identifying inner feelings exists in varying degrees, and the concept was subsequently recognized as applicable to patients fitting many diagnostic categories. Characteristically, these individuals are referred to treatment by a significant other or by a physician who has been unsuccessful in treating the various physical complaints they present. Patients may complain of feeling isolated or misunderstood, even though there is an external facade of sociability. In dyadic treatment they are frustrated and frustrating as sessions are often bland and affectless. Referrals to group therapy are sometimes made when therapists become discouraged because progress in the dyadic work has been minimal or nonexistent; thus, these patients often come to group feeling they have failed. For some such patients, however, the group provides an opportunity to directly participate in the affective experience of others, which assists in their identifying their own feelings.

Intimately associated with the problem of alexithymia is the difficulty some patients have in empathizing with others. Difficulty in identifying others' feelings, in linking behavior with affects, and in understanding the emotional meaning of members' interactions are some manifestations of deficits in empathy (Kleinberg, 1991). Swiller (1988) recommends that these patients be treated in concurrent group and individual therapy.

GROUP THERAPY AS TODAY'S
TREATMENT OF CHOICE

At this time, accumulated experience indicates that almost all patients are potential candidates for group psychotherapy. The pathologies of the modern era are primarily difficulties in gaining and tolerating authentic intimacy. The majority of our patients come with complaints about the lack of fulfillment in their lives (see Chapter 1). "Group therapy, by its very format, offers unique opportunities to experience and work on issues of intimacy and individualization. In . . . groups, the community is represented in the treatment room. It is usually impossible for individuals to view themselves as existing alone and affecting no one when in a group therapy situation over any significant period of time" (Rutan & Alonso, 1979, p. 612). Group therapy seems to be a natural antidote to the predominant disorder of our age. Since groups focus on individuals as relational beings and rely on relationships for growth, learning, and change, this treatment offers a response to modern mankind's fragmented ability to relate. Groups offer the hope of relatedness in the context of appropriate limits, an opportunity to gain autonomy *through* intimacy, not at the expense of intimacy.

Thus, if group therapy is the treatment of choice for our modern dilemmas, we should be concerned primarily with inclusionary rather than exclusionary criteria. The two major groups that are excluded are patients who refuse to enter a group and those for whom group is not the treatment of choice. The first instance, while seemingly obvious, requires emphasis. No patient should be forced, overtly or covertly, to join a group. If a patient does not willingly join, no matter how convinced the therapist is that group is the treatment of choice, that patient is a poor candidate for successful treatment. Frequently, we find that such patients will join a group at a later date.

The final success or failure of therapy will depend upon the complex interaction between members, therapist, and the treatment process itself. There can be little doubt that different therapists have varying levels of comfort with different patients and pathologies. Therefore, the therapist's affective reaction certainly affects the group's capacity to help particular patients. Some therapists, for example, are uncomfortable with homosexual or alcoholic or overaggressive patients, and such patients ought to be excluded from the groups of *those* particular therapists. Moreover, much of the material in the professional literature about who can and cannot be included probably has been influenced by personal bias and countertransference.

SPECIAL CONSIDERATIONS IN DIAGNOSING AND EVALUATING PATIENTS

It is our contention that group therapy should be considered as a viable option for most patients seeking treatment. Just raising the prospect of joining a group often evokes a powerful reaction. It is not unusual that a patient reacts to the idea of joining a therapy group according to his/her primary presenting problem. A patient coming to treatment with anxiety, for example, often gets anxious at the prospect of joining a group. To the degree that a patient's reaction to joining a group mirrors the presenting problems, group might be seen as an exceptionally valuable therapeutic experience because the primary problems will be immediately apparent for examination and exploration. When patients see the connection between their presenting concerns and their interpersonal relations, they often willingly enter groups.

A great many patients who are potential group candidates spend a considerable amount of consultative time preoccupied with interpersonal difficulties. For instance, they might complain about their spouse, boss, children, or friends in a seemingly endless litany. However, no change takes place and the troubles persist. Before group therapy can be effective, it is often necessary to help these patients begin to accept some personal responsibility for the interpersonal difficulties that beset them. As long as they project all problems onto others, they remain uninsightful and resistant to change. When this ego-syntonic behavior is not quite so ingrained, a group can help such patients begin to see their contributions to their interpersonal impasses. In all diagnostic evaluations it is important to listen for and focus on a patient's interpersonal transactions. When it seems clear that this arena is central to the presenting concern of the patient, group therapy should be actively considered as the primary treatment.

In cases where the patient becomes *too* involved with the therapist, the transference becomes unmanageably powerful. In the past these patients were labeled "overly dependent," but more modern formulations emphasize the need such patients have for an idealizing transference in order to recommence an interrupted developmental process (Kohut, 1971, 1977; W. Stone, 1992). By virtue of the presence of the other patients, groups provide a helpful distance from the therapist for such patients. In many cases this allows them to examine more objectively their feelings about the therapist and to compare and contrast their responses with those of others. An exception to this is the patient for whom jealousy and possessiveness are so strong that the presence of other people in the therapeutic arena is simply overwhelming.

As we review the criteria for selecting patients for group therapy, we would also suggest that the psychopathology of the prospective group member is not the only consideration in the selection process. A therapist who rejects several successive group applicants might review the cases with a colleague to determine if the decisions, in part, were based on countertransference. Such decisions might be based on reactions to common characteristics of the patients or to the referral source. Clinicians also need to take into account systems issues impacting upon their decision making. In today's economy many therapists are pressured to begin groups and to keep them full in order to decrease waiting lists or increase productivity. Referrals from colleagues who have been frequent suppliers of members may be difficult to turn down, even though the therapist recognizes that particular patients present with a number of high-risk characteristics.

Factors related to functioning of the group also require scrutiny. If the census is low and the therapist fears that members' morale will deteriorate or that the group will disband, there is a greater tendency to accept new members, in part to reassure those already present. An opposite situation occurs, often in clinic settings with relatively inex-

perienced therapists, when clinicians reject suitable candidates because
they fear the response of those already in the group; the common rationalization for this decision, which is based in part on more specific
countertransference, is that the prospect is too ill and will disrupt the
group.

EXAMPLES OF THE PATIENT
EVALUATION AND SELECTION PROCESS

Example I: Sister Annette

Sister Annette was a 33-year-old nun who sought psychotherapy for
her heightened anxiety. She felt her anxiety was rooted in her flagging
dedication to the church and to her religious beliefs. However, she could
not gain any precision in describing what doubts she was having about
her faith. As was the custom of the evaluating therapist, the prospect
of group therapy was mentioned. Sister Annette immediately became
very anxious and stated that she could *"never* be in a therapy group."
When the therapist inquired why, she said, "There would be all those
men there talking about sex. It would be no place for a nun." Using
the projected data gained from her guesses about what a group would
be like, Sister Annette was soon able to see that her anxiety was actually stemming from heightened sexual feelings and corresponding guilt
about them. In light of this she decided to enter a therapy group to
see what she could find out about her sexuality in the safety of a therapeutic setting. In the course of several years of group therapy this patient was able to own, explore, and become comfortable with her
sexuality. Eventually, she decided to retain her vows of chastity and
to remain in the convent, and she was able to continue her career without
the anxiety that had brought her to treatment.

This case illustrates how the mere mention of a therapy group can
evoke powerful and important affects that can assist in the diagnostic
and dispositional process. When the specific affect aroused is closely
connected to the presenting complaint, group therapy can be seriously
considered. Even if there is no obvious connection between the two,
sometimes the feelings stimulated are of sufficient importance that patient and therapist agree that group could be very helpful.

Example II: Bill

Bill was a young man who seemed psychologically minded. He complained that he was a 28-year-old virgin in a social milieu in which

dating leading to intercourse was the norm. Bill felt blocked in his understanding of why he could not date successfully. The external focus of his individual therapy, which was fascinating and rewarding for the therapist since Bill vividly described his inner world in a creative and captivating manner, was on Bill's continuing conflict with bosses at work; there was an absence of discussion of peer relationships and no mention of dating. When the therapist initially suggested that group therapy be added to his individual treatment, Bill engagingly described that the suggestion had evoked feelings as powerful as an avalanche in his mind. The anxiety that he experienced was so intense that he declined the suggestion. Nevertheless, no change in his life was occurring, and several months later the therapist again suggested group treatment, explaining that Bill rarely spoke about troubles with dating and his social life, despite these being his initial reasons for seeking treatment. Again Bill refused, but with less anxiety and vehemence. Six months later, he himself raised the question of his entering a group, saying he felt his individual therapy was at an impasse. In the course of his group treatment Bill was able to examine his anxiety about sexuality, his competitiveness with men, and his seductiveness with women. After joining a group, he made important personal gains.

This example indicates how group can be added to individual therapy to assist the patient. Bill shifted from interpersonal to authority problems in the individual treatment and subsequently became stuck in a transference impasse that seemed to preclude examination of the presenting peer and social problems. The referral to a group loosened that therapy impasse. It should also be noted that the referral did not occur quickly and that the therapist's willingness to raise the issue, offer the suggestion, and accept Bill's refusal was ultimately rewarded when Bill himself was able to initiate the referral.

Example III: Carl

Carl was referred as a candidate for a group because of his anxiety and depression over his wife's threats to initiate a separation and divorce. Carl, though a very successful executive businessman, had almost no awareness of his inner world. Indeed, his history was so bereft of any close relationships that it was remarkable that he had managed to marry. Group therapy had been suggested to him by a previous therapist because of the barrenness of his interpersonal world. However, the evaluating therapist did not accept Carl into a therapy group. Rather, it was determined that Carl was not well suited on at least two counts: First, he was in immediate crisis; he was reeling from the prospect of losing his only viable relationship, and he was quite desperate. He would not find it easy to put that desperation aside long enough to meet, trust, and negotiate some relationship with a series of strangers in a therapy group. Second, Carl's interpersonal skills appeared so impoverished that it was likely he would be overwhelmed, not assisted, by a group. Carl was referred again for individual psychotherapy when he began to gain insight into how disconnected from his feelings he had been and how that meant that he was dramatically shortchanging his wife in their marriage.

This example highlights a case where the screening therapist decided group therapy was not the treatment of choice. The patient in this case quite willingly accepted the referral, but the group therapist, after evaluating the patient's crisis around the divorce, recommended a period of individual therapy before exposing him to the more stimulating interaction in a therapy group.

Example IV: Duane

Duane was referred for severe headaches that had forced him to take a leave of absence from work. He had consulted numerous physicians in an attempt to find a definitive diagnosis, but to no avail. Two psychiatrists were consulted, but both were unsuccessful in engaging Duane in self-exploration. The third psychiatrist he found was able to initiate a usable alliance, and Duane was able to begin looking into interpersonal stresses in his life. History revealed that just prior to the onset of his headaches, Duane had learned that his supervisor would be changing jobs and that he himself was in line for a promotion. To Duane a promotion meant giving up his old relationships and joining the ranks of management. Even more important, during the same time period, Duane's wife had taken a full-time job outside the home and was no longer devoting herself exclusively to the housework and care for their 12-year-old son. Duane recognized that these were both important events, but he could see no connection between them and his headaches. Despite repeated suggestions for group therapy, Duane maintained his conviction that his was a biological problem. He was referred to a pain clinic.

This example is cited to indicate the importance of negotiation in referring a patient to group therapy. If any modality of psychotherapy is to work, it is almost mandatory that the patient have some understanding of, and agreement with, the reasons for selecting the modality chosen. Duane could never accept the rationale for group therapy, and thus he was not referred to a group.

SUMMARY

In this chapter we have examined guidelines for the evaluation and selection of applicants for group psychotherapy. Historically, economic considerations have been paramount in selecting patients for groups. In more recent times a great deal of attention has been devoted to exclusion criteria and much less to inclusion criteria. Diagnostic classification systems that might assist in formulating inclusion criteria were reviewed. These systems utilize both intrapsychic formulations and interpersonal behavioral criteria. However, no single current system fully accounts for the complex situation of an individual with strengths and weaknesses entering a particular group with its own values, norms, history, and interacting individuals. In this chapter we have also presented brief vignettes illustrating some of the more common problems for which patients are referred to group therapy; they also demonstrate the initial resistances, contradictions, and steadfast refusal with which patients may respond to suggestions that they consider the treatment modality of group therapy.

Once individuals have been selected as suitable for treatment in group therapy, three tasks remain for the therapist: One is to determine which group will be best for the patient and which patient will be best for which group; issues of group composition will be explored in the next chapter. The second task is to prepare the patient for entrance into a therapy group, and the third task is to negotiate the group agreements with the patient. The last two tasks will be explored in Chapter 7.

6

Issues of Group Composition

Successful psychotherapy groups require careful planning. The task is not simply to gather six to ten individuals together, set a time, and commence. Rather, the enterprise requires a substantial foundation. In this chapter we will examine issues related to one part of that foundation, the composition of the group. The first step is to ascertain whether there is a need in the community for a therapy group and whether it can be supported by patient referrals. After he finds that the need and the support exist, the therapist can turn his attention to how to form the group most effectively.

A SYSTEMATIC APPROACH
TO PATIENT RECRUITMENT

Patient Availability

All too often new groups are formed in response to the enthusiasm of the therapist without regard to the realities of patient availability. It is very disheartening to have a new group with only two or three members and no referrals in sight. Thus, it is necessary at the outset to assess whether or not there is reasonable expectation that a flow of patients will be available. It is not enough to ask if there are sufficient patients currently available to begin a group. One must also determine if there will be sufficient referrals in the future to guarantee successful continuation of the group.

Even if the therapist determines that there is an ample supply of patients who need a group, this does not mean there will be a sufficient number of patients who choose to join! Helping patients overcome their fears and join a group is a delicate task (see the description of research by Budman et al. and by Klein and Caroll in Chapter 5). Ultimately, it is much easier to find patients for preexisting groups than for new ones, since both the therapist and potential referring sources have some "feel" for the existing group and have confidence that a potential new member will fit comfortably in that group.

The Treatment Milieu

Even if it is determined that a group is *needed,* this does not ensure its success. It is important to make certain that the referring community will support the enterprise. If group treatment is a new modality or is not actively supported in a particular setting, important preliminary steps have to be taken to create a favorable atmosphere.

Historically, group psychotherapy, as compared with individual psychotherapy, has been perceived as a second-class modality. Such devaluation highlights the first task of the clinician: to educate his or her colleagues about the efficacy of group therapy. Similarly, if the social milieu emphasizes behavioral or pharmacological treatment approaches and is not attuned to psychodynamic/analytic modalities, the possibility of obtaining referrals will be limited unless the therapist demonstrates the potential of group therapy to help patients. It is not only good practice but also good public relations to give feedback to clinicians who have referred patients to your group.

Clinic Settings

In a clinic the therapist needs to understand and relate to the administrative and authority structures (McGee, 1969), and the institution must be prepared to support a group program. Such preparation includes consultation with those in authority as well as with colleagues and associates who may directly influence the availability of patients. Discussions should allow for expressions of both positive and negative responses. It is important to develop sensitivity to the administrative problems posed by therapy groups, such as the need for larger interviewing and waiting rooms, for greater soundproofing, and for clerical support. Subtle administrative resistance may emerge if these details are not openly discussed.

Clinics in which groups do not enjoy a ready-made acceptance will also benefit from an educational program for the staff. Although the program may consist of didactic presentations at staff meetings, a better approach is for the therapist to permit a small number of staff members to actually observe a newly formed group in operation for a number of weeks. With patients' consent it is possible to have observers without adversely affecting the treatment (if there are to be observers, consent should be included in the initial group agreements). The observers can be introduced as members of the clinic staff who wish to learn more about group therapy. Such direct involvement typically engages staff in an immediate and active interest in the program, but if it is not practical, the therapist should speak often with the referring therapists so that everyone continues to feel involved with the workings of the group.

It is particularly important to ensure that persons with the power of referral support the program, since the flow of patients has an enormous impact upon the formation of groups (Johnson & Howenstein, 1982). The classic study by Yalom (1966) on dropouts is a striking testimonial of this: At the outpatient clinic of Stanford University, Yalom was able to start nine new groups within a period of 8 weeks simply by administratively closing off the option of individual treatment and routing all new patients to group psychotherapy. The fact that nine groups could be started in such a short time is ample evidence of the effectiveness of administrative clout. (Furthermore, follow-up research indicated that these patients reported satisfaction with their treatment equal to that expressed by patients who had been carefully selected and referred.)

Availability of patients can also be influenced by broad social factors. For instance, recent public policy has sharply reduced the number of long-term patients hospitalized in state facilities, leading to large numbers of patients being referred into the community for continuing care. Clinic administrators often see group psychotherapy as a solution to the increasing press of patients upon limited clinic resources, but groups for this population are often slow to develop. As concerns over containment of medical services costs mount, expensive long-term individual treatment is being limited. It is uncertain if group therapy will provide a substitute therapeutic modality, but a report by the Group for the Advancement of Psychiatry (1992) predicts that in the future most psychotherapy will be brief and conducted in groups. Nevertheless, external pressures may then interfere with the therapist's ability to properly screen and select patients.

When all is said and done, economic hardship and increased regulation of psychotherapy by third-party payers make the present age very conducive to the practice of group therapy in clinic settings.

Private Practice

The private sector is not insulated from psychosocial forces nor from the need to educate and support a referral network. Insurance coverage has become limited. HMOs, PPOs, and a variety of managed care systems increasingly monitor and limit the type, duration, and cost of psychological treatment. The impact of these practices on actual practice remains uncertain. Group therapists quickly find that they need to develop a sizable network of referral sources. Some communities do not value group therapy as much as others do, and in those communities the flow of patients is negligible unless the therapist is willing to actively promote his or her group. In such a situation the therapist may occasionally feel pressured to select unsuitable or inappropriate patients in order to sustain a slim referral network or even to keep a group alive. This usually results in dysfunction in the group.

The opposite situation also has its difficulties. An established group therapist may be inundated with referrals and lack places in groups for new members. However, too frequent rejection of referrals tends to stem the flow of referrals and keeping the spigot flowing at an optimal rate is a problem. A therapist can often keep the referral network intact by locating an opening in some other group as a service to both the patients and the professionals who make referrals. Therapists who provide an ombudsman function keep their own referral network flourishing.

THE THERAPIST'S EMOTIONS

Beginning and running groups is a highly emotional experience for therapists. Sometimes the emotions involved in forming a group adversely affect the group's beginning. For example, therapists beginning a group can obtain patients from their own individual caseloads. While there is debate in the field as to the advisability of seeing the same patient in both individual and group therapy, we are convinced this is both a viable and extremely powerful modality; the chance to see our patients in both the dyadic and interpersonal setting offers comprehensive treatment opportunities. The shift in treatment modality involves either giving up the individual sessions or providing combined individual and group treatment, and either situation can stir potent feelings in the therapist. Ironically, therapists sometimes have difficulty shifting patients from individual to group treatment, whether or not they plan to continue the individual sessions. Exploration of this difficulty often exposes countertransference problems. Therapists beginning a group should review their own individual cases in search of members. If they are reluctant to refer a number of individuals for similar or identical reasons, a countertransference reaction may well underlie the decisions. For example, a therapist sometimes feels protective of a particular patient and does not want to expose the patient to potential criticism in a group. Or perhaps the therapist is unwilling to put a patient who is in the midst of a powerful negative transference into a group lest that patient stimulate similar negative feelings toward the therapist in other group members. Consultation or discussion with coworkers can help resolve these countertransference problems. Occasionally, the result of the clinician's increased self-awareness is increased patient flow, as the therapist comes to recognize and alter those subtle communications to colleagues that previously interfered with their making referrals.

One argument against seeing one's individual patients in group therapy is that it causes undue rivalry and competition among the members. In fact, in all groups there is *always* great competition and rivalry and great concern over whom the therapist prefers and to whom he or she grants most attention. The addition of one's individual patients to a group does not *cause* this dynamic and in fact often facilitates its exploration.

There are instances when therapists should *not* accept a patient referred from an individual therapist. Often, for example, there are overlooked countertransferential reasons for the referral. One frequent countertransference reason entails the individual therapist referring a patient to group therapy in order to avoid the unrecognized, intimate *warm* and *loving* feelings that exist in the dyadic relationship. Since many patients are referred to the group principally because they have difficulty in establishing or maintaining tender relationships, a referral under these conditions represents an unconscious collusion by the individual therapist and the patient to avoid the intensity of their affect.

Another manifestation of countertransference is dumping unattractive patients into groups. Many times when an individual clinician finds it impossible to treat a patient, he or she concludes, "This patient needs a group," when what is really meant is, "Perhaps other patients can say directly to this patient what I, as a professional caretaker, do not feel I have a right to say!" Such a referral to a therapy group and the termination from individual therapy will be very complicated. It is not unusual for patients referred to group therapy under such circumstances to have an extremely difficult time making the transition to group treatment.

Ironically, the patient who cannot even establish a viable relationship in dyadic therapy is typically *not* a very good candidate for a group. Further, such patients sense that they are being dumped, it is often an experience in life about which they have some expertise. When the referral is an attempt to avoid dealing with unpleasant sides of the individual therapy, the patient often retaliates by quitting the group prematurely. Whenever a group therapist receives a referral of a patient who will be terminating individual therapy, it is important to fully assess the individual therapy relationship to ensure that this does not represent acting out on the part of the individual therapist or the patient—or both. The group therapist can often be a valuable consultant to the individual therapy by anticipating the dynamics of the individual termination process and the transfer to a group. In most instances frank discussion of the termination and how future individual contact should be handled will aid in smoothing this sensitive phase of treatment.

The reason for considering some of the less complimentary reasons for group referrals is that knowledge of these reasons, which are very often unconscious or not discussed, will help both individual and group therapists in the ongoing treatment of patients. For a great many group patients termination of the individual session is not indicated, and a combination of group and individual therapy is the most useful treatment format. This combination is explored in depth in Chapter 13.

Once patient flow has been established, the therapist next faces the problem of how to decide which patient is best seen in which group and, in addition, which patients are best for which groups.

DETERMINING THERAPY GROUP COMPOSITION

The composition of a group may be viewed from two perspectives: The referring therapist wants to determine whether there is a group best suited for his or her patient. The group therapist has to determine which patient is best suited for a particular group. In this chapter we will look at the issues of group composition from both perspectives.

Which Group Is Best for the Patient?

A few authors (e.g., Bach, 1954) suggest that it is not helpful to place patients in groups according to some notion of which groups are best for them. According to this point of view, groups should model life and patients should therefore be referred solely according to who comes along next. While the pragmatics of private practice sometimes make this more the rule than the exception, such a practice is nonetheless far from optimal. One of the fundamental screening tasks is to determine the best fit for patient and group. Questions such as "Should the patient be in a group with a male or a female leader or with coleaders?" are important. Often, if a patient is currently in ongoing individual psychotherapy, it is helpful if the group therapist is of the opposite sex from the individual therapist.

More frequent considerations are the level of functioning of the group and the characteristics of specific members. Prior to adding a new member, the therapist should review the group's predominant themes. Some groups deal with fundamental issues of trust for years, others characteristically struggle with anger, and still others might be concerned with intimacy, individuation, or competitiveness. The presence of a patient who is working at a different level may even catalyze particularly painful but important sectors of pathological functioning in group members that could otherwise go unexplored, but the therapist should not count on this happening. The screening therapist should always judge whether potential new members for a given group are similar enough to the others so that they can connect with one another and yet different enough so that they can help one another gain perspective on the problems with which they struggle. In the following paragraphs are suggested ways to assess the compatibility of specific groups for specific patients.

Preliminary Formulations

By attending to the presenting problems and listening to the interpersonal history of a potential group member, it is usually possible to generate several viable hypotheses as to the origins of the problems. These data can be discussed with the patient as a part of the negotiation about choice of treatment modality; the formulations will also be useful to the therapist in predicting the patient's probable course in the group. For example, many patients unknowingly are unable to form relationships because they suffer from insufficiently mourned losses. It can be hypothesized that in the life of the group someone important to the patient will terminate and that this will offer the patient an opportunity to relive loss experiences.

In many cases the major source of data about the interpersonal life of a patient is the dyadic relationship. If therapists will pay special heed to their affective responses to the patient, they will gain access to a veritable gold mine of information. For example, if the therapist is bored or easily distracted and feels "alone" in the office or wishes the clock would speed up, the chances are that he or she is sitting with a schizoid, obsessional, or primitive narcissistic patient (excluding the obvious alternative that the therapist is struggling with personal issues of his or her own that are not evoked by the patient at all). Alternatively, a borderline patient is almost never boring; he or she may be frightening, stimulating, enraging, entertaining, or demanding—but rarely boring. In the first instance the individual therapy can founder on the rock-hard defenses of intellectualization and isolation of affect, and with a borderline patient the therapist may be held at a distance by the aggressive, hyperactive self-presentation. For many of the former patients, eventual exposure of the underlying conflicts reveals that noninvolvement is a defense against perceived terrors and dangers of intimacy. A very important component of this is the fear of a nonresponse by an unempathic significant person (Wogan, Getter, Anidur, Nichols, & Okman, 1977).

Sometimes patients can be assisted in joining a group by helping them link their affective reactions to the prospect of joining the group with the affects that trouble them in life. It is rare that patients have brand-new responses to the thought of joining a group, rather, they usually conjure up expectations honestly earned from their personal history and have affective reactions to them.

Hypotheses About Patient Roles and Reactions

Using the data from the pregroup evaluation, the therapist can make inferences about how the patient may respond to various stimuli in the group. Through generation of such hypotheses and observations of the subsequent behaviors and feelings of the patient, formulations can be either validated or disproved. If major revisions are necessary, this may be the result of new information or faulty empathic connection between therapist and patient. At the same time, the therapist can gain a historical vantage point that may be utilized in helping the patient understand the connections between in-group responses and those from the past (Rutan & Alonso, 1978).

CLINICAL EXAMPLE

Elaine came to group to work on her terror of intimacy with men. Successful individual therapy had given her much insight into the roots of her difficulties, but she wanted to join a group in order to gain actual opportunities to meet and relate to men at an intense level. In her individual therapy she worked on accepting the reality that the women in her family were flawed, her mother being psychotic and usually mute and her sister being retarded. Elaine, though raised by a loving aunt, nonetheless had an image of herself as defective and inadequate. The therapist, after having interviewed Elaine and negotiated the group agreements, decided to place her in a particular group because he hypothesized that a woman in that group, Francine, would stir very important, though painful, feelings for Elaine. Francine was a seriously depressed and very silent member, often not speaking for months in the group. Within 2 or 3 weeks, Elaine stated that she was leaving the group because she found it was not helping and because she was getting more anxious. She stated that she was having difficulty sleeping the night before the group meeting. In this case the therapist, having made a preliminary hypothesis, simply said, "A family with women who are silent when you need them to be helpful is a familiar problem, Elaine." Despite the fact that Elaine had never mentioned Francine, she instantly began weeping and yelling at Francine for being so "hostile." In the ensuing weeks both Francine and Elaine worked very productively on the meaning of their interactions.

This represents an example of a therapist carefully selecting a group for a patient based upon hypotheses about how the specific group might be of assistance.

In assessing an individual's "fit" for a particular group, several areas should be explored. First, the patient's ability to experience and reflect upon his or her interactions, an indicator of ego capacity, must be considered. Some patients become emotionally enmeshed in the group interactions and have very limited ability to focus their observing ego on the affect stirred in the therapy. Other patients are so intellectualized in their defensive structure that they never allow themselves to spontaneously "be" in the group. The goal of the therapist with respect to the first subgroup of patients is to help them develop the ability to move from experience to observation and intellectual understanding whereas the goal for the second subgroup is to help them experience the impact of the interactions before using their intellect. The therapist should be wary of having too many patients representing either end of that continuum simultaneously in the same group.

A second consideration is the patient's ability to take on a variety of roles. Traditionally, the roles of leader and follower are explored. The leader role is linked to an individual's relationship to authority and developmental experiences with parents, the follower role to peer relationships in which collaboration, cooperation, and intimacy are associated and can be traced to early sibling or educational experiences. In addition, a series of other significant roles may be productively explored in the pregroup interviews. Benne and Sheats (1948) distinguished among roles that facilitate group progress and problem-solving capacity, maintain or build the way the group is working together, or satisfy individual needs. The applicant's capacity to work effectively or ineffectively within organizations and social settings provides clues as to potential group roles. Both leader and follower roles are available for all members. Taking a detailed history of the patient's functioning on committees, teams, work groups and other social groups will provide predictive information regarding the role the patient will likely assume in a therapy group. More often than not, individuals seeking group therapy have histories of functioning poorly as leaders and followers in other groups. Thus, we usually find individuals who have proclivities toward being harmonizers, compromisers, standard setters, opinion givers, moralizers, and so forth.

A third consideration is the patient's capacity to acknowledge a need for others. Following the tenets of object relations theory, we believe that *everyone,* irrespective of pathology, wants and can profit from the experience of intimacy, that is, of loving and being loved. One accurate means of diagnosing individuals may well be to assess how much they try to deny the reality of that need.

The emphasis on experiential training groups in the 1960s highlighted an additional criterion particularly relevant to group therapy: the ability to give and receive feedback appropriately. These twin abilities are a central part of the experience in a therapy group. Ormont (1967) places the task of giving feedback in a traditional psychodynamic frame. He succinctly states that patients may express how they feel but may not attack others. His emphasis is on educating members for an appropriate interpersonal role, although he realizes that the ineffectual interpersonal behavior is part of the problem for which a patient seeks help. By highlighting this ground rule Ormont sets the stage for analyzing the difficulty of remaining in the role. We do not recommend making this a part of the group agreements, because it is unfortunate but true that some patients need to work on issues of sadism and rage. However, we are very attentive to sadism in groups and move quickly to interpret it. On the rare occasions when this is insufficient to diminish sadism we take a more active stance, including pointing out the sadism and its effects and stating that such behavior is not useful in the group. (Refer to Chapter 10 for a discussion of extreme cases in which members must be removed from groups.)

Equally important is the patient's ability to listen in an open fashion, without defending or justifying a feeling or position but being able to consider what has been said. Again, such behaviors are not typically part of the repertoire of most patients. By their very nature, groups provide growth-producing experiences for patients to genuinely feel helpful to others and to develop the capacity to listen nondefensively to other people.

A fifth consideration in assessing a prospective patient's "fit" is the patient's empathic capacity, which is a corollary of the capacity to shift roles (Abse, 1974; W. Stone & Whitman, 1980). The ability to empathize, that is, to temporarily put oneself emotionally in the shoes of another, implies that the individual has been able to reach a stage of development where others are experienced as separate, with needs and wishes of their own. Some prospective members possess only rudimentary empathic capacity, and their inclusion in group treatment mandates that this missing function be filled by others — a task that most frequently falls to the therapist. Empathic capacity includes not only empathy for individuals but empathy for the group itself. One aspect of empathy for the group is the requirement of maintaining confidentiality. Some individuals are either too gossipy or need to utilize group information as a base for power or to gain attention and thus cannot adequately respect the tenet of confidentiality. For such patients it is not a question of which group is best; no group is suitable, since their inclusion unduly risks harming the other patients.

A criterion of a different sort is that the applicant have no preexisting relationship with other members that would inhibit the work of the group. It is important during the screening to learn enough about the patient's life and activities to be reasonably certain that a stranger is being introduced into the group. Exploration of a prospective member's work or recreational activities may expose a situation where that person has continuing and significant contact with someone already in the group. Usually awareness of the patient's home address and place of work alerts the therapist to the possibility. If the therapist has reason to believe that a preexisting relationship exists, considerable tact is required to elicit sufficient data on which to base the decision to accept or reject such an applicant. It is clear that certain relationships are of sufficient importance as to limit the freedom to share. This is especially true in work-related situations, where, for example, one member might have administrative responsibility over another member or where a minister might find himself in a group with a parishioner. Many variations of this problem exist, especially in smaller communities, and it is a part of the therapist's responsibility to take reasonable care in protecting the members' anonymity.

Despite precautions, sometimes acquaintances or friends will be placed together in a group; quick decisions must then be made regarding the nature of the group's composition. Once a new member has walked into the room and thereby breached the confidentiality of the others, the decision regarding his or her continuing membership is part of the group process, though the responsibility for such a decision usually rests with the therapist.

CLINICAL EXAMPLES

Following a careful evaluation, a man joined a mature group only to be confronted at the end of the initial meeting by a woman saying that one of her best friends was the new member's steady girlfriend. The woman had realized this part way through the session but had been uncomfortable and had not revealed it until just prior to the end of the session.

The new man then asked what to do, and the therapist stated that the task of the group would be to decide whether this unexpected complication would compromise the therapy of either the new patient or the woman in the group. In the remainder of that session and in the next the group actively discussed the pragmatic difficulties this situation posed as well as a myriad of feelings elicited by it. For example, the woman associated to the lack of privacy she experienced in her home. Ultimately, the group decided this was not a tenable treatment situation, and the new patient accepted the therapist's offer to join another of his groups.

Handling this delicate problem in the group setting modeled for the members of the lesson that nothing is beyond the scope of the group. Further, the full exploration of the feelings evoked by this situation allowed the new member to leave without feeling injured or rejected, and he was able to join a new group quite successfully.

A different situation occurred when a new man entered a group only to discover that many years ago he had been engaged to marry a member of the group. (To add to this surrealistic meeting, it happened that the electricity was out and the meeting was held by candlelight!) Not surprisingly, the two were very surprised to discover each other again after so many years. (This relationship had occurred in another state and there was no way the therapist could have known of it.) That relationship had ended very painfully when the man simply disappeared without a word. The woman was in therapy to deal with her depression, and one significant stimulus for that depression was the failed engagement. She had never married. The man came to therapy because of his terror of intimacy and his lack of contact with his affective life. Ultimately they and the group decided it would be most productive for them to remain in the group. The woman wanted to learn more about what happened in their relationship, and the man felt it would be useful to him to have someone in the group who knew his family and history well in order to help him remember and make connections to his history. They remained in the group many years, and aside from a brief attempt at acting out and resuming their romance (they went out to dinner one evening), they both made excellent progress in their group therapy.

Not every preexisting relationship precludes placing people in the same group in the creation of an optimal therapeutic environment. However, our experience indicates that putting persons with any degree of prior relationship in the same group usually results in havoc and should be avoided. In the event that it is determined that the therapy is untenable, the new patient is always the one to leave.

Which Patients Are Best for the Group?

The therapist has to be concerned with both the individual and the group itself. Ultimately, care should be taken to ensure that the maximum effectiveness of the whole group benefits each individual. Ideally, groups are finely tuned organisms, not conglomerates of randomly selected individuals. Whereas in the previous section the concern was with which groups are best for which patients, in this section the focus is on which patients are best for which groups.

Groups may be established for a variety of reasons. Time-limited groups are often formed on the basis of demography (e.g., women, adolescents, gays), crisis (e.g., divorced or bereaved individuals), or symptom (e.g., alcoholics, anorexics). In such groups the emphasis is upon universality and sameness. The fact that individuals begin with the knowledge that in some fundamental ways they are similar to others means that the initial, trust-building stage will be shorter.

In ongoing treatment, however, the goal is to meld together individuals who are sufficiently alike that they can understand and empathize with one another but sufficiently different that they can offer different perspectives and different strengths to each other. The optimal composition for an ongoing psychodynamic group is for members to be similar in terms of ego development but different in terms of interpersonal style. Furthermore, it is important that each individual have at least one other person in the group with whom he or she can identify, a premise that will be elaborated shortly.

It should be underscored that we are discussing issues of composition for newly forming groups. Mature groups can tolerate and benefit from greater heterogeneity among members; indeed, different levels of ego development become assets. Specifically, the addition of patients with early developmental concerns allows the higher-level patients access into primary process whereas the higher-level patients help the more disturbed patients translate their inner chaos into secondary process. In new groups, however, major disparities in ego development simply frighten the members and make the development of cohesiveness very difficult.

Level of Ego Development

The initial task of any group is to establish enough trust among the members so that the developmental process of the group may commence. Individuals approach trust building from very different perspectives, depending on their psychological health. Healthier patients approach a new group with fundamental trust in others; less healthy patients enter with clear ambivalence about trusting others. The most disturbed pa-

tients enter with an absolute conviction that others are not to be trusted. Individuals from these three separate perspectives would have great
difficulty even understanding one another, much less arriving at some
acceptable level of trust that would allow the group to work.

The same could be said about the primary defenses utilized by
different patients. Healthier patients rely on reality-respecting defenses
(like intellectualization, rationalization, undoing), while sicker patients
rely on reality-distorting defenses (such as projection or reaction formation). Our most primitive patients, on the other hand, utilize reality-
denying defenses (including denial, splitting). Again, mixing these patients will make the task of forming a group quite difficult.

Patients at different developmental levels are attempting to accomplish different tasks in their groups. The healthiest patients are typically working on issues of intimacy and authenticity whereas the most
primitive patients need to work on simply sitting in the room with other
human beings, and developing, to begin with, the most minimal connectedness to others without resorting to splitting.

Age

Newly formed groups should also not span too wide an age range. Individuals in their fifties by and large have different life concerns than
individuals in their twenties. While a wide age range can be beneficial
in more mature groups, it typically makes it more difficult for members of new groups to cohere and have a sense of belonging. New groups
of younger adults ideally should have an age range of approximately
a decade; for older adults (mid-thirties and older), a broader age range
is workable. Further study is needed regarding the issues of adult development and life transitions in order to help us conceptualize age factors more precisely.

Gender

Though women's and men's groups offer a great deal, it is advisable
that ongoing psychotherapy groups be mixed in gender. Because ongoing groups are concerned with helping their members learn as much
as they can about living in the real world, they should include both
men and women. Why rule out half the human population from the
therapy experience? It may be a reasonable alternative for individuals
particularly frightened of the opposite sex to enter a single-gender group
before joining an ongoing mixed group.

Many clinics find that their patient populations are notably skewed with regard to gender. The most usual situation is for clinics to have many more female patients. Under such circumstances, groups may form with all women, with the stated plan that men will be added later. The goal of equal gender distribution may not be attainable, but the situation where there is only one man (or woman) in the group is to be avoided. It is preferable that the group include at least three members of each gender. If one's referral network is such that this is difficult to accomplish, leave chairs open for men or women and wait until there is an appropriate patient; for example, if the desired group size is eight members, then no more than five seats should be filled by one gender.

Interpersonal Style

Whatever the ego development, age, or gender, each patient also has an interpersonal style, which is the external presentation of the person's psychic organization. Patients at any developmental level can be domineering or retiring, gregarious or shy. For purposes of an optimally functioning group, a variety of styles is mandatory; it may well be that a good mix is the single most important aspect of group composition.

Leary (1957) has conceptualized the variety of interpersonal styles in terms of the four quadrants of a circle, with domineering versus submissive styles forming the vertical axis and outgoing versus shy and withdrawing forming the horizontal axis. It is our contention that effective groups have members representing all four interpersonal styles. A group filled with shy and retiring individuals will not have the emotional electricity of one with a variety of interpersonal styles. As the psychic organizations underlying these self-presentations are exposed, individuals have an opportunity to learn about aspects of themselves that have been hidden. We assume that much interpersonal conflict is based on the tendency of group members to disown aspects of themselves that are present in others. Inclusion of patients with diverse styles gives each member the opportunity to learn from the comparisons and contrasts that will inevitably take place.

Thus, in forming a new group, care should be taken to make sure that each interpersonal style—outgoing, shy, dominant, and submissive is represented. If a therapist is filling a vacancy, he or she should take the interpersonal styles represented by the existing members into account in selecting the new member.

SUMMARY

No two groups are identical. As the classical Gestalt psychologists noted, the whole is greater than the sum of the parts, and this is certainly the case in an effective therapy group. The effectiveness depends upon the subtle interplay between the members. Therapists have long noted how dramatically the atmosphere in a group can change when just one member is changed. Thus, therapists must be very sensitive to the twin issues of "Which group is best for each individual patient?" and "Which patient is best for any particular group?"

Once an applicant has been selected and assigned to a group, there remains the task of preparing the applicant to become a member. That issue will be discussed in Chapter 7.

7

Patient Preparation
and the Group Agreements

PATIENT PREPARATION

Controversy exists about the nature and goals of preparing patients for group therapy. By the very existence of a variety of schema, it is evident that no one method has been accepted universally. We believe the process should begin with one or more individual interviews. It is not possible to adequately assess a patient's suitability for group therapy in general or for a particular group without at least some individual time with the patient. Further, it is imperative that each new group member receive and accept the group agreements prior to entering. Finally, patients entering group therapy usually benefit from some preparation, which accomplishes the following:

1. Establishes a preliminary alliance between patient and therapist
2. Establishes a clear consensus about the patient's therapeutic hopes and goals
3. Imparts information and instruction about group psychotherapy
4. Deals with the patient's initial anxiety about joining a group
5. Informs patient about the group agreements and gains patient's acceptance of them

The time required to accomplish these tasks varies according to the therapist's personal preference and experience, and according to the patient's needs. Experienced therapists usually can accomplish them in one visit, especially if the patient comes referred specifically for group therapy (i.e., some of the working through of the idea of group therapy has already been accomplished.) W. Stone and Rutan (1984) found that the number of pregroup interviews does not correlate with patients remaining or terminating prematurely. Some patients need several weeks of preparation whereas others can be prepared in one meeting (see Bader, Bader, Budman, & Clifford, 1981). If a patient has not had prior psychotherapy, it seems wise to arrange a series of individual interviews before the patient joins a group. This helps orient the patient to what psychotherapy is about. Individuals who have not had prior treatment and are not in concurrent individual therapy are at unusually high risk of prematurely dropping out (W. Stone & Rutan, 1984).

Frequently, the response of patients to the referral process and preparatory interview raises questions about their motivation for change. Motivation may be the least rigorously used word in our field since it can be presumed that any patient who seeks therapy is motivated for change. The question is often "What *kind* of change is desired?" Sometimes the wish is simply for symptomatic relief or to satisfy some external pressure; sometimes it is for a magic solution to life's problems. Many times a patient will accept a referral to group therapy out of a wish to please the referring therapist or to avoid some difficult therapeutic impasse in the individual therapy. As therapists discuss elements involved in joining a group and negotiate the group agreements with the applicant, careful attention must be paid to what the patient wants and how the desired goal is to be accomplished. This is the essence of motivation.

Establishing Preliminary Alliances

The minimum task in the screening and evaluation process is for the therapist and patient to meet each other and establish a preliminary working alliance. Given the power of stranger anxiety, many patients experience groups as the most difficult form of psychotherapy to begin. Entering a group is stressful and stimulating, and it is very helpful for entering patients to have at least a minimal alliance with the therapist. For more primitive or frightened patients, this rudimentary alliance is a necessity if they are to get past the early anxiety.

Establishing Consensus on Goals

Misalliance in therapy is often founded on a lack of agreement between therapist and patient as to what the patient really wants (example of Duane in Chapter 5 is typical). Some therapists would have referred Duane to a group because *they* were convinced of its efficacy, despite Duane's unwillingness or inability to see its usefulness. If Duane had

entered a group, it can be assumed that he would have become a "premature terminator."

Any good recommendation for treatment is the result of a negotiation with the patient (Lazare & Eisenthal, 1979; Lazare, Eisenthal,
& Frank, 1979). Group therapy, where the immediate gratification
of contact with and the undivided attention of an individual therapist
is diminished, is all the more dependent upon the patient's understanding and agreeing to embark upon the rigors of the treatment. The
patient who feels forced or seduced into this therapy may find it very
easy to forget the agreements and to look for more gratifying help.
If the patient is a part of the negotiation, a willing and active participant, the times of stress are less likely to result in revoking group
agreements.

Imparting Information About Groups

While many prospective group members have had previous experience
with one or more individual therapists, not many have had prior group
therapy experience. Moreover, since groups evoke intense affect quite
rapidly, patients need to feel grounded by having specific concrete information about how groups work and what they can expect from being in one.

Information can be transmitted in a variety of ways. In addition
to describing the general structure and rationale of group therapy
(Yalom, 1985), some authors suggest giving reading material to prospective members (Gauron & Rawlings, 1975) or didactically explaining
the group process (Wogan et al., 1977). Others have suggested permit-
ting the prospective member to either observe a session behind a two-
way mirror or actually participate in a session, which is then followed
by a discussion (Wogan et al., 1977). Truax and Wargo (1969) studied
the effect of having applicants review excerpts of a tape recording of
a "good" patient in group therapy; those who participated in this
pretraining session showed greater improvement in the three months
of the study than those who had not received the training.

Although good arguments can be made for all the procedures
cited, there is no evidence that any one format leads to fewer early
dropouts or to greater or more rapid success during treatment. Nevertheless, the ideas embodied in the pretraining studies emphasize the need
to prepare patients for the special conditions existing in a psychotherapy group.

Typically, the information about group therapy that applicants are given includes the group agreements, specifics about how the group works, and answers to realistic questions that the patient might raise (e.g., "How many men and how many woman are in the group?"; "How long do people typically stay in your groups?"; "Will I know any of the members?"). Although questions can represent metaphorical statements about deeper concerns, patients have a right to know specifics of the venture they are about to undertake. Bader et al. (1981) note that the group therapist is more active during the screening process than in the group itself and that applicants should be forewarned that the therapist will be less active in the group and, consequently may seem unavailable and distant.

Physical and practical arrangements also should be explained. Patients need to know the day, time, and place of the meeting, along with the fact that these variables are not flexible. Inability to make the time commitment eliminates a patient from further consideration. The day and time of the meeting, as well as fee information, should be mentioned during the initial telephone contact in order to ensure that the applicant can conform to these basic requirements. It is best to provide the remaining orientation material during the presentation of the group agreements.

When members enter existing groups, the veterans quickly take on some information-giving functions, telling the newcomer by word and deed how the group works and what is expected. For example, within a few weeks a new member will likely learn that intense affect is permissible and valued, that dreams are relevant material, and that honesty and self-curiosity are esteemed qualities. In a newly formed group the treatment process and the evolving norms usually provide the data at a pace the members can use.

Dealing with the Initial Anxiety About Joining a Group

Patients are typically quite anxious about joining groups. The therapist should help those whose anxiety is conscious understand that anxiety about joining is universal and should encourage them to explore the specifics of their own anxiety. For patients whose anxiety is unconscious, the therapist should help in raising anxiety to the level of awareness.

Exploration of dreams is one useful approach. If asked, a surprising number of patients will report having had bad dreams just before the initial screening session or between screening sessions. These dreams may be used to bring into focus some of the anxieties that the patient has about the forthcoming treatment.

CLINICAL EXAMPLE

Hedda, a nurse who was consciously very enthusiastic about entering a group, reported that after the initial screening interview she had developed a headache, which she linked to her fear that the group would evoke more feelings than she could manage. She then related a dream she had the evening following the first screening session: "I was in intensive care. I said to the mother of a patient, 'Go ahead and cry; your son has been through a lot, but don't be upset.'" Exploration of the dream revealed some of its meanings: Since group therapy was being added to her individual sessions, this meant an intensification (intensive care) of her treatment, which further stimulated her fears. The end of the dream referred to two of her habitual defenses: supporting someone else ("A lot of people talk to me about their problems") and minimizing or denying anxiety. Further associations were elicited that indicated how physical complaints were used in her family to manipulate others and how during childhood her parents were particularly unavailable to the patient or her siblings because of illness. Ultimately, the children had turned to one another for support, but Hedda was unaware of how competitive they had been for parental attention. The dream brought all this material directly into her awareness as Hedda prepared to enter the group.

Often, useful material about patients' anxieties may be gleaned by directly inquiring into their fantasies about the group or their feelings about joining. The history of an applicant's entry into social groups or organizations will further elucidate typical anxieties and defenses. Therapists need to be sensitive to any subtle communication from prospective members that might inform us about the nature of their anticipatory anxiety.

Presenting and Gaining Acceptance for the Group Agreements

If the individual members are the bricks that make a group, the group agreements are the mortar that binds those parts into a therapeutic whole. As early as 1920 McDougall indicated that the single most important means of harnessing the potent forces residing in groups was the establishment of an overt, mutually agreed upon set of goals and guidelines for rules of behavior.

Unfortunately, the word *contract* is often used by clinicians. This leads to the perception by both patients and therapists that these preconditions to joining a group are a collection of hard-and-fast laws. Our position is that we are trying to establish the structure that will be the most therapeutic. Because patients are expected to take responsibility for their agreements, not blindly adhere to them, we prefer the term *group agreements*. Patients are asked to cooperate with this arrangement; this is a conscious agreement that reflects the level of ego functioning and the therapeutic alliance. However, in the course of therapy both conscious and unconscious forces will result in patients attempting to alter or circumvent the agreements.

The group agreements are not only between the individuals and the leader; although they are established by the leader, they are also between each individual and the entire group. A breach of the agreements affects everyone. We will now present a set of group agreements that has worked well, in our experience, with all psychodynamic therapy groups. Except in the case of some time-limited, homogeneous groups that do not have pregroup sessions, these agreements should be presented to each potential member prior to joining a group and acceptance of these agreements should be a precondition of joining a group.

THE GROUP AGREEMENTS

Members Agree to Be Present Each Week, to Be on Time, and to Remain Throughout the Entire Meeting

We try not to make agreements that are impossible to keep or are inherently conflictual. The first agreement places a high priority on attendance. It is true that there will be occasions when one cannot attend. Some therapists include the provision that a member who is planning to miss a meeting must tell the group in advance or, if that is not possible, must notify the therapist. If patients notify therapists when they will miss a meeting, therapists may simply reveal that they have been notified of the absence or they may also give the reasons cited for the cancellation. In either case the important norm is that absences are discussed and, if possible, the individual and/or groupwide meanings of the absence are explored. When patients miss meetings without prior notification, a different dynamic ensues — and that too can be explored. Through repeated experiences in groups members learn that absences have multiple levels of meanings.

CLINICAL EXAMPLE

In one meeting both a man and a woman were absent. Both members had a conflicting commitment to attend a Cub Scout meeting with their respective sons. In the following session the therapist reflected on the different meanings of the absences. In the man's case he considered the absence a healthy, adaptive choice. This man had come to the group to deal with his distant relationship with his son, and taking time to be with him at one of his activities represented a visible sign of therapeutic growth. The woman's absence was understood very differently; it was seen as a resistance to therapy. Her presenting issue had been symbiotic overinvolvement with her son, and forfeiting her commitments to the group represented another reenactment of the initial problem.

Patients also should understand that the therapist will not be present each and every week. Therapists take vacations, get sick, and go to professional meetings, but they too have a responsibility to notify members appropriately when they will be away. A therapist's planned brief absence generally should be announced at least 2 or 3 weeks in advance, preferably at the beginning of a meeting. It is not unreasonable for therapists to routinely announce absences as soon as they are aware that they will occur, even if this is months prior to the event. The amount of notice given by therapists for upcoming absences is directly tied to theory. A more traditional psychodynamic therapist might allow only 2 or 3 weeks, not wanting to introduce agenda into the group process until absolutely necessary. A therapist relying on object relations theory might notify the group as soon as he or she knows of the upcoming absence out of a conviction that the therapist is altered by the knowledge of the absence and that the patients deserve accurate information about that alteration. What is important is that the members are provided ample opportunity to fully respond and explore their reactions to the upcoming interruption. Moreover, group members soon learn to identify with the therapist and eventually discontinue the all too frequent "Oh, by the way, I won't be here next week" announcements made at the end of a meeting. If members continue a pattern of announcing absences at the last moment, this subtle action becomes easier to discuss when the therapist has initiated a more appropriate model.

The therapist's extended annual vacations might be announced a year in advance, and members might be reminded again 3 or 4 months in advance of the interruption. Some therapists expect patients to schedule vacations to coincide with their own. While this is the ideal arrangement because it results in the least disruption in continuity, it is unrealistic in most circumstances. This option is viable only when the therapist takes the same vacation time each year and members have sufficient flexibility in their own work and personal lives to schedule vacations accordingly.

The essence of this agreement is to encourage as much continuity as possible. Each time a single member is absent, something is lost. Nonetheless, comings and goings are an important part of life, and there is much to be learned by how individuals manage the inevitable absences.

Different kinds of groups can modify this agreement for their specific needs. For example, in a time-limited group, this agreement can be changed to "Members agree to attend all of the meetings."

Members Agree to Work Actively on the Problems That Brought Them to the Group

Ideally, people who join a therapy group do so in order to make substantial changes in their lives. This agreement specifically asks patients to share the internal reactions that they have during the meetings, including feelings about one another, feelings triggered by others and by group interactions, memories awakened during a meeting, and associations. The stimulus is presumed to be the group, and members are expected to discuss openly as much of their inner world as possible.

This stipulation serves at least three valuable purposes. First, merely talking about one's inner responses may be therapeutic. Keeping old fantasies and feelings bottled up adds to the individual's isolation. Self-revelation can appreciably alter that state of affairs. Second, once feelings are shared publicly, they are open to exploration. Members also have the chance to confirm or deny assumptions held regarding what will happen if others know what they are really experiencing. Third, they also have an opportunity for consensual validation of affective responses. If an individual becomes angry at another member and expresses it, that individual can discover whether or not he or she is the only one experiencing anger; if others are also angry, it is likely that in this instance the individual's emotional gyroscope is properly aligned. However, it is also possible for several members in a group to have a similar affective response owing to the fact that they share a common defensive stand. For example, individuals may at times unconsciously provoke angry responses in others in order to keep others at a distance or to expiate guilt.

Finally, if the member is the sole individual experiencing a particular affect, most frequently anger, he or she can entertain at least two hypotheses: Either he or she is the only one aptly responding to the situation, or he or she is responding to a cue in an idiosyncratic way based on personal history and not on the reality of the situation. If it is the latter, the member has the opportunity to explore the specific and parallel situations in order to see if he or she is routinely distorting in this area.

Members Agree to Put Feelings into Words, Not Actions

Patients agree that membership in a group means expressing feelings verbally, not behaviorally. Traditionally, this agreement proscribes violent behavior such as striking others, throwing objects, or damaging property. But violence is masked in many ways, and verbal violence, as distinguished from an expression of anger, falls within this part of the agreement. Violence in the form of virulent verbal attacks by one member toward another is thus prohibited. Patients can learn to put even their angriest feelings into words without violating others.

The matter of affectionate or soothing physical contact among members is a problem area for many therapists. It is not unusual for one member to reach out and touch, or perhaps embrace, a weeping colleague. Since this is a socially acceptable way of expressing feelings, such actions are often unexamined or even congratulated. Some therapists may rationalize such contact as solely therapeutic, since they see no harm coming from warm touching in the group. However, ambivalence, terror, dislike, or even hate may be hidden behind the behavioral facade. There is a place in therapy groups for a gentle touch or hug as an authentic expression of communicating deeply felt emotions, but these acts should always be examined for their full meaning and impact.

CLINICAL EXAMPLE

Ruth began to cry as she said she felt she simply could not change. The members sat silently for a few minutes, and then Sylvia said that she would like to hug Ruth. Ruth became very angry, stating, "I could not tolerate that!" She expounded about the insincerity of social hugs and linked this to her narcissistic mother always telling her that she loved her but behaving in a very different way. Sylvia felt responsible for Ruth's escalating discomfort; she felt confused because her attempt had genuinely been to soothe Ruth. Tom pointed out that they knew each other well enough to distinguish between what was genuine and deep and what was unauthentic, and superficial. He added that if he hugged Sylvia, she would know if it was a sexual advance or an expression of platonic affection. Ursula said that she felt just like Ruth but that she would have accepted Sylvia's hug and not said a word about her discomfort. Victor pointed out that it was a sign of Ruth's trust in the group that she could tell the group her feelings about the proposed hug. He pointed out that she was probably more trusting of the group than she let on. A great deal of important data surfaced as the members talked about their feelings rather than using the shortcut of action. In the end, Ruth felt very comforted by Sylvia.

Some therapists specifically prohibit eating or drinking during groups (Ormont, 1967). (These days everyone prohibits smoking!) A common rationale for this stance is that such behaviors diminish useful anxiety and tension that could more profitably be experienced. Each therapist must decide how specific to be with regard to the behavioral prohibitions, since many actions can be handled through interpretations. (The therapeutic management of some extreme instances of acting rather than verbalizing will be discussed in Chapter 10.)

Members Agree to Use the Relationships Made in the Group Therapeutically and Not Socially

How patients may utilize the relationships made in their groups is a matter of divergent opinion among therapists. At one extreme are those therapists who absolutely prohibit out-of-group contact; at the other, those who openly support, reinforce, and all but require it.

The fundamental use of the group is for therapeutic, not social, purposes; in the long run the two are mutually exclusive. As patients express their feelings for one another, including their yearnings to socialize, a considerable pressure to act emerges. The wish (on the part of both therapist and patients) for patients to use the relationships gained in the groups outside the group is understandable. For many patients the contacts with their group colleagues represent their most viable and authentic relationships. Restricting their use and enjoyment may feel unduly harsh and withholding. Nevertheless, it is more therapeutically profitable to discourage extra-group socializing, since doing so reduces the variables affecting group behavior and increases the likelihood of spontaneous revelation of affects in the group. Further, if the use of in-group relationships for social purposes is thwarted, patients tend to gain their own social networks outside the group more quickly. They feel less dependent and more autonomous when the social network utilized is really their own and not one provided by the group.

The language of this agreement contains room for creative debate. Members are left to discuss and decide what constitutes therapeutic as opposed to social interaction. All groups do have relationships that extend beyond the actual meetings. Even the moments before and after the group session represent opportunities for important interactions. Group members can be told that any extra-group interactions may well represent important ways of managing feelings evoked in the therapy and that they should therefore discuss emotionally meaningful extra-group contacts in order to enhance learning. Within this framework of dynamic understanding, patients can be reminded that the primary use of all interactions with group members is therapeutic.

Members Agree to Remain in the Group Until
the Problems That Brought Them Have Been Resolved

This agreement is often seen as problematic by applicants. Patients are invariably anxious about entering a group, and they often attempt to master their anxiety by envisioning their early weeks as a trial period. Some therapists deal with this by asking that entering patients agree to remain for a specified period of time, generally 3 months. This practice presumably helps new patients remain through the early difficult period and is long enough for them to develop a strong therapeutic alliance.

The trial period is inadvisable for two reasons. First, any newcomer breaches group confidentiality, and if there is an agreed-upon trial period the group process likely will be skewed toward caution rather than openness until that trial period has expired and the patient has committed to joining. Second, some patients simply stay for the duration of the trial period and then leave. In this situation the therapist is left with little or no therapeutic leverage, since the patient has indeed fully adhered to the group agreement.

Acceptance of this agreement does not prevent premature quitting, but it does remind patients that they agreed to remain until they resolve their presenting problems. In addition, many patients experience this agreement as an initial source of hope and are comforted by the clear expectation that group therapy can help them resolve their problems.

This agreement also serves to set the norm about how appropriate terminations occur. As patients consider termination, it is very useful for them to make their decision in light of this agreement by asking themselves, "Have I resolved the problems I came with?" The subsequent discussion of presenting problems is one element in the review process that is essential to successful termination. Patients learn that they should not abruptly stop therapy but should spend time examining the changes they have made and their feelings about ending treatment.

Members Agree to Be Responsible for Their Bill

In this day of third-party payment for psychotherapy, group therapy often seems to exist in a financial vacuum. That is, group therapy is sufficiently inexpensive that some patients find that nearly all of their bills are paid by insurance. This diminished fiscal responsibility may be detrimental to patients who correlate expense with emotional commitment. At the very least, patients should be responsible for their bills. If possible, patients should pay the therapist directly and then receive the insurance money themselves. If there is a problem in insurance payments, the patient, not the therapist, should negotiate with the company. Finally, the therapist should fill out insurance forms only the first time. Thereafter, where possible, the patient should be responsible for completing the forms, using the same repetitive data (including diagnosis) and the proper dates and amounts, with the therapist simply checking for accuracy and then signing the form.

It is wise to stipulate further that statements will be handed out during the first meeting of the month and that members are expected to pay in full before the next bill is distributed. There are certainly other ways of implementing these principles. What is important is that the fiscal elements of the agreement be spelled out in detail and that patients understand that financial matters are also group business.

Patients should be charged for scheduled meetings whether or not they attend. In individual therapy if a patient misses a meeting, the therapist can choose to fill that hour and therefore not suffer a financial loss because of the patient's absence. In groups we do not have the option of temporarily replacing an absent member. Thus, no matter the reason for absenteeism, members are charged for their seats. If this agreement is used, patients need to be reminded that third-party payers do not reimburse for missed meetings.

Some therapists prefer a less rigorous approach to fees and do not charge patients for vacations or unavoidable absences caused by illnesses or required business trips. In these cases the therapist is placed in the position of having to work with the patient to determine which absences are instances of acting out and which are unavoidable. For the therapist choosing this approach, the key variable is consistency, so that patients can gain the most from analysis of how they choose to attend meetings and handle payment of fees.

The important principle is the separation of the therapist's financial interests and the patient's therapeutic responsibility. In whatever manner therapists manage fees, part of the group agreements relate to their expectable earnings. Further, the agreements are a structure that patients might use for their own internal needs; for example, a patient might use the financial agreement as an opportunity to rebel or to deprive the therapist of real or imagined gratification. This principle enables the therapist to comfortably examine absences whether or not a fee is charged.

In modern America it often seems easier to discuss intimate sexual experiences than financial matters. Therapists face more than a strong social taboo when they bring up a member's overdue fee; extremely strong feelings of shame, embarrassment, narcissistic injury, and rage are mobilized. Yet to avoid dealing directly with the meaning of money and the payment of fees runs the considerable risk of colluding with patients' resistances. Financial matters are not private matters because there are invariably groupwide meanings and reverberations when a patient falls behind in paying fees.

As a part of the continuing emphasis that everything can be discussed in the group, the therapist must deal forthrightly with fees. We prefer that statements be distributed and payment be received during sessions. This simple practice invites candid discussion of financial matters in the group.

Members Agree to Protect the Names and Identities of Their Fellow Group Members

This agreement is saved for last because there is usually an input overload when the group agreements are discussed and members often do not recall all the elements. Mentioning the requirement to protect other members' anonymity last gives it a deserved special emphasis.

Confidentiality is the cornerstone upon which group therapy relationships are built, and yet it is rarely completely maintained. Therapists often ask patients to agree to "keep in confidence all that is shared within the group." We believe this is a troublesome way of handling the issue for at least two reasons. First, it is an agreement not likely to be kept. As the group becomes important to people, they will talk about their experience with others. Sessions can be very stimulating, and talking about what happened is a reasonable way to begin to integrate strong emotions. Every therapist will recognize his/her propensity to seek out a colleague after an affect-laden meeting in order to blow off steam and further process what happened. Obviously, such discussions go on as a matter of course between cotherapists. It would be unreasonable not to expect the members to do the same. Second, to ask patients not to speak of their group experience is to place them in a double bind. On the one hand, by virtue of being treated in a group, they are told overtly and covertly that it is healthy and helps them to grow to share intimately with other human beings while on the other hand they are told, "But don't tell anyone about this!"

In fact, we hope our group therapy patients do talk with their significant others about their group experiences. If they are in concurrent individual therapy, it is therapeutically imperative that they discuss the meetings. It is also enriching to share some of what is learned in a group with loved ones. The end point of group therapy, after all, is not that individuals merely become intimate and honest with other group members but, rather, that they gain authenticity with those with whom they share their lives.

The fundamental concern with confidentiality is that the anonymity of the members be protected; hence, the agreement is worded so as to protect names and identities rather than to prohibit members from discussing with others outside the group the lessons learned during group interactions.

SUMMARY

Entering a therapy group is a difficult task for anyone. Group applicants come to us because they have more than the usual amount of anxiety in interpersonal situations; thus, careful preparation for their entrance into a group is a necessity if successful therapeutic work is to follow.

It is important in the proper preparation of patients to introduce them to the treatment goals and to gain their acceptance of them. If there appears to be a significant discrepancy between the patient's motivation or goals for therapy and those of the therapist, it is wise to delay the patient's entrance into a group until those issues can be clarified. Often a therapist, anxious to have a new member, will avoid dealing with these conflicts in the hope that they can be resolved by the group. Such conflicts, however, inevitably lead to problems and are best resolved before the applicant joins the group.

The presentation of the agreements, along with examining the overall response of the patient to the idea of entering a group, offers an important opportunity for the therapist to gain information about the patient whether or not the latter ultimately chooses to join the group. Patients exhibit a variety of responses, such as compliance, acceptance, anxiety, rebellion, rejection, and so forth. These responses should be viewed as more than just overt responses to the agreements themselves; they should be seen as potential windows into the inner world of the patient.

The group agreements are not a formal, written document; rather, they are a verbal agreement between patient, therapist, and other members regarding the ground rules of the group's operation and are repeated each time a new member joins. The agreements are the foundation for a productive and safe therapeutic environment. The specific elements we have presented should be mutually agreed upon treatment guidelines.

The following elements constitute the agreements for ongoing, open-ended therapy groups. The patients agree[1]

---

[1]If the therapist has a procedure for dealing with his or her own absence (such as making up the meeting or providing a substitute leader), this should be one of the original group agreements. (See Chapter 10.)

1. To be present each week, to be on time, and to remain through-out the meeting
2. To work actively on the problems that brought them to the group
3. To put feelings into words, not actions
4. To use the relationships made in the group therapeutically, not socially
5. To remain in the group until the problems that brought them to the group have been resolved
6. To be responsible for their bills
7. To protect the names and identities of fellow group members

We are convinced that any group needs a clear set of agreements in order to be effective. Furthermore, the agreements become a powerful tool in analysis of various resistances and character traits.

8

The Role
of the Group Therapist

One of Freud's more famous remarks was his comparison of psychotherapy to chess. Of the latter he observed, "Anyone who hopes to learn the noble game of chess from books will soon discover that only the opening and end games admit of an exhaustive systematic presentation and that the infinite variety of moves that develop after the opening defy any such descriptions. The gap in instruction can only be filled by a diligent study of games fought out by masters." (Freud, 1913, p. 128). The beginning and end of therapy can be taught — less so the middle. If the comparison with regard to the role of the individual therapist holds, it is even more pointedly true for the group therapist, who shifts among group, interpersonal, and intrapsychic perspectives. Group therapists are continually confronted with a richness of data, and great skill is required to sort through it in order to focus upon and use the most relevant and powerful material. It is this very complexity that contributes to the therapeutic potency of groups.

There are only a few attempts in the literature to offer specific assistance to therapists in organizing and assigning priorities to group data (Rutan & Alonso, 1978). We will elucidate a number of principles that should provide assistance in determining when and how to intervene. For heuristic purposes we separate leader activity into *role* and *focus,* each composed of several continua (see Figure 8.1).

The three continua that represent the *style* dimension are considered in parallel. That is, each leader is continually and concurrently making decisions about how active, transparent, and gratifying to be. The six continua of the *focus* dimension may be considered a hierarchy. The therapist's attention should first be focused on the past–present

ROLES for the Group Therapist

ACTIVITY ◄————————————————————————————————► NONACTIVITY
TRANSPARENCY ◄————————————————————————————► OPAQUENESS
GRATIFICATION ◄———————————————————————————► FRUSTRATION

FOCI for the Group Therapist

PAST ◄——————————————►(HERE AND NOW) ◄——————————► FUTURE
GROUP AS A WHOLE ——————— (INTERPERSONAL) ——————— INDIVIDUAL
IN-GROUP ◄————————————————————————————► OUT-OF-GROUP
AFFECT ◄——————————————————————————————————► COGNITION
PROCESS ◄—————————————————————————————————► CONTENT
UNDERSTANDING ◄——————————► CORRECTIVE EMOTIONAL EXPERIENCE

FIGURE 8.1. Leadership dimensions of the group therapist.

continuum, then on the group-as-a-whole–individuals continuum, and so on. While the complexity of group interactions does not allow for hard-and-fast rules about how to attend to group data, considering the focus dimensions hierarchically will often help clarify material.

Where any therapist operates on the *style* and *focus* dimensions is in part related to his or her theoretical persuasion (Christ, 1975; Kauff, 1979; Lieberman et al., 1973; Rutan, 1992a; Wolf & Schwartz, 1975; Yalom, 1985). A therapist who adheres to group-as-a-whole processes generally will choose to *focus* on the in-group, affect, and process ends of the respective axes. A traditional psychoanalytic therapist may high-light transference aspects of interpersonal transactions, fantasy life (content), and the importance of the past. Of course, these same therapists may both eschew transparency, gratification, and activity on the *role* dimension.

Although on some occasions it is most therapeutic to operate from an extreme pole of any continua, it is important for therapists to understand that there are consequences to these decisions.

THE LEADERSHIP ROLE DIMENSION

Members are very watchful of their leaders, heeding what they say, how they say it, what they reveal about themselves, and how they relate. The warmth in the voice, the eye contact, and the feelings exhibited are elements to which patients pay close attention. Further, the leader serves as a model (through both imitation and identification) for observing and using group phenomena. Therefore, it is important that therapists thoughtfully assess the manner in which they relate in order to understand fully the implications of their style on the treatment process.

Activity Versus Nonactivity

Groups, particularly in early phases of development or at times of high stress, are likely to be preoccupied with the therapist's activity. Members complain about the quantity or the quality of the therapist's participation, creating considerable pressure in the therapist to respond. The therapist is continually balancing the issues of silence versus verbal activity. Overactivity may result in infantilization of members, while underactivity or excessive withholding may result in narcissistic injury followed by withdrawal and rage.

In general, the most useful activities for leaders are internal ones — feeling, empathizing, and hypothesizing in order to further understanding. Overt activity for the leader is primarily verbal. How much does one speak? How cryptic or extensive should one's interventions be? This issue is separate from the *content* of the activity. The therapist's role is essentially reactive rather than initiating. The dynamic therapist waits for the group process to occur and then comments on it.

It is unusual for a dynamic therapist to initiate discussion. Any agenda the therapist needs to bring to the group (e.g., the announcement of a vacation or of an increase in fees or the news that a member has notified the therapist that he or she will not be attending a meeting) should be announced at the beginning of a meeting. This procedure provides the members with the opportunity to respond with their own associations, secure in the knowledge that the leader has no additional significant agenda to introduce.

The patients' roles on this continuum are also primarily verbal. The therapist tries to establish the norm that change occurs most effectively when members feel, express, and talk rather than *do*. Therefore, expressing a yearning to physically embrace another member is considered more therapeutic and beneficial than actually embracing that person. This stance is obviously quite different from the more active therapeutic techniques, and it flows naturally from psychodynamic theory. In dynamic therapy the goal is to help the patient feel, identify, and give voice to the feelings.

The place of touching and doing in therapy is strongly contested. However, if we want to reassure our patients that the therapeutic arena is a safe place to experience and explore *all* affects, then it is imperative that they be assured that no physical action will follow. (It is one thing to sympathetically touch someone when one has warm feelings, but it is quite another if the affects being experienced are strongly sexual or aggressive.) When groups are allowed or encouraged to act on warm and affectionate feelings, a lingering question remains about what actions might follow when members are feeling angry, sadistic, or even homicidal.

Usually the therapist can set the norm for "talking, not doing" by flagging and commenting on even the most benign physical touching. If a member reaches to comfort another, the therapist can inquire, "What feelings were you expressing through the touch?" On those infrequent occasions when an actual threat of physical violence exists in a group, the therapist must not rely on interpretation alone but must clearly and promptly set limits on any potential action. Every effort must be made to avoid physical harm. It is reassuring to note that despite the affective power of groups actual physical violence within them is extraordinarily rare.

Transparency Versus Opaqueness

The transparency–opaqueness variable highlights the distinction between the members and the therapist. It is expected that members will allow themselves to be as transparent as possible, expressing their associations, emotions, secrets, histories, and thoughts. Therapists, however, should be transparent only in limited ways. It is usually helpful to reveal only that which is in the service of the treatment process. Even within the rather narrow confines of the dynamic tradition, however, there are differences in how therapists conceptualize their role on this axis. Strict traditionalists rarely give much hint about their own inner feelings while practitioners with an object relations point of view often find it useful to share an emotional reaction to a patient or the group in order to facilitate exploration of projective identifications.

Therapists need to be particularly alert to avoid responses arising from their own inner needs or from pressures from the members. To the degree that patients are not burdened with the therapist's personal data, their task of transferring meaning and attributes is easier; conversely, the more members know about the therapist, the more difficult it is for them to fantasy.

No matter how strictly a particular therapist holds to the opaque pole of this continuum, after a time members come to know a great deal about the therapist. As an actively engaged participant in the group, albeit in a role different from that of a member, the therapist reveals a great deal in nonverbal ways. Patients learn to read body language and facial expression; they know when the therapist is pleased or displeased. It is not necessary or useful for group therapists to be blank screens. Groups are intensely human encounters, and it is often impossible (or inhuman) for a therapist to avoid laughing at a funny moment or feeling tearful when a group is struggling with sadness. If therapists are empathically attuned to their groups, they are not immune to the affect that engulfs everyone. It is through the therapist's steadfastness to the task, through the concern, caring, and, thoughtfulness, and through the ability to be introspective, to tolerate affects, and to move forward in a therapeutic manner that the group members come to know a great deal about their therapist. The group process, complete with the consensual validation that this multiperson arena affords, means that the veil of secrecy of the therapeutic role is considerably lessened. Though patients will sometimes deny how much they know of us, they nonetheless know a great deal. For some therapists this reality is uncomfortable; for most, however, it is a not unenjoyable aspect of leading groups.

Much therapeutic benefit can accrue if the therapist is aware of this element of transparency and can respond if the members comment on it. Patients will occasionally pick up and comment on the affective state of the therapist, sensing sadness or anger, for example. Moreover, a mistake or slip of the tongue can expose the therapist's unconscious just as surely and accurately as it can expose the patient's. Since one goal of psychotherapy is to help patients become more empathic, it is counterproductive for therapists to refuse to acknowledge patients' accurate therapist-directed empathy. To acknowledge that a patient has correctly sensed something is quite different from gratuitously offering personal information.

Sometimes aspects of the therapist's personal life are public information and therefore come into the group. This can occur, for example, when the therapist gets married or divorced, a new car is in the office driveway, the therapist is injured, or something about the therapist's career is published in the newspaper. A therapist's pregnancy represents a particularly powerful and public piece of personal information that becomes known to the group. Furthermore, if one group member discovers some personal information about the therapist, it is soon known by all. When patients comment about such aspects of the therapist's life, there is no reason not to indicate that such information is correct, although the precise timing of confirming the information will vary according to the situation and the theoretical orientation of the therapist.

Despite the exceptions, patients do not come to hear about their therapist's successes and failures, joys and sorrows. Since groups so often take on a very familial feeling, group therapists are uniquely prone to the temptation to share irrelevant personal information with patients. Further, there may be some magical wish on the part of the members to hear how the therapist solves a problem or to know the therapist more personally in the hope that this will somehow solve their own problems. Requests by members for personal information about the therapist should be explored to understand their roots, not gratified under the notion that for the therapist to be considered human personal information must be shared. Opaqueness should never be confused with emotional distance or lack of personal warmth.

Gratification Versus Frustration

An artful balance should be made between gratification and frustration in therapy, whether it is group or individual therapy. Too much gratification results in insufficient anxiety to promote change. Too much frustration results in a relationship insufficient to promote the trust, caring, and safety necessary for personal revelation. In groups the therapist is freed to adopt an empathic observer role because the members can provide gratification when the leader does not. Thus, even more than in dyadic therapy, the group therapist can use the observational posture without unduly distressing a patient. Overgratification by the therapist may take the form of too much activity, self-exposure, or even too-frequent interpretations. Yet too much frustration or too austere an environment can stifle group effectiveness. For example, some therapists inappropriately avoid eye contact when speaking to a specific member or when making group-as-a-whole interpretations. Indeed, when group members avoid eye contact, that behavior is usually a subject of exploration.

Therapists face an ever-present danger of falling prey to a countertransferential need to be central at all times in their groups. Through excessive gratification they may retain their centrality and make the group leader-dependent rather than balanced between leader-focused and member-focused tendencies. The goal in working on this axis is to allow the maximum usable amount of anxiety for each patient and for the group as a whole and not to interfere with the members' abilities to work with their feelings and relationships.

THE LEADERSHIP FOCUS DIMENSION

Leader activity involves not only a particular leadership role but also the leader's focus of attention. The continua on the role dimension are to be considered in parallel, that is, the therapist's role can be defined by all of them simultaneously. In the leadership focus dimension leaders can vary their attention among the various axes. Indeed, it is possible for the therapist to conceptualize an order in which these axes may be considered in order to use them as aids in the task of understanding the multiplicity of data arising in a group. Though the elements are presented separately, there is obvious overlap and therefore no rigid hierarchy. Different therapists may choose to order the importance of the axes differently, but systematically considering each of them will often bring clarity to what otherwise seems chaotic.

Finally, we stress that there is no "right" place on these continua. The weight given a particular point on each of the continua reflects a therapeutic judgment about how best to help members change. We would suggest, however, that it is unduly limiting for therapists to restrict themselves to particular points on the axes. The art of being a group therapist is at least in part knowing when to focus on different points on these continua.

The Past–Present–Future Axis

All dynamic psychotherapies include consideration of an extended time dimension, one from the past, through the present, and into the future. A particular theoretical orientation may emphasize one point more than another, a fact exemplified by the particular importance existential therapists place on the end of life and our ultimate finitude. In psychodynamic therapy all points on this axis are important, but the initial focus of attention and exploration is on the *here and now,* that is, the present intragroup responses, interactions, and feelings. There is a mistaken notion that dynamic therapy focuses on history, the "there and then," but transference is a here-and-now phenomenon occurring between patient and therapist and between patients and patients (Michaels, 1981). The past is relevant to the extent that it informs or distorts the present.

Indeed, two important pasts develop in therapy: the treatment and the personal. In the treatment past are the events that have taken place in the therapy. Groups develop rich legacies, and members will often recall events or issues from the group's history that help clarify current events. The personal past brought by each member also becomes known to the group over time, and the exploration of each person's idiosyncratic reactions to current events takes on a new perspective when the uniqueness of each history is understood. As each member relives and remembers his or her past, new associations and memories are evoked in the other members.

Often what is happening in the present is unclear and can be understood only with reference to the past. For example, a member has an excessive emotional reaction to what appears to others to be a mild stimulus (what might be called a hundred-dollar reaction to a one-dollar event). This is often an indication that the member is responding to data from history, not the present. The precise timing of when to link the present with the past through interpretation depends on the clarity of the associations as metaphors and on the state of the therapeutic alliance (Katz, 1983). The personal past emerges in the stereotyped roles patients adopt. These roles usually are ways of managing anxiety and conflict that have worked in the past. If members can become aware of patterned behavior and the meaning of that behavior, associations from the past will add to overall insight.

As with all elements in therapy, the past may be used defensively to avoid the present. The therapist is not immune to this tendency, and a common error is to prematurely shift the focus to the past in order to contain intense affects in the present. Patients also revert to the past as an intellectual or obsessional defense, and such flight should be considered in light of its use in maintaining both group and individual equilibrium.

Therapists can often use their own affect responses as indicators of the need to explore the past or stay with the current interactions. Feelings of boredom, lack of interest, or a sense of repetitiveness may suggest that the members have mobilized defensive patterns. These defenses might represent a response to an unattended group conflict, a product of individual character styles (roles), or newly emerging transferences. The past, either near or remote, may then shed light on the present conflicts. Often the therapist's anxiety is a reliable guide: If it feels more anxiety provoking to allow the current interactions to continue, then continuing is probably the course where the most therapeutic value resides. Conversely, if the therapist experiences anxiety over the prospect of linking current interactions to historical material, then making those links is likely the proper course.

Finally, the future is also always present. Patients come to therapy in order to make their futures better. They plan, think, and feel about what is in store for them. Many in-group behaviors can best be understood as predicting or trying out new responses. Fantasies about what someone will do or feel or how they may react in some outside situation are commonplace and are clearly future oriented. As patients near termination, they become more future oriented, wondering about their ability to be different from what they were before entering therapy. Furthermore, it is one of the goals of therapy to help patients gain ability to predict the outcomes of their behaviors.

Any debate about where to focus—past, present, or future— has been largely resolved: All three have an important place in treatment.

The Group-as-a-Whole–Interpersonal–Individual Axis

Leaders must move back and forth flexibly between observing the group as a whole, attending to the interpersonal interactions within it, and analyzing individuals. A primary focus on group-as-a-whole phenomena provides an opportunity for members to understand their shared, universal concerns and to gain understanding from their participation in the powerful conscious and unconscious group processes. The focus on interpersonal interactions assists in understanding communication blocks and distortions as well as the impact on others of one's personal style. The focus on the individuals within the group gives members the opportunity to examine their uniqueness and enhances a sense of potency in the world. To focus on one element to the exclusion of the others is to lose touch unnecessarily with powerful therapeutic forces.

Typically, one can give dominance to group-as-a-whole observations at those times when members are responding to the same stimuli, such as when the framework of the group is affected, for example, when the group is forming, a new member is being introduced, a member is terminating, or the vacation of the therapist is imminent. At these times when the group's boundary is altered or forming, attention to the groupwide reaction, and therefore to the individual contributions to that reaction, is most useful.

Groupwide reactions occur rather silently much of the time. Within the group there may be a subtle thrust for greater intimacy or increased expression of difficult affects; in this process the members may be working to change old group norms toward greater spontaneity. Conversely, if the stress is too high, there may be movement toward restriction of feelings. When a group is feeling a powerful regressive pull, it is often best for the therapist to offer group-as-a-whole interventions. From this perspective, the notion of enabling or constricting solutions to group focal conflicts highlights the group-as-a-whole perspective (Whitaker & Lieberman, 1964). That is, generally not one individual who interferes with the expression of feelings or the discussion of a stressful topic but two or more individuals with the covert cooperation of the others.

Kernberg (1975) suggested that the group-as-a-whole–interpersonal–individual perspective might parallel developmental stages, maintaining that those groups composed of individuals with preoedipal personality configurations can best use the group-as-a-whole focus whereas members with oedipal personality configurations learn more from an interpersonal focus. However, this formulation overlooks the oedipal (and specifically sexual) attractions and rivalries that involve the whole group and that could be clarified for all members through group-as-a-whole interpretations. Furthermore, the more primitive patients are often unable to profit from the lack of personal meaning in an exclusive group-as-a-whole approach.

The most productive interventions take into consideration the varying involvements of the members in any meeting. For instance, an intervention to one member working on competitive feelings at an oedipal level in a group struggling with preoedipal issues of basic trust would miss the main focus of the group. The individual might gain from the intervention, but the group focus would rapidly shift away from competition and back to the central focus. Thus, the intervention would not lead to elaboration or working through. On the other hand, the same intervention in a group that was dealing with oedipal competitive issues may be powerful and therapeutically enabling not only to the particular individual but to the others as well since the comment would likely stimulate relevant associations in several members. When a particular member is working at a significantly different level than the rest of the group, the therapist can often take note of it and refer to it later at a time when the group and that member are working at comparable levels.

There are occasions when one or several sessions might be devoted almost exclusively to a particular member's problems. This is appropriate in times of crisis, and the other members can learn from their inner reactions to the situation and responses to the distressed member. However, the therapist needs to maintain a broad perspective to ensure that the focus on one or two members does not become a pattern and thereby a detriment to free interaction.

There are staunch and avid practitioners of both the group-as-a-whole and the individual approach to group therapy. In fact, both aspects of group functioning are vitally important and work well in concert. The goal is not to select one or the other but to know how to use both effectively.

The In-Group–Out-of-Group Axis

The same principles hold for the in-group–out-of-group axis as for the past–present–future axis. It is certainly true that individuals sometimes associate to out-of-group events as an avoidance to powerful in-group affects. Even in these instances it is important that the therapist not imply that the out-of-group material is irrelevant. It is preferable if the therapist can tactfully link the out-of-group and in-group material. Here again, the therapist's affect may provide a guide in determining where to ultimately bring the focus of attention.

Members have their in-group and out-of-group lives. Patients often talk about their relationships with group members, and they equally often speak of their relationships with important others out-side the group (such as loved ones, parents, bosses). The theory of group therapy assumes that individuals are presenting the salient elements of their personalities and their conflicts in the group; thus, where possible, attention is focused on the in-group action, where the elements are more available for direct analysis. As with the here-and-now continuum, there may be many roadblocks in accomplishing this task. In the vast majority of situations, however, when patients use their interactions with one another or with the therapist or analyze their perceptions of the group, they gain important affective and cognitive appreciation of their problem.

Though the therapist should welcome and scrutinize all out-of-group material for its relevance to in-group matters, it is helpful to remember that not everything is a metaphor for some group transaction or feeling. The birth of a child, a wedding, a relative's divorce, a death — all are examples of important external events that probably have meaning that transcends whatever metaphorical analogue there may be in the group relationships. Members can profit from the opportunity to talk and feel about such events in the company of valued others. Only a naive therapist slavishly adheres to the belief that such events are primarily transferences. It is not farfetched to believe that a neophyte therapist could interpret a story about a serious automobile accident involving a member's family as solely a metaphor for a damaging event within the group. Usually the introduction of powerful out-of-group stimuli does result in in-group associations that are profitably explored. The therapist needs to maintain a "both and" rather than an "either or" mentality in these situations. That is, even if the therapist relates external events to in-group matters, he or she should imply that *both* are important rather than reject the external material as pure resistance.

The fundamental guideline is that most productive therapeutic work in the long run arises from the affective experience in the group itself. Some therapists attempt to mandate that groups will discuss nothing but their in-group relationships. Nonetheless, it is an oversimplification to see these as the exclusive focus, since individuals learn about themselves in their own ways and at their own rates. The therapist needs to monitor and reinforce the norm that examination of in-group transactions is the most productive but not the exclusive way of learning.

The Affect–Cognition Axis

Because psychodynamic theory began with the notion that understanding unconscious material would free individuals of their neuroses, conscious understanding was at first the mainstay of the curative effort.

Rather quickly it became apparent that cognitive insight is an incomplete avenue to change, and therapists began including an emphasis on freeing affects and on "emotional knowing."

The exclusive attention to either extreme of this continuum is generally ineffective. What transpires in effective psychodynamic psychotherapy is a combination of feeling and understanding resulting in affective and cognitive integration. Emotional knowing arises from having deeply experienced a situation and fully felt the affects involved. The building blocks of psychological learning are affects, both felt and shared. To that degree, the first and most important focus of therapeutic attention is affect, not cognition. Often, cognitions are viewed as resistances to experiencing strong emotion. Nonetheless, therapeutic change is not a function of pure affect or pure catharsis. Once the affective data have been made available to the patient, a cognitive integration is very important. It is not enough that our patients feel; they must then understand as well. In research some data are "necessary but not sufficient"; the same is true for affect in psychotherapy. However, as with most principles, there are exceptions, and some patients change after gaining cognitive understanding that then forces them to experience affects.

Therapists have to balance their wish to provide cognitive closure with the need of patients to first explore, bear, and fully express their affective experiences. Typically, therapists err on the side of moving to cognition too quickly, presumably to reduce their own discomfort.

The Process–Content Axis

Communication in groups is simultaneously occurring verbally and nonverbally, consciously and unconsciously, and as a response to immediate and distant stimuli. Each meeting is fueled by each member's personal history, which evokes wishes, needs, transferences, distortions, and affective attribution of meaning. It is also fueled by the group history, by the relationships between members, and by those between each member and the leader. At all times members are negotiating their relationships with one another and with the leader.

The content (the overt meaning) of any given meeting cannot be divorced from the process (the covert meaning) because in almost every instance there is a connection between the two. The content might be a symbolic representation of a groupwide issue or an interpersonal transaction, or it might be a direct commentary upon the process within the group.

The therapist should keep an ear finely tuned to the process. The question "Why is this association or series of interactions emerging at this time?" provides perspective. Is the current discussion a direct result of what occurred a few moments ago, is it related to a general issue in the group, or is it idiosyncratic? The content of associations can be highly symbolic or a metaphor of the group process. Through a judicious combination of both elements, the therapist can help members gain understanding of unconscious functioning. The unconscious is just that—out of awareness; furthermore, it is designed to remain that way to provide protection. Unless we steadfastly hear all content as potential process, unless we are aware of the interplay between process and content, we run the risk of missing important unconscious material.

CLINICAL EXAMPLE

During a meeting members found themselves involved in intense rivalry. Several began bragging about various personal exploits. The therapist initiated examination of the interaction by exploring the feelings of the members and by trying to understand the meaning of each exploit, thereby sharpening the sense of showing off or competing. The members understood that each story was an example of a personal triumph, and they could then recognize that they had become competitive with one another.

The therapist then noted that he began this meeting by announcing that a new member would be joining the group in 2 weeks. He pointed out that the initial response to his announcement had been muted, with a general tone of, "Oh, good, the empty chair will be filled." However, the process then immediately shifted to the relating of exploits. While not specifically stating how he understood the meaning of the sharing of exploits but by simply indicating instead that he suspected there was a connection, the therapist enabled the members to emotionally connect the two processes. There followed an elaboration of the content as the members recognized that they had much more feeling about the prospect of a new member than they had been willing to acknowledge at first or even to know consciously. The members could then deal more directly with the competitiveness they experienced (process leading to new content), and in some cases they were able to make genetic reconstructions (understanding more fully the advent of rebellious behaviors as children during the time of mother's pregnancy).

Psychoanalytic theory suggests that nothing is random. Thus, a primary tool of psychoanalysis is free association. The assumption is that if analysands are able to reduce ego control and simply speak of whatever comes to mind, therapists can follow the unconscious connections between associations and help patients gain insight into their inner world. Group therapy expands this notion by asking that all patients speak freely of whatever comes to their minds or hearts. This is group process.

Self psychologists (Ornstein, 1978) use process in a particular way. In working with patients suffering from disorders of the self, the emphasis is placed on interpreting specific sequences, for example, a narcissistic injury and the subsequent response to that injury. The content is used to highlight the process, including the precise empathic understanding of the injury (which is usually buried in the unconscious) as well as the details of how the patient (or group) tries to regain an inner equilibrium. For example, members may respond to a therapist's interpretation as a criticism, with associations suddenly turning to religious themes. The interpretation of this behavior could then highlight the process of having felt criticized (and hurt) and then turning to a higher authority for more nurturance and protection. More typical is the sequence of individuals feeling hurt, repressing that feeling, and then quickly finding themselves enraged.

The Understanding–Corrective Emotional Experience Axis

The roles of understanding and corrective emotional experiences in the curative process have often been polarized and thought to be mutually exclusive. Does healing occur through insight and understanding or through the experiencing of life in different and more wholesome ways than before? In fact, both are necessary for effective psychotherapy. The notion of a corrective emotional experience is inherent in the nonjudgmental, empathic, supportive, investigative stance of the therapist. The benefits of such an experience in group psychotherapy have been emphasized by Yalom (1985), who stressed the therapeutic effect of group cohesion. The experience of belonging to a cohesive, functioning group, an environment in which wishes and needs are acknowledged and responded to positively, has a soothing, calming, and growth-producing impact. For almost everyone this is a corrective emotional experience. For some this is sufficient treatment; these individuals can stabilize themselves in the group setting and continue to grow on their own after terminating. For most patients, however, this fundamental building block needs to be supplemented by knowledge of unconscious inner conflicts or structural deficits.

Understanding and insight are useful in helping patients integrate and consolidate what they have experienced. A sense of knowing one's own sensitivities and vulnerabilities helps one master everyday stresses. Insight enables the patient to spot a troublesome area or behavior pattern and, hopefully, avoid what would previously have become a problem situation. Certainly, it is not that all conflicts disappear, but many can be short-circuited through self-awareness.

Kris (1956) stated what most therapists have experienced, namely, the discovery that insight, either cognitive *or* emotional, is often insufficient to bring about real change in our patients. Fried (1982) suggested that "what matters clinically is that insight into most conflicts, be they preoedipal or oedipal, does not rectify deficits and malformations. They have to be corrected through the very repetitive experiences and challenges that groups offer in abundance" (p. 420).

Groups provide uniquely therapeutic opportunities to acquire both understanding (emotional and cognitive insight) and corrective emotional experiences; they provide opportunities to build new psychic structures via better, more authentic, and more nourishing relationships and to try out and practice new behavior patterns. Group leaders need not choose between the ends of this continuum; they need to ensure that both ends are operative and that patients are receiving both information and experiences.

A CLINICAL ILLUSTRATION
OF THE LEADER ROLE AND FOCUS DIMENSIONS

In the following illustration the leader's role is examined across both role and focus dimensions. As usual, to best use these dimensions the therapist must have an awareness of the process that has been occurring in the group as well as of the presenting problems and personal histories of the members.

> A mature group had been proceeding very nicely for a period of months. There had been, for example, the successful and moving termination of a patient the month before. Suddenly, in one meeting the members became moribund and depressed. After a prolonged period of silence, Sarah, who had experienced a long period of warm and affectionate feelings for the therapist (feelings the therapist also felt for her), exploded in a fury. She accused the therapist of not appreciating her gains, of not caring for her, and of giving all his attention to the other women members. Everyone present was confused by the unexpected depressed silence at the beginning of the meeting and by Sarah's surprising outburst, which seemed unwarranted to them.
>
> The therapist, knowing the group process and Sarah's presenting problem and family history, was able to hypothesize about the seemingly strange responses. The process was initiated by the loss of the loved member, and the group was depressed because they had not sufficiently

mourned that loss. Instead, with the leader colluding, they had focused on sad, warm and loving feelings to the exclusion of envy and rage.

Sarah's initial presenting problem was her "insane jealousy" of other women, and her outburst toward the leader was a replay of her primary symptom. The etiology of her problem, in large measure, had to do with the loss of self-esteem she experienced at 6 years of age when a baby sister came into the family. As the group was saying its final good-byes to the departing group member, Sarah inwardly turned her attention to the future and the expected "new baby" in the group who would come to fill the empty chair. Because of her history, she anticipated rejection from the leader and acted as if it had actually happened.

The understanding of current group process seemed sufficient for understanding the depressed response of most of the members. However, Sarah's reaction did not fit, and there was no overt stimulus. It was unclear what had precipitated her outburst until the therapist reviewed for himself the presenting problem and the significant historical events in Sarah's life. Indeed, the precipitant turned out to be a group event, but not the one that had been affectively important to the others. With this material raised to consciousness, the therapist could then make decisions about his interventions based on the dimensions in Figure 8.1 as well as his clinical judgment. Let us examine the therapist's handling of the situation first in terms of the role dimension and then in terms of the focus dimension.

Activity Versus Nonactivity

The therapist chose to remain quiet to allow both the group depression and Sarah's attack to reach a crescendo before offering any overt responses. Had he not had some sense of what was transpiring, he might have felt compelled to intervene sooner in order to calm both the group and himself. Yet he was not inactive. He made a series of active choices: He did not interfere with the attack and the full expression of negative feelings; he did not offer a defense or a correction of Sarah's distortions about his warmth for her; he determined that all the members of the group could profitably bear the strong affect for at least 60 minutes before any closure was considered. Only then did he make a clarifying interpretation.

Transparency Versus Opaqueness

The therapist chose to remain opaque, having determined that it would not serve Sarah to correct her distortion about his warmth for her. He felt Sarah would be better served if he helped her understand her distortion, and a full understanding required that she be allowed to experience it more fully. The therapist did not confuse the patient with contradictory data but, rather, kept a neutral position and accepted her attack.

Gratification Versus Frustration

The leader was experienced by the group as somewhat frustrating early in the meeting when he simply accepted and encouraged the depressive feelings of the members. However, this was a mature group and there was sufficient alliance with the leader that the members were able to persevere, secure in the knowledge that he would sooner or later offer his observations. That is, they were secure in their conviction that his nonresponse, his failure to do anything to relieve the discomfort, was neither sadistic nor humiliating in intent.

The Past–Present–Future Axis

The therapist's full interpretation moved through the past–present–future axis and included references to the recent past (the termination), the distant past (Sarah's history), the present (the group's current reactions), and the future (the coming of the new member). To have focused exclusively on any single aspect of the time line would have been to miss important material.

The Group-as-a-Whole–Interpersonal–Individual Axis

When he did respond, the leader made both a group-as-a-whole and an individual response. He first responded to the whole group, commenting that Sarah's powerful response and the group's depressed silence had been linked, that both were indications of the members working through the termination of the lost member. He then helped Sarah understand her idiosyncratic reaction, how her reaction to him was a response to history and not to current reality. He helped her understand (through her own associations) how her sudden loss of self-esteem was connected to the forthcoming "baby" in the group family. Sarah readily accepted this interpretation and confirmed it by reporting a dream. In her dream the new member was female (as was the infant in her history), despite her rational conviction that a man would replace the man who had terminated.

In this situation the therapist chose to focus on the individual in order to help the group as a whole. This decision was predicated on the leader's observation that Sarah was filled with the most overt affect and on his conviction not only that she was experiencing a powerful replay from her history but also that in some important way she was probably a spokesperson for affects that were relevant for the group as a whole.

The In-Group–Out-of-Group Axis

In this illustration the members did not bring out-of-group material the session. Interestingly, this time it was the *therapist* who ultimately introduced out-of-group material, linking the in-group affects to the now-departed member and to Sarah's family history. This process of first experiencing affects *in* the group and then placing them in relevant context outside the group is the ideal process.

The Affect–Cognition Axis

As usual in psychodynamic therapy, both the affective and cognitive aspects of insight were important in helping Sarah and the group learn from the exchanges in this meeting. Also as is usual in psychodynamic therapy, the affective elements of learning precede the cognitive. That is, the therapist allowed a full expression of the feelings without prematurely bringing cognitive closure (i.e., linking the behavior to Sarah's past). It is a tenet of psychodynamic therapy that the most important learning occurs emotionally, though that is rarely sufficient for change without a cognitive component as well.

The Process–Content Axis

The axis of process and content is a particularly important one in this scenario. The leader both accepted the content as content and interpreted it as a coded communication about the group process. That is, Sarah *was* furious and convinced that he did not care about her. The leader did not deny that overt content, but he attempted to view it in the light of recent group process as well. Giving primacy to the process allowed the leader to help the members explore very important hidden feelings about the recent termination. Had the leader not looked to the process and linked the present content to the ongoing process, an important opportunity for learning would have been missed.

The Understanding–Corrective Emotional Experience Axis

Finally, understanding alone was considered important but insufficient to help Sarah and the group grow. It was necessary for Sarah, over the ensuing weeks, to put aside her intense rivalry with other women and try out new behaviors and perceptions of herself. Finally, when some months later a woman did join the group, Sarah responded very differently. She commented, "For the first time in my life I feel free to enjoy women rather than just experience them as competitors."

SUMMARY

The focus of the group therapist's attention should vary, not remain static. In each meeting there are allusions to current in-group issues, historical antecedents, emotionality and cognition, and so on. Therapists are often bewildered by the amount of information that confronts them, and in some cases they become paralyzed or simply focus on the most obvious or superficial data.

The two dimensions of leader activity and their component continua provide a way of ordering the plethora of data generated in every group. With this framework therapists are better prepared to make decisions about the use of self (the leadership style dimension) and to organize their thinking and make appropriate interventions (the leadership focus dimension). We suggest that therapists view the data in the order in which the leadership focus dimension continua have been presented here, beginning the sequence with examination of the here and now and continuing with the group-as-a-whole, in-group, affect, and process continua. One can move across the continua as needs dictate.

9

Beginning the Group

APPROACHING THE FIRST MEETING

At some point after all the preparatory work has been completed, the therapist and patients prepare for the first meeting. Typically, everyone approaches this first meeting with a great deal of apprehension and anxiety. Therapists wonder whether the patients who have been screened, selected, and prepared will actually arrive and mesh well together. Members worry about meeting strangers, but their anxiety is vastly increased when they remember that interacting will include sharing the most intimate details and secrets about their life. All the usual concerns about trust and safety are, quite appropriately, central in the minds of the participants. This anxiety and apprehension regarding the initial meeting represents the first shared experience.

Everyone, including the therapist, approaches the unknown situation with his or her own particular fantasies, defenses, and coping mechanisms. Prior experience does not seem to matter—even senior therapists are filled with anticipatory anxiety. If therapists minimize the intensity of their anxiety, their capacity to utilize their own emotional life as a barometer of the group members' experience is diminished. Both therapists and patients are concerned about how group members will work together, how members will respond to them, and how patients will respond to the group. The anticipatory anxiety patients experience may exaggerate coping patterns, but their very exaggeration exposes them all the more clearly.

PRELIMINARY DECISIONS

Prior to the first meeting, the therapist has certain gatekeeping functions. The degree to which these have been accomplished will help con-

146

tain anxiety and influence the patients' confidence and trust in the enterprise.

Before the first meeting the therapist must clearly inform the patients of the time, day, duration, and location of the group. Furthermore, each member should agree to the group agreements prior to meeting the other members.

Ideally, a psychodynamic psychotherapy group would probably meet once weekly for 90 minutes and have eight members, four men and four women. It is certainly within the realm of traditional practice for a group to meet twice a week, from 75 minutes to 120 minutes, to have up to ten members, and to be composed primarily of members of one gender. These parameters must be carefully thought out and decided upon before a new group is formed.

THE TIME FRAME

Frequency of Meetings

Though the usual frequency of group sessions is once a week, groups that meet twice weekly are not rare. Some therapists are beginning to experiment with even more frequent meetings. Birk (1974) reported that patients who failed in other extensive and intensive treatments demonstrated marked improvement when seen in a therapy group that met five times per week.

The optimal frequency of meetings depends upon the capacity of the patient population to hold a memory trace of the group from meeting to meeting. If the patients consistently "seal over," that is, lose contact with the affect from the previous meeting, the leader might consider increasing the frequency of the meetings. However, for most outpatient populations, once a week is sufficient. If meetings take place less frequently than once a week the process seems to get lost and the therapeutic usefulness is diminished.

Some therapists increase the frequency of group meetings by utilizing the technique of alternate sessions, meaning that the group meets a second time each week without the therapist present (Kadis, 1956). The rationale proposed to support this practice is that by meeting without the therapist, members can learn to work without his or her presence, can begin discussions of their negative feelings about the therapist with diminished fears of retaliation, and can, in essence, become less dependent.

It is precisely the reasons put forward in support of alternate meetings that lead us not to recommend this approach. Members need to develop the capacity to feel secure in their affects and thoughts and need to develop independence in the presence of an authority figure. The therapist's task is to analyze resistances and difficulties along that path. If a patient needs to idealize a therapist, the basis for such a response is best worked through in the presence of the therapist. Testimonials by satisfied individuals indicate that there is value to the alternate session, but there has been no research into the processes, dynamics, or the overall efficacy of this format.

Length of Meetings

The range of clinically productive time for psychodynamic psychotherapy groups is between 75 and 120 minutes. Sessions shorter than 75 minutes usually do not provide sufficient air time for the members. In sessions of more than 2 hours' duration, fatigue sets in, a condition that may harden or loosen defenses. Some therapists utilize marathon time formats specifically to invoke fatigue as a therapeutic element (Yalom, Bond, Bloch, Zimmerman, & Friedman, 1977). In psychodynamic groups, however, the object is not to defeat defensive structures but, rather, to examine and understand them. We find little use in extending the time frame to the point where undue fatigue, on the part of either the patients or the therapist, occurs.

The sole exception to this approach to the length of meetings is the option of using a "double-length" meeting after a week in which the group session has been canceled. This alternative will be discussed in Chapter 10.

Time of Meeting

Given the logistical problems involved in gathering eight to ten individuals together weekly, most therapy groups meet before or after usual working hours. Arranging sessions when there is less likelihood of time conflict increases the potential for referrals. Therapists must continually weigh the disadvantages of sacrificing a time convenient for their personal lives against the advantages of offering a time that creates the best opportunity for the group to survive and flourish. In major metropolitan areas it is possible to run groups during the day. Even in such settings, however, the referral network is notably narrowed. Daytime groups typically draw from nonworking, self-employed, professional, student, or night-working populations. Early morning groups can avoid work conflicts but are a problem for parents of infants or school-age children. In the vast majority of instances, groups meet in the late afternoon or early evening.

GROUP SIZE AND GENDER DISTRIBUTION

The choice of group size should be predicated upon the number of patients with which a leader feels comfortable. The usual range is from six to ten members. For some therapists the dynamics that unfold with groups of ten feel comfortable and understandable whereas for others ten in a room feels unmanageable. There is often a connection between the number of members and the length of each meeting, with larger groups meeting for somewhat longer periods.

Clinically, ten members seems to be the upper limit for productive work in a psychodynamic group, although Winick, Kadis, and Krasner (1961) reported on groups having up to twenty-five patients. Beyond ten, less assertive members rarely have sufficient opportunity to discuss their issues. Fewer than six members creates difficulty in effectively utilizing the group process and diminishes the richness of interpersonal input. In smaller groups there is a great temptation for the therapist to focus on the four or five individuals and lose sight of groupwide processes. Further, certain members may feel overexposed or prematurely forced into a type of intimacy for which they are not prepared. Finally, there is some indication that for groups of four or less the group becomes so concerned with survival that other issues become submerged (Fulkerson, Hawkins, & Alden, 1981).

If at all possible, groups should begin with at least seven patients. Since research indicates that most new groups will suffer from one to three dropouts within the first few months, it is important to have sufficient membership so that there is a workable cadre remaining when dropouts occur. When groups begin with insufficient numbers, this is usually a reliable indication that appropriate referrals are in short supply and that the therapist will have continuing difficulties in maintaining a satisfactory census.

Some therapists, in anticipation of members dropping out, begin their groups with more patients than they consider optimal. This strategy, though protecting against the possibility of dropouts threatening the group's survival, ultimately forces some patients to leave. We believe therapists should never begin a group with more than the number with which they are comfortable, since they will remain uncomfortable until the group reaches optimum size and will be less able to make optimal therapeutic interventions.

Ongoing groups should have a balance of men and women. Often, women seeking treatment significantly outnumber men. In such instances it is possible to begin a group with a preponderance of women. For instance, if the therapist's goal is eight members, the group might begin with five women and whatever number of men are available. The remaining seats would be reserved for additional men.

GROUP SPACE

Groups differ markedly from dyadic therapy in space requirements. Too small or too large a room alters everyone's level of comfort and ability to work. Furthermore, the presence or absence of a waiting area affects where and how members assemble prior to the meeting time and has significant impact upon the range of choices they have in relating to one another. For example, in a clinic setting members may have to sit in a communal waiting area with other patients, an arrangement that diminishes pregroup exchanges.

Optimally, the group room itself can be made available at least 15 minutes prior to the beginning of a meeting so that the members may convene there. Some patients enjoy the socialization prior to the meeting whereas others avoid it. These are not chance behaviors, and the subgrouping patterns and conversations that begin prior to the meeting are often important therapeutic material.

The seats themselves connote a great deal about how the group works and what is expected. How a therapist decides to set up the room with sofas and chairs is variable. (Sitting on pillows or on the floor is to be discouraged in adult groups.) Some therapists set a group size and leave a chair for the leader and for every potential member of the group. This arrangement emphasizes that members are absent and that there will be newcomers entering in the future. Furthermore, an empty chair looms large in a group after a significant member has terminated and is a powerful stimulus to the group's mourning process. An alternative procedure is to set up chairs only for those expected to attend a meeting; no chair is present for a terminated member, for someone on vacation, or for someone who called and announced an absence. In this case it is assumed that patients will remember the absent member. The general principle in either approach is consistency.

The seating arrangement should be comfortable enough so that individuals can easily sit for the duration of the meeting. Individuals select seating based on conscious and unconscious determinants. These choices are often connected to the patients' character styles or to dynamic processes taking place within the group. Observations about patterned choices help patients gain valuable insight. For example, who chooses the more comfortable-looking and the less inviting seats? Who sits near other people and who sits farther away? Who sits near the leader and who sits far away? We learn not only from the type of seat chosen but also from its position. In some groups patients become rooted to particular chairs; in others the seating arrangement is flexible. It is best for the leader to sit in the same chair each week. This not only serves to underline consistency, but it provides the opportunity to glean meaning from the members' choice of seating vis-à-vis the leader. (For a more complete discussion of nonverbal communication, see Chapter 11.)

Some group rooms include a table in the middle of the group. Indeed this is standard practice for clinicians trained in the group analytic model. In the United States it is a less common practice. The main principle is that the group setting be such that members are not physically hidden from one another.

A particularly important aspect of the group space is the door, a boundary that must be regulated predictably. On occasion, patients and even inexperienced therapists will leave the door open after the session has begun with the expectation that a tardy member will soon enter. Obviously, an open door has considerable impact upon members' sense of freedom and privacy. Further, such an open door symbolizes an open acceptance of the tardiness. It is preferable that the door be closed when the group session begins in order to demonstrate this fact conclusively.

THE FIRST MEETING

The moments just before the start of the first meeting are a time of great excitement and anxiety, a common state of arousal shared by therapist and patients. When the door is closed and the first meeting has begun, patients look around apprehensively and almost always fix their gaze on the therapist. Later in the life of the group the therapist will enter, sit down, and begin observing, but the first meeting represents an exception; in this case the therapist does have a responsibility for beginning the meeting.

The therapist starts by making it clear that he or she has met previously with each individual, that all have agreed to the same agreements, and that all have significant personal issues they wish to resolve. At this point the therapist should repeat the group agreements. In the case of homogeneous groups, the therapist also makes it clear that the members share the common variable. Typically, he or she then suggests that people get to know one another, leaving the exact manner of that introduction to the members themselves. The leader should then sit silently (but not impassively) and observe the developing interactions.

From the moment the group begins, we have an opportunity to observe the approaches our patients utilize to cope with stress. The initial data available for observation and analysis are the various styles used by the members to cope with the groupwide anxiety. How the members handle that common anxiety depends on their personality structure, their historic defense mechanisms, and the specific interactions that actually occur in the group. Therapists beginning groups should be thoroughly acquainted with the formative phase of group development (which is explored in depth in Chapter 3).

The Therapist's Role

When a group meets for the first time, there is an enormous pull on the therapist to reduce the initial anxiety by becoming active. The therapist wants the group to begin comfortably and certainly wishes to avoid such intense anxiety that members never return. The members also want relief from the terrors of the unknown. The fantasy arises that the leader can reduce the anxiety. Nonetheless, therapists should resist the impulse to be overactive because a style once established is difficult to break. In groups where the therapist is quite active in introductions and agenda setting, patients feel disappointed in subsequent sessions when he or she becomes less active and they, seemingly without the leader's protection, are faced with the unknown. Contrary to the intuition of the therapist, even new groups of primitive patients can survive and profit from a first session in which they are left largely to their own devices.

After the initial comments, the therapist's task is to begin to show the members how their fantasies and interactions in the here and now can be valuable in learning about themselves and the problems they came to resolve. The main issue is that members should feel that they have *learned* something from their initial anxiety.

The Patients' Roles

The first meeting usually begins with rudimentary introductions. Names, ranks, and serial numbers are given, after which the members will often fall silent. It is important that the therapist wait for the group to break the silence (it only *seems* like it is going to last forever!). If the therapist indicates an early discomfort with silence by intervening too quickly, he or she will quickly teach the group that they can get the therapist to respond by being silent.

If the therapist remains quiet, the members will begin to talk, sometimes about the problems that brought them, but mainly they will test the water by feeling out the others in an effort to access the safety and comfort they might expect from the group. There are rare exceptions when the therapist has misjudged the members' capacity to interact; rather than sit in prolonged silence, the leader should intervene to protect members from the fears the silence evokes.

Eventually, though by no means necessarily in the first meeting,

someone in the group will offer the first group "gift," revealing information or feelings that make that individual truly vulnerable if the
response is insensitive. Perhaps a member begins to weep or to tell in
more detail why he or she is in the group. At this point the other members may or may not join the new level of sharing. If the gift-giving
member has not revealed something entirely foreign or too personal
for a first meeting, others will inevitably tell more themselves. In the
first meeting, *what* is shared is much less important than the fact that
something *is* shared and that the response is not threatening. The group
is beginning to test out what can be said in this room, and they are
very watchful and wary of the reactions of the other members and especially of the therapist.

Ending the First Meeting

The ending of an initial group meeting should accomplish several objectives: First, if the agreements were not restated at the beginning of
the session, such a restatement should be made at this time. Second,
the group leader should make some contact with each member. In this
first meeting it is especially important that all the members know they
were noticed and attended to by the leader, who might say, for example, "We noticed a variety of ways in which people dealt with this common anxiety about the initial meeting," and might then relate the
responses he or she observed.

Sometimes mere eye contact between therapist and member is sufficient to let a member know that some connection is being made. Beginning a group is difficult and, ironically, a very lonely experience for
patients. It is unlike beginning individual therapy, where there is some
cultural expectation that the therapist will listen attentively, will not
be hurtful or vengeful, and will give undivided attention. In groups the
patients must struggle for time and attention, and they have no assur-
ances about how their fellow members will respond to personal ex-
posures.

Despite the initial anxiety, almost all first sessions are judged a
success by the therapist and the members. There is a feeling of exhila-
ration and pleasure that the enterprise has gotten off the ground. Before the first session members were so concerned with personal survival
that the reality of the meeting is quite mild by comparison. Indeed,
simply the recognition that others are just as worried is very helpful
to each member and evokes a positive feeling.

There are few meetings in which the themes can be as accurately
predicted as in the first one. For example, the therapist will be helpful
and almost always on target if he or she closes the meeting by saying

"The group has been testing to see how safe it is going to be to share what is most important in your lives with these people and with me." Or "People have been saying 'hello' in a variety of ways."

THE EARLY WEEKS

After the initial meeting patients generally resurrect their defenses and characteristic patterns of interacting. Caution is an important dynamic, and an underlying behavior in the early weeks is testing to see whether the group and others can be trusted (W. Stone & Gustafson, 1982). Members are experientially trying to establish group norms in order to institutionalize safety. However, conflicts inevitably arise since not everyone has the same safety requirements. The tensions between the differing needs fuel the interactions, but the pace is generally slow because dealing with these tensions directly involves the central pathological conflicts of many of the members. Often patients become disheartened and disillusioned about the group during this time.

Therapists have a number of important tasks to help group formation. They must monitor boundaries and norms. The primary boundary is between the group and the outside world. For a variety of reasons, members will come late or be absent. The therapist must draw attention to these violations of the group agreements in order to establish both the norm of exploring boundary violations for their potential deeper meanings and the norm of valuing the importance of the here and now. What complicates matters is the extensive use of denial at this stage. Members generally ignore or minimize the deeper meanings of others' behavior. Therapists may feel they are swimming upstream. Members will create all sorts of pressures to keep the therapist from bringing boundary violations to their attention and especially to keep him or her from interpreting the meanings of these violations. Nevertheless, the therapist, with as much tact and therapeutic creativity as possible, must point out what is happening.

Being addressed are not only the external boundaries, but also the boundaries within the group. Individuals erect barriers to giving and receiving information about one another. Usually no one person blocks development of trust and openness; instead, a collusion exists in which members avoid difficult affects, use anger as a defense against involvement, switch topics, and so on. While the content that is discussed might be quite revealing as to the hidden conflicts or fears of the speakers, the focus for the therapist at this stage is the process, that is, how members deal with anxieties and conflicts rather than the content of a particular conflict. The anxieties aroused in the early weeks tempt the therapist to close off affect prematurely with summarizing interpretations. Instead, the therapeutic task is to help members tolerate and face the anxieties generated by the process.

During the early phases of a group, therapists sometimes become discouraged with the lack of progress and with the defensiveness and resistance of the members. It is well to remember that resistance is not a process designed to resist treatment; rather, it is a defensive process designed to resist emotional pain. Typically, patients in group therapy have not had histories of sustaining, healing, and comforting relationships. It would be unnatural for them to assume that group relationships are different. In sum, it would be much more pathological and aberrant if the patients suddenly adopted new behaviors in the group rather than relying upon the tried-and-true (albeit deficient) behaviors from the past.

In this opening period a number of interactive patterns emerge with regularity. In almost every group there is a period when advice giving is a common modus operandi. Members will present a problem or a conflict in their lives, and others will make direct suggestions about solutions. Analysis and understanding is not the goal; problem solving is. A number of dynamics may be functioning in such advice-giving behaviors, such as a desire to remove problems that make people uncomfortable; to use tried-and-true remedies rather than recognize a sense of helplessness; to focus on external problems so that the more difficult task of dealing with the in-group interactions can be bypassed; to compete with the therapist for fantasied acclaim; or to demonstrate the members' ineffectiveness with one another (only rarely does a suggestion have the potential to solve a problem inasmuch as patients have already received lots of advice and suggestions before they enter the group). When confronted with a period of advice giving, the therapist must help the members understand its function with regard to the group's development.

A similar situation occurs when a group focuses on one member as "sick." Overtly, all are altruistically working to help solve that individual's problems. However, by focusing on one member the pathologies of others are obscured. The parallel with family interactions, in which a child may be labeled as "sick" and thus the scapegoat for all the family's difficulties, is evident. In a variation on this pattern members seem to be taking turns: "Last week we talked about Adam; now it's Betty's turn." Seldom is this process explicit, but it subtly becomes established and serves to limit intragroup transactions.

These are but a few examples of the ways members and therapists attempt to manage the problems of developing group trust and cohesion. The analysis of resistances, character traits, and emergency defenses all can be used for therapeutic gain, but sometimes in these early weeks the therapist and members become discouraged, primarily because the group is not meeting their expectations. Under such circumstances the therapist's countertransference may be mobilized to scapegoat members who seem to be obstructionistic, or the therapist may become defensive and less open to hearing his or her patients. These problems affect the group atmosphere and promote dropping out, a problem we will discuss in the next section.

The patients' discouragement often leads to depression, exacerbation of symptoms, or a futile attempt to arouse optimism about the group through reaction formation. The critical consideration for patients and therapist during this time is to remember that the reawakening of primary defenses and pathologies is a sign that the group is in fact becoming effective; that is, as these behaviors are displayed, the members begin to experience their problems in the group itself.

DROPOUTS

Almost all new psychotherapy groups have one or more dropouts within the first few weeks. Such dropouts, while disconcerting and disappointing, should be considered an expectable part of beginning a group. A number of reports in the literature indicate that 20% to 45% of charter members leave within the first year. The data seem valid for both clinic and private practice settings and for both inexperienced and seasoned group therapists (W. Stone & Rutan, 1984).

The reasons given for leaving are varied. Sometimes no reason is given at all. On occasion patients will suddenly find they have a time conflict, perhaps even pleading that the group time be changed to accommodate them. However, any change in the group structure is contraindicated. Many a well-meaning therapist has changed the time of a group to help a particular member avoid a time conflict only to find that the very member in question drops out of the group anyway. Time conflicts, while certainly real in many instances, are nonetheless best understood dynamically, that is, as a communication about the patient's experience of his or her participation in the group.

The fact that the early life of groups involves people leaving prematurely dramatically reduces the members' optimism. It is not unusual for new groups to develop an atmosphere of hopelessness and discouragement and to begin questioning the efficacy of group therapy and the competence of the leader. The leader should encourage the open expression of these fears and doubts, thereby reassuring the members that all feelings can be honestly shared.

VERY SMALL GROUPS

For a variety of reasons there will be weeks when only one or two patients come to a meeting; running a session with such a small group
is a problem. Unfortunately, this is not unusual early in the life of a
group, before cohesiveness has set in.

Inexperienced therapists often wonder whether they should reduce
the amount of time or cancel the meeting if only one or two group
members arrive. The press to cancel or shorten the time is the therapist's countertransferential attempt to avoid the affect (hurt, anger,
disappointment, fear, and so on) stimulated by such a small group.
However, to curtail or cancel the meeting would be to punish the very
members who kept their group agreements and would certainly institute nontherapeutic norms. Furthermore, one is never certain that other
members won't come strolling in late.

Leading the very small group is awkward for the inexperienced
therapist. There is a temptation to revert to therapy techniques for individuals or couples. However, the group still exists in the minds of
the members who did come, and the particular meeting occurs in the
context of the failure of several members to honor their agreements.
It is not unusual for these sessions of very small groups to have a significant impact on those who attend. The technical key for the therapist is to remember that this is still a *group,* albeit a very small and
fragmented one. One of the major issues needing attention is the feeling on the part of those who came of being let down by their colleagues.
Old feelings of separation, loss, abandonment, divorce, and family dissolution all may be awakened. On the other hand, for some patients
the very small group means that they have more "air time." How the
attending members respond to the situation is potentially quite important.

NEW MEMBERS

In ongoing groups the coming and going of members has great meaning. Each good-bye and hello means that the group itself changes. The
therapist should encourage members to explore personal and groupwide meanings associated with the anticipation of newcomers prior to
their introduction. Considerable pressure may arise within the group
to avoid change, even at the cost of maintaining a lower census. Members will talk openly about their anxieties with the intent of coercing
the therapist into delaying new additions. An alternative strategy occurs when they attack the therapist for making poor choices, hoping

to influence him or her to reject some acceptable applicants. Finally, some may threaten to quit rather than face a newcomer, and on occasion a member actually leaves.

The various pressures may influence the therapist's decisions. It is not easy to decide when a group could benefit from more time to work on a loss or on the feelings surrounding the advent of new members. The repeated thought "This is not a good time to add members" is often a manifestation of countertransference, and therefore acting on it may be an error. On the other hand, therapists can collude to cover over patient feelings by prematurely filling an empty chair.

New members should *never* simply arrive at a meeting without warning. Old members need a period of preparation so that they may explore their reactions to the idea of a new member, but it is also important that they be able to come to each session without the concern that strangers might be present. The usual procedure is for the therapist, at the beginning of a meeting, to announce that a new member will be joining the group on a particular date. It is advisable to provide only the fact that a new member will be entering. Fantasies about the age, sex, marital status, and other details about the coming member all contain useful material from which the old members can learn. The length of time between the announcement and the actual arrival of the new member depends upon many variables. If a group has had an open chair for some time and has been awaiting a new member, 2 weeks can be sufficient lead time. If, on the other hand, the empty chair is the result of a particularly important or painful loss (a highly valued member who terminated or one who suddenly died), the time required to sort through feelings about another person joining should be longer. All other factors being equal, 2 weeks' notice seems optimal. This provides members the opportunity to work on their reactions immediately and in the following week as well.

From a practical perspective a new person can be admitted when the appropriate preparation has been completed. There has been some support for the suggestion that new members be added in pairs, not singly, in order to protect them from being victimized by latent or overt hostility from the members. This practice is presumed to reduce the chances of newcomers dropping out prematurely. W. Stone and Rutan (1984) found that adding patients singly did not lead to unusual numbers prematurely stopping, and in fact the data suggest this approach diminishes the number of dropouts. By adding members individually, each new member has a time of separate introduction and the norm becomes established that empty chairs will be filled as they are vacated.

At times the therapist will be confronted by the situation of having two or more simultaneous openings and an equal number of applicants. The question at this time is "Should the new patients be added singly or together?" There are pros and cons to either answer. Ideally, each member has the opportunity to enter the group alone. This provides each new patient with a brief individual introduction, allowing for more individualization and affording a clearer view of the introductory dynamics of that person. On the other hand, if multiple openings are filled at the same time, there is the real advantage of closing the group boundary more quickly. Furthermore, the new members often experience a powerful and immediate alliance with those who join with them. The exception is when the new patients being considered outnumber the members already in the group. In that instance the entrances should be sequential so that there are never more new than old members. Naturally, on those occasions when groups have diminished to a membership of one or two, even that rule must be broken.

Each group develops initiation rites (Kaplan & Roman, 1961). The therapist sets the tone by restating the group agreements, which also reminds the existing members of those agreements. Frequently, the agreements are remembered incorrectly, and this habitual restating allows for corrections as well as explorations of the meanings of the distortion. Repetition of the group agreements puts everyone on an equal footing in this area.

Some groups appear to greet newcomers warmly and enthusiastically, and only through closer scrutiny is ambivalence exposed. Retention of the fantasy of the old group, which subtly excludes the newcomer, may be expressed by reminiscing or by cryptically referring to prior events. Another common initiation procedure is for groups to have dramatic and highly emotional meetings. In part such meetings can be understood as exhibitionistic demonstrations of how much emotion, personal revelation, and confrontation can be tolerated. These dramatic meetings often have another unconscious element as well—an attempt to frighten off the newcomer or at least to test his or her mettle. Questioning new members about their histories and reasons for coming to group is yet another initiation pattern. The questioning can vary widely in its form and intent, ranging from courteous inquiry of a new member, thereby offering him or her an opportunity to make connections with the other members, to sadistic grilling with no altruistic motivation. Impressions at this time of change in group composition are valuable data and are available only briefly. Whatever initiation rites are used to greet newcomers, the therapist must help the group learn from them.

10

Special Technical Considerations: I

A number of leadership issues arise with sufficient regularity to warrant special attention. In the next four chapters we will deal with a variety of these recurring and important leadership issues. In this chapter we will attend to issues of (1) cotherapy, (2) leader absences, (3) transferring of groups, (4) removing patients from groups, and (5) the affect of the therapist.

THE USE OF COTHERAPISTS IN GROUP PSYCHOTHERAPY

It is not unusual for groups, especially in clinics and training settings, to have coleaders. Rabin (1967) has even suggested that most therapists prefer working with a colleague. Eliot (1990) has taken the concept so far as to do cotherapy using some of the mothers of anorexic and bulimic patients.

Various advantages are cited for a cotherapy model. Dual leadership allows for a fuller and more complete view of the group and protects against blind spots in either therapist (Demarest & Teicher, 1954). Furthermore, each therapist has the opportunity to move in and out of active and passive (or observational) modes (Gans, 1962). Parallel to this is the advantage of watching a colleague at work and learning from that opportunity (Solomon, Loeffler, & Frank, 1953). Cotherapy offers the pragmatic advantages of providing ongoing coverage at times of sickness or vacation, increasing limit-setting capacities in working with certain patient populations (e.g., children, severely acting-out patients, geriatric patients), and making work with large groups possible. It also provides an opportunity for peer consultation and support (Getty & Shannon, 1969; Yalom, 1985).

The treatment process of group psychotherapy may be enhanced by cotherapy inasmuch as this model theoretically offers a replication of a two-parent family. Even in cases where the therapists are of the same gender, it has been reported that patients respond transferentially as if to a male–female pair (Lundin & Aronov, 1952). Other authors stress the unique value of having a male–female cotherapy team that stimulates parental transference (Demarest & Teicher, 1954), and also offers each patient a same-gender therapist with whom to identify (Mintz, 1965). Another advantage of cotherapy stems from the manner in which cotherapists relate to each another, handle conflict, and communicate acceptance. Their relationship (if it is a healthy one) provides a model that patients may use for imitation or identification (Getty & Shannon, 1969, p. 769; Yalom, 1975, pp. 421–422).

Despite all these suggested assets, cotherapy is primarily used as a vehicle for training group therapists. The presence of a cotherapist lessens anxiety for the trainee (Yalom, 1985, p. 418), provides a sense of support, and allows for a shared responsibility. The presence of cotherapists, especially when their leadership tenures do not coincide, softens the impact of loss on group members when student therapists terminate their leadership as they leave their training. There is also the reality that most training programs do not have sufficient groups to allow each of their trainees to lead a group individually. It is something of an irony that we rarely ask our group therapists to experience in training what we ask our group patients to experience—the anxiety of entering a group alone.

Despite the aforementioned advantages, cotherapy is not the preferred leadership model in most situations. In fact, many of the arguments *for* cotherapy turn out to be arguments *against* it. For example, is it really advisable to reduce the therapist's anxiety? Should not the therapist confront anxieties about entering the group alone that are similar to those our patients must face? Middleman (1980) agrees that dulling therapist anxiety is neither in the service of training or good clinical care. Likewise, the argument that cotherapy allows the therapist to drift in and out of focus, relying on the cotherapist to remain attentive, is weak because at times of highest stress *both* therapists simultaneously would likely want to back away. In the treatment process the therapist is stimulated by the variety of passionate affects in the group. Optimally, the therapist can bear this affect and use it diagnostically and to guide technique. For example, if a therapist is feeling rageful, it is useful to determine if the feeling represents the containing of a projective identification, the reasonable human response to outrageous behavior, the empathic attunement to a rageful patient, or pure and simple countertransference. However, in cotherapy situations these passionate affects often become part of the cotherapy relationship, reflecting the truism that children can encourage parents to fight or love each other. Finally, in an era when mental health delivery costs are under close scrutiny, it seems hard to justify doubling the cost of group therapy by doubling the number of therapists.

Cotherapy is actually a more difficult model to follow than is solo leadership because it entails having to maintain the cotherapy relationship itself. Working in the intimate arena of a therapy group, cotherapists are exposed to highly stimulating situations and affects. As a result, it is not unusual for cotherapists to become rivalrous — or to become lovers. In one sense cotherapy is like a marriage, and the cotherapists who may have been courting before the cotherapy began are placed in a marriage-like relationship once it does. The ordinary adjustment period is stressed by an immediate task, namely, the equivalent of raising needy and (hopefully) outspoken children. But no cotherapists automatically work together smoothly. They cannot. What makes cotherapy succeed is the maturity and willingness of the two leaders to continually work on and attend to their own relationship so that tensions in it do not filter into the group. Cotherapists must be willing to devote considerable time to maintaining *their* relationship. They must achieve a degree of comfort in disagreeing with each other, and they must determine the extent and nature of the disagreements they wish to air in the group (Lang & Halperin, 1989).

MacLennon (1965) noted that transferences arise between cotherapists, and add to the complexity of sorting out the members' "real" and transferential relationships. The traditional boundaries between therapists and patients prohibit socialization, but there is no such prohibition for cotherapists. Indeed, since cotherapists are encouraged to use one another to unwind and to review the meetings, they have considerable informal, semisocial contact. The stimulation, or arousal of affect, in the therapist role requires that cotherapists be especially alert to the potential for acting rather than talking. We have seen significant therapeutic and social complications arising from cotherapists' acting on their feelings for one another, be they warm or hostile. Furthermore, the transferential relationship between cotherapists is often exaggerated by splitting defenses employed by the members (Greene, Rosenkrantz, & Muth, 1986).

Patients may experience difficulty with a cotherapy format. Many patients find it harder to confront or disagree with two therapists presenting a united front. Others, rather than learning from differences between the therapists, are frightened by the cotherapists' inevitable conflicts. The notion that a cotherapy team represents an ideal mother–father pair is somewhat grandiose, since few cotherapy teams we know suggest such maturity or perfection in their relationship.

Rutan and Alonso (1980) have suggested an intriguing training alternative to the traditional model of cotherapy, an approach they term *sequential cotherapy.* In this approach two leaders are employed, but each leads the group separately for a prescribed number of weeks while the nonleading cotherapist becomes a silent observer. This model offers some of the advantages suggested for cotherapy (such as binocular vision, peer consultation, sharing of responsibility, covering at times of illness or vacation) while neutralizing some of the competitive features of traditional cotherapy. This model has particular advantages as a teaching tool, since the observer therapist can more easily lead a didactic session with trainees who have observed the group session. At the time of this writing Rutan and Alonso have sequentially co-led a group of very disturbed patients for almost 20 years, and they report increasing conviction that the model holds promise.

Overall, the disadvantages of cotherapy outweigh the gains. In training situations there may be no alternative if trainees are to gain experience as group leaders, but supervisors of these groups should be attentive to the increased problems cotherapy imposes on trainees. With certain patient populations, particularly the chronically mentally ill, the disadvantages of cotherapy are outweighed by the necessity of having two therapists in the room if therapy is to proceed at all.

LEADER ABSENCES

Therapists take vacations, attend professional meetings, become ill, and occasionally have competing priorities that mandate their not being present to lead their groups. Absences should be rare, and the decision to miss a group session is not one to make lightly. Nonetheless, even the most conscientious group therapist cannot be present every week. The question then becomes "How is the group best served in this situation?" There are several options available, including the following:

1. Canceling the meeting
2. Providing a makeup meeting
3. Holding a double session before or after the leader's absence
4. Inviting the group to meet without the leader
5. Providing a substitute leader

Given the paramount importance of continuity and cohesion, any breaches in the schedule are matters that threaten the effectiveness of the group. Any absence of the leader is an important event, and the members' feelings concerning this event must be fully explored and used to enhance learning. There should be no attempt to blur the affects connected to the leader's missing one or more meetings.

As Rutan, Alonso, and Molin (1984) have pointed out, there is a theoretically valid rationale for each of the aforementioned options. The advantages and liabilities of each are explored in the following paragraphs.

Canceling the Meeting

Advantages

Time lost is lost forever. When the leader is absent, and the group is forced to lose time with him or her, canceling a group reinforces that reality. The cancellation of a meeting forces the members to fully face the absence of the leader and all the implications of that loss. For example, one ramification of the leader's absence is that it is not only the leader but also the group that is lost to the members for that period of time. Canceling the meeting is an option that does not offer false restitution. The search for painless solutions to life's dilemmas is one source of pathology for many patients. Thus, for most members this response to a leader's absence holds great promise.

Liabilities

Patients do not always learn best by actually experiencing the full deprivation that may have led to developmental arrests. Some patients need a time of idealizing their group therapist (Rutan & Rice, 1981), and the treatment may be adversely affected by premature de-idealization of the leader, which would result if the meeting is canceled. The reexperiencing of painful affect, resulting from canceling the meeting, which may simply reactivate the repetition compulsion without any working through. Also, especially when faced with a rather long absence of the leader, there are some groups, or specific members, who may not survive the loss of continuity. It is not unusual for vulnerable members to drop out of a group in anticipation of a disruption in continuity.

Providing a Makeup Meeting

Advantages

If leaders provide an opportunity to make up the lost meeting or meetings, this can demonstrate a commitment to the group and can heighten awareness of the mutual responsibilities involved in relationships. This option allows the members to avail themselves of the healing power of the group even though the regularly scheduled weekly meeting will not occur. If this option is used, the time should be negotiated with the group rather than imposed by the leader. However, this negotiation should be based on a limited number of times (no more than three) offered by the leader. This period of negotiation often highlights character styles and issues of motivation for the members. (By the way, unless a makeup meeting policy was part of the original group agreements, the therapist should not charge members who do not attend the atypical meeting.)

Liabilities

One major problem with the makeup option is that it may suppress angry feelings. How can one be angry at an abandoning therapist who goes out of his or her way to make up the meeting? Indeed, therapists may invoke this option out of a need to please or avoid anger rather than out of a more thoughtful consideration of the pros and cons. If the makeup meeting option is used, the therapist needs to listen carefully for the members' negative affects linked to the original cancellation (and to the inconvenience that the makeup meeting may entail). Patients should not end up feeling grateful to the exclusion of other feelings about the lack of agreed-upon consistency.

A second problem with this option is the difficulty in finding a suitable alternate time. Anyone who has tried to arrange a meeting for six to ten people knows how complex and frustrating this can be. Almost invariably someone is unable or unwilling to meet at the time agreed to by the majority. To meet and exclude one or more individuals creates another array of problems and affects (specifically, feelings of exclusion, competition, and favoritism). If the makeup option is used, the therapist must decide in advance what to do if all the members cannot agree on an alternate meeting time. To meet without some members causes problems but to allow a deviant member to force everyone else to do without is also a problem. The leader should also retain final decision power over when the meeting will be since to open this to a democratic process raises more issues than it solves.

Holding a Double Session

Advantages

If one meeting is canceled, it is sometimes useful to meet for twice as long the week after the absence. Such an extended session should occur *after* the missed meeting rather than before it since double sessions often stir up considerable affect and the members should not have to wait for a prolonged period before meeting again. Furthermore, holding a double session after a missed session does not interfere as much with the experience of the missed week. Holding a double session is similar to holding an alternate session since it indicates the therapist's willingness to be responsible to the agreements, even while altering them; while not meeting at the agreed-upon time, at least the therapist is offering to meet for the allotted amount of time.

A particular advantage to this option is that the extended time frame allows for more sharing from some members. Other theoretical modalities (notably those that use marathon formats) have demonstrated the power of extended sessions. While we do not propose to defeat patients' defenses through sheer fatigue, the extension of time permits greater self-exposure. The danger of overwhelming defenses is minimized by the fact that the double session occurs in the context of an ongoing group.

Liabilities

The problems with the double-session option again include the possibility that the patients may not experience or express their feelings about the leader's unavailability or lack of dependability. Further, there is the danger that more fragile patients may be endangered by the expanded time. There is also the possibility that members may infer that twice as long is twice as good, which would then lead the group to wonder why all sessions are not of the extended format. Finally, as with the makeup meeting option, there is the thorny question of whether there is to be a double session for every missed meeting or just for some, as well as the issue of what to do if not all members can stay for the extended period.

Inviting the Group to Meet Without the Leader

Advantages

Some therapists use the format of the leaderless meeting as a routine part of the therapeutic agreement (the alternate meeting). Even in groups where the alternate meeting is not used, members frequently express the wish to meet during the leader's absence. Usually such a proposal dies during subsequent discussion. The response may be different if the therapist initiates the idea. A host of dynamics related to authority, power, and safety are mobilized, and marked emotionality generally results as members vehemently support or oppose the idea. An especially difficult situation arises if one or more members choose not to attend an alternate meeting: The leader will not be present to hear what may be said about the absent members. If this option is used, the therapist must make the usual group room available and discourage the group from meeting anywhere else. It should further be stipulated that the group begin and end at the usual time. This structure enhances continuity, discourages using the alternate meeting as a social encounter, and provides symbolic support. The alternate meeting also supports independence and implies that the leader has confidence that the group can function without him/or her.

Liabilities

Of all the options available to deal with a leader's absence, we view the leaderless format as the least helpful and the most likely to result in problems. For one thing, there is really no such thing as a leaderless group. Therefore, the group will inevitably elevate one member to the leadership role for that meeting. This has complicating implications for subsequent meetings. For dynamic groups members give themselves permission to freely and spontaneously express forbidden affects as a consequence of their conviction that the therapist will provide safety.

Providing a Substitute Leader

Advantages

An unusual and yet viable response to a therapist's absence is to provide a substitute leader. Where possible, a consistent substitute leader should be available to be called upon whenever a primary therapist is absent. A substitute leader allows for continuity and predictability for the boundaries of therapy groups without implying that the group leader is all-giving or idealized. In the course of time, groups begin integrating the substitute leader as an important transferential figure. This model offers the following unique opportunities:

   1. The group can actively explore the meaning and effect of the leader's absence without having to endure the loss of a session. The

substitute leader can be facilitative in helping the group explore their reactions to the leader's absence.

2. The group not only gains from the different perspective of the substitute therapist but also has the opportunity to explore the different transferences that leader may evoke. Ideally, the substitute leader should be of the opposite gender from the ongoing leader in order to enhance these effects.

3. A group is able to continue functioning in those rare instances when a leader must be absent for a prolonged period of time, such as when illness, injury, or pregnancy occurs.

4. Peer consultation between the therapists is especially valuable. Since the substitute leader has the opportunity to meet with the group on different occasions, he or she has the overview perspective of seeing the patients periodically and can therefore help the ongoing therapist assess the progress of the members and of the group itself. Further, the substitute therapist might view particular members or group dynamics quite differently from the ongoing therapist, thus broadening the latter's perspective.

Liabilities

Providing a substitute leader also has its disadvantages. The introduction of a second leader occasionally invites splitting and other regressive defenses resistant to interpretation. Further, the introduction of a second therapist means that a form of cotherapy has been initiated, along with all the complications of cotherapy mentioned earlier in this chapter. Moreover, as is the case when a patient sees one therapist in individual therapy and another in group therapy, the therapists in the substitute leader arrangement are not seeing the patients together; this adds a level of complication and requires that the therapists communicate actively in the service of the treatment. Finally, the substitute therapist option becomes even more complicated if the substitute therapist is not available when the primary therapist cannot meet with the group. The group is now faced with a double disappointment.

Conclusion

If there is any plan to deal with leader absence other than the usual exploration of feelings and memories evoked, this must be made clear to the group members from the beginning, preferably as part of the original group agreements. Generally, groups can tolerate leader absences very well, and unless there are extenuating circumstances we prefer not to hold a meeting or make up the time, thereby allowing the group

to experience and learn from the therapist's absence just as they do
from the absence of individual members.

TRANSFERRING LEADERSHIP OF A THERAPY GROUP

Though therapists move, get ill, or retire, most commonly groups change
therapists when a leader (or set of coleaders) finishes a period of training. Since beginning a new group is an arduous and often lengthy
process, training programs, which are dependent upon there being
groups for students to run, attempt to maintain ongoing groups that
change therapists. Whatever the reason, loss of the group leader is a
difficult challenge for the group (Chiang & Beck, 1988; Long, Pendleton, & Winter, 1988; McGee, 1974).

Changes in leadership can be divided into those that are planned
and those that are unplanned, the latter being cases of illness and death.
Sharpe (1991) suggests that the degree of difficulty in the transition period can be correlated with the length of the group's association with
the previous therapist, the similarity in theoretical orientation of the
two therapists, and the new therapist's potential for ensuring the group's
survival. To this we would add that each clinician's personal characteristics and style set the stage for comparisons and contrasts to be made
between the therapists. In the case of a therapist's death, attention to
the mourning process is crucial.

A change of therapists is never easy. Often, a planned transition
becomes a crisis so filled with affect that the group suffers rather than
learns from the experience. It is not unusual for one or more members
to drop out instead of making the transition. Occasionally, a whole
group is destroyed in this process. A number of strategies are available
to make this crisis an opportunity for learning rather than a trauma.
Each clinical situation requires close examination because each model
has its strengths and liabilities.

Models of Transition of Leaders

How the new leader(s) is introduced to the group is a major concern.
There are several options available to accomplish this transition.

No Overlap

In one model a departing therapist leads the group until the announced
termination date and the succeeding therapist does not meet with the
group until the following week. (There should never be a gap between

sessions led by an outgoing and an incoming therapist! Losing a therapist is a crisis for a group, and it is often difficult for the group members to contemplate "beginning all over" with a new therapist. If there is a gap of time between losing the old therapist and beginning with the new one, there are a disproportionate number of dropouts and groups often do not survive the transition.) This rigorous model focuses on the issues of the loss of the old and the impact of the new and maximizes the affective response. It offers the maximum focus on the feelings regarding the loss of the leader and is the option of choice when the ego strength of the members or the group's developmental level is judged adequate to manage the intense affects aroused. This model promotes fantasies about the incoming therapist since there is no concrete data about him or her (other than perhaps a name, which usually implies gender). Patients face the unknown collectively, but they each have fantasies about the benevolence or destructiveness of the new therapist. Sometimes these fantasies can be terrifying. Even when this approach is handled well, some patients may be overwhelmed and flee treatment.

Minimal Overlap

In the minimal overlap model the incoming therapist is simply introduced to the group 2 or 3 weeks prior to the outgoing leader's termination. Typically, the group is notified that the new therapist will be present for a few moments in the next group meeting. At that meeting the incoming therapist simply introduces himself or herself and says something like "I am looking forward to working with you." He or she also specifically mentions the date the new leadership will begin (the new leader should avoid engaging in a question-and-answer period). The new therapist then leaves, and the group continues. This model provides a bridge so that the group actually sees and meets their new therapist, but it does not unduly interfere with the group's saying goodbye to their exiting leader.

Observation

In the observation model (used primarily in training centers) incoming therapists begin by silently observing the groups they are to lead (W. Stone, 1975). This model promotes continuity and bridging of leadership, and members can begin to develop a relationship with the new therapist. Although there may have been only minimal or nonverbal exchanges, the members have an opportunity to assess the new leader and the new leader gains valuable information about the group and therefore comes to the task of leadership with knowledge. This is also an important training opportunity for the new therapist, for whom leading a group may be a new adventure. The opportunity to watch a group in action without having responsibility for leadership is a fine way to gain experience. In training programs the observer also participates in postgroup meetings with the retiring leader and attends supervisory sessions on the group, thereby increasing his or her knowledge of the group history and functioning. An optimal observation period is from 3 months to 1 year.

There are also problems with this model. Pragmatically, an extensive time commitment on the part of the observer is required. Further, the observer must eventually move from the role of student to therapist in the eyes of the group, and this has powerful transference and countertransference implications.

Stage Phasing

In the stage-phasing model the incoming therapist becomes known to the group in stages prior to becoming the leader, appearing first as a silent observer and then functioning as a cotherapist during the final weeks of the outgoing therapist's tenure. The advantages of this approach are that it smooths the transition, decreases stranger anxiety, allows for overt comparisons between the two leaders, and provides leadership opportunity for the new therapist. The main problem of this model is that it blurs the good-bye to the old therapist with the hello to the new one, often leaving both tasks only partially complete.

Conclusion

How the transition of leaders is handled is a complex and important consideration. Each model suggested has assets and liabilities, and each has implications for the treatment. Some models emphasize comfort, both to the group members and the incoming therapist, thereby maximizing the chances that the group will survive the transition while minimizing the options for affect and complete learning. Whichever model is chosen, it is strongly suggested that incoming therapists routinely attend supervision of the group for some months prior to becoming the group therapist.

The central issue in transferring leadership remains how to maximize learning while minimizing unproductive anxiety and stress. As we will discuss in the final chapter, terminations reactivate feelings associated with all previous losses, deaths, and new beginnings. Members' responses to individual absences or group interruptions might prove useful predictors of the feelings and behaviors evoked by the therapist's departure. However, the change of therapists can awaken significant and unexpected unconscious material, perhaps stemming from the separation-individuation stage of development or from specific traumatic events such as a parent's remarriage or the sporadically available parent.

Throughout the transition process it is useful to remember that one must say good-bye before one can fully say hello. The group is best helped in this difficult transition by ensuring that they explore as fully as possible the feelings evoked by the loss of their therapist. In addition to transference, there are the realistic and conscious feelings of loss that must also be managed. Not everything is transference, and members experience a genuine loss when a therapist leaves. The incoming therapist should continue the group focus on the loss, even while the members are beginning to establish a relationship with him or her. Incoming group therapists must suffer through the realization that it will be many months before the group is really theirs.

Another aspect of the problem of transferring leadership is that of maintaining a healthy working alliance (Zetzel, 1956). Due to their public nature groups provide more opportunity than does individual therapy for establishing good working alliances (Glatzer, 1978). Members can compare their perceptions and experiences to those of their colleagues and can use consensual validation as one means of discriminating valid from distorted perceptions. This is not to suggest that affects are suppressed by reality or that consensual validation can defeat transference, but members are able to use their trusting relationships with each other to explore and assess affects as they arise. Group therapy might thereby also be more able than individual therapy to retain working alliances even when therapists change because the important relationships among the members are retained.

Our experience in training centers suggests that a minimum 2-year tenure as group therapist is preferable for both student and group. It is not unusual for members to spend a considerable amount of time preparing for the departure of a therapist, dealing with the departure, and building an alliance with the new therapist. At a minimum, it takes 3 or 4 months for an incoming therapist to truly become the therapist of a group. When feelings are especially intense, it may easily require twice that amount of time. The time consumed by too-frequent leadership shifts diminishes the opportunity for undisturbed work on areas other than separation and loss. It is not unusual in training centers where trainees routinely leave in June or July for veteran group members to begin inquiring in January if their leaders will be leaving in the summer. These considerations should be viewed in light of the fact that the usual length of time for a patient to finish a substantial piece of therapeutic work can be 2 to 3 years even in an ongoing, leader-constant group (Stone & Rutan, 1984).

Guidelines for Transferring
Leadership of a Therapy Group

Whatever strategy is chosen, using the following guidelines will facilitate the therapeutic transferring of group leadership.

1. The departing leader needs to examine thoroughly his or her own feelings regarding the leaving. Frequently, departing therapists experience significant guilt about abandoning their group in order to go on to the greener pastures that a posttraining life predicts. The patients have given a great deal to the therapist, have contributed to his or her training, and their reward is to be abandoned and left in the hands of a neophyte whom they must train. Not infrequently, the outgoing therapist also experiences feelings of competition with the incoming therapist. In training settings, where the new leaders are almost always less experienced, outgoing leaders might gain perspective by recalling how little they knew when they took over a group.

2. The change of leaders may be usefully considered along Bowlby's (1973) continuum of protest, despair and detachment. These reactions, which Bowlby observed in infants suddenly separated from their mothers, aptly describe the reactions that group members experience when faced with a forcible separation from their group therapist. We must help the members avoid detachment by giving them the opportunity to rage and weep over this act of abandonment and to connect it to all the similar acts in their histories. This will enable the patients to say an effective good-bye, to own the gains and loves as well as the rages and disappointments with the outgoing therapist. Such work allows the members to test reality and demythologize the departing therapist, thus allowing them to reconnect to someone new. Even if this is not possible for each individual, the natural differences among members will call forth a broad spectrum of responses to the loss, verbalization of which will help the group as a whole tentatively move forward. It is often difficult for the outgoing therapist to hear and bear all the discomforting affects aroused by the departure. This might lead the therapist to prematurely accept a diminution of negative affect as a sign that the loss has been worked through. Typically, the outgoing therapist will need to continually invite expression of the rageful and disappointed affect.

3. Incoming therapists must work on their anxiety about becom-

ing a group therapist. Typically, group therapists have been trained in dyadic therapy first. There the therapist is protected by the therapeutic role, and the therapy is couched in privacy. It is often unnerving and uncomfortable to "go public" and begin to operate as a therapist in the public arena of a group. To complicate this matter, incoming therapists are often neophytes and worry that they will do the group harm (patients, sensing this anxiety, may inquire, "How many groups have you run before this one?"). One part of incoming therapists' anxiety typically includes feelings about the therapist they are replacing. It is important for new therapists to use supervision to work on the uncertainty and anxiety that accompanies becoming a group therapist; the same is true for experienced therapists who are taking on a new group. Transference looms large, and new therapists often lose sight of the fact that the beloved outgoing therapist knew just as little about groups when he or she began. Further, it is important to know that groups, no matter how abusive they might appear, want the new leader to succeed. Finally, the affects that fill the therapist are shared by the patients; they, too, wonder and worry that the new therapist will prove inept. And they worry that they will appear inept and unlovable to the new therapist.

4. Both the outgoing and incoming therapists need to examine their narcissistic vulnerabilities and their competitive strivings so that they are able to tolerate the patients favoring one over the other. No matter how experienced they are or how clearly they understand the transferential basis of members' angry and diminishing feelings, therapists are vulnerable to feeling hurt and defensive under continuing attacks and criticism. It may be useful for therapists to remind themselves that such attacks may represent a positive sign — the patients feel comfortable enough to forgo politeness and they have somehow determined that the therapist is tough enough to withstand their attacks. Furthermore, a common defense against the sadness of saying good-bye is to go away mad rather than sad. Incoming therapists will have the role of step-parent for a time, while the members continue the work with their "natural" parent who has left. The feelings of being ignored or belittled are never easy, and new therapists have trouble maintaining their therapeutic balance under such conditions. It may be helpful for incoming therapists to project into the future and realize that in a short period of time the members will likely be struggling over losing them and that a new incoming therapist will be bearing the brunt of those feelings.

5. It is important that the incoming therapist receive a great deal of information, not only about the lives and pathologies of the patients but also about the history of the group itself. It is very useful if the

incoming therapist can participate in the group supervision for some weeks or months prior to assuming leadership. Furthermore, it is important that the incoming leader receive quite specific information about how the group works: such as where the group meets, how members assemble (in the waiting room or in the group room) or if the therapist goes to get them, where the leader traditionally sits, which patients sit regularly in which seats, and so forth. The incoming therapist is not bound by these traditions, but it is important to know them.

6. In training settings, supervision should bridge all changes in leadership. When leaders change, if at all possible the old supervisor should continue during the transition. This is especially important in groups with one leader. In this way group continuity can be borne by the supervisor.

7. The incoming therapist should make individual appointments with all the group members. The individual history for each patient that is provided by an outgoing therapist is insufficient substitute for reviewing such data directly with the patient. Furthermore, these appointments provide opportunities to accelerate the alliance between new therapist and group members; they can also give members a chance to review their progress in group and to clarify goals they have for the future. If particular members refuse to accept the invitation to meet with the incoming therapist individually, they need not be pressed to do so. Rather, this behavior can be a source of curiosity and exploration within the group.

8. It has been our experience that more mature groups (groups that have been in existence for several years and have experienced previous changes in leadership) are likely to gain from a no-overlap or minimal overlap model. Indeed, for those groups the transition is often a time of accelerated growth. In newer groups, the baton of leadership must be handed over more cautiously, probably invoking one of the bridging techniques. In groups with the most damaged patients, the primary goal is to transfer the leadership, not to enhance affect in the members; for these patients issues of basic trust (or basic distrust) are so powerful that they can profit from rather extensive contact with the incoming therapist prior to the actual change in leadership.

REMOVAL OF PATIENTS FROM GROUP THERAPY

Members of groups are invited to speak the unspeakable, to present their least acceptable selves. Yet this at times leads to a situation where a member is perceived as damaging to the process of the group. More often than not, this situation can be handled through the power of interpretation, and the therapist should not move from affect to action (i.e., banning the patient from the group). To remove a patient from a group is a serious matter; it may provide a sense of protection in the other members, but it also stirs in them the worry that they too might do something so awful that they will be thrown out. The decision about whether or not to remove a patient from a group must also be distinguished from the therapist's *wish* that the patient would leave or could be evicted. The latter is not at all unusual and represents an important opportunity for learning for the patient, since it is likely that the therapist is experiencing a common reaction to the interpersonal style of the patient.

At the risk of implying that the removal of a patient from a group is a more common experience than in fact it is (the authors, whose combined experience in running multiple groups per week exceeds 40 years, have removed a total of two patients from groups), nonetheless it is important to consider how this important event should happen if that rare circumstance that warrants it arises.

There are two types of removal of a patient from a group: temporary (with the expectation that the member will return) and permanent.

Temporary Removal

A patient may be asked to leave a group session because of a temporary loss of self-control. This loss of control might result from an exacerbation of psychotic process (usually in the form of uncontrolled mania) or, less frequently, a relapse into an acute schizophrenic state. In most instances the deterioration is apparent over a number of sessions, during which the decompensation can be addressed and various approaches, such as individual appointments or hospitalization, can be explored. If at all possible, the individual should be allowed to remain for the duration of the meeting.

However, if the patient becomes so disruptive and out of control that removal during a meeting is required, the therapist is faced with the decision of whether or not to accompany the patient and make immediate arrangements for additional treatment or hospitalization. If the patient is so out of control that it is not safe for him or her to remain in the group, there is little reason to believe the patient is capable of suitable self-care. In such a situation the therapist must be the one to accompany the patient to whatever protective treatment might be available; this is too potent a situation in which to place a group member. If it occurs that the therapist must leave with such a patient, it is assumed that the group will continue the meeting until the usual time of completion even if the therapist does not return.

Another situation calling for temporary removal is a sudden display of dangerous acting out. In the face of violence, where there is a threat of physical harm to another, the initial response of the therapist is a forceful reminder that the group agreements call for talking, not acting. This should include a statement that inability to adhere to this agreement would be grounds for exclusion from the group meeting. In almost all circumstances, this reminder of the group agreements is sufficient to bring renewed self-control. Failing that, the therapist can attempt an interpretation, linking the present situation to some important aspect of the patient's history.

CLINICAL EXAMPLE

John had a history of criminal activity and violent acting out. His father had been a violent man who often beat John and all the members of his family. John hated his father and yet had modeled his life after his father's. He came to therapy when he found himself truly in love with a woman who would not tolerate his rageful outbursts.

In a particular group meeting John became incensed at the criticisms he perceived coming from a female member. He stood menacingly and walked across the room to her, screaming at her. The therapist was alarmed and suggested that John return to his seat and talk about the feelings he was experiencing. He also reminded John that the group agreements were that he talk, not act. John, however, would have none of it. His rage escalated, and he raised his fist, clearly poised to strike the female member. The group leader, in a last desperate attempt to salvage the situation before he had to simply physically intervene and pay the consequences, said, "John, you are now behaving just like the father you profess to detest."

John looked stricken, dropped his fist, and sank to his knees weeping. He apologized to the female member, stating that he knew exactly how terrified she must have felt because he had experienced that fear during most of his youth.

In this instance reminders of the agreements were insufficient to intervene in destructive behavior, but the power of interpretation did work. These moments in group are exceedingly rare, probably rarer than in individual therapy because the holding environment of the group serves to contain acting-out behaviors. Had John struck the female member, he would have been banned from the group permanently. That breach of the group agreements would have been too egregious to allow continued membership. Furthermore, the other members would forever be fearful that the act might be repeated. If John had remained on the brink of control but had not actually acted, it would have been appropriate for the therapist to suggest that he leave the meeting and return the following week so that the incident and feelings could be explored without the danger of violence. Of course, one would hope that patients on the brink of losing control of violent impulses would leave of their own volition, thereby retaining some self-respect.

A situation that occurs with unfortunate regularity is when a patient attends a meeting while intoxicated. Some therapists routinely ban intoxicated individuals from group sessions, suggesting that they return when sober. This, however, is akin to barring depressed patients from attending when depressed or psychotic patients from attending when psychotic. If substance abuse is a presenting problem, it should not surprise us that it will occasionally enter the therapy. Nonetheless, the behavior of some individuals when intoxicated is so disruptive as to guarantee that no productive work in therapy can be accomplished during that session. Even in such an instance, it is suggested that the member be allowed to stay, the premise being that this is a communication to and about the group (Munzer, 1967). If, however, the behavior continues over several weeks, the therapist will have no choice but to ban the member until he or she demonstrates the ability to bear affect and attend the meetings sober.

Permanent Removal

Obviously, removing a group member on a permanent basis should be a last resort. One of three circumstances is usually the basis for deciding that a patient cannot return to the group. The *first* is a significant and continuing inability or unwillingness to comply with the group agreements; the *second* is an unrelieved lack of progress in the therapy; and the *third*, which is rare, is when a patient makes such progress that he or she outgrows a particular group and would benefit from a higher-functioning one. In all cases the situation is not acute and does not require immediate attention but, rather, is the result of careful deliberation over time.

Inability or Unwillingness to Comply with the Group Agreements

Sometimes patients' life circumstances are altered, and they can no longer attend group meetings on a regular basis. Naturally, alterations in attendance should be explored for resistance and unconscious operations, but there are real-life changes that are not resistance. The final decision in such cases rests with the therapist, and each case must be considered separately. A temporary change (for example, an overseas assignment, a required class in school, a new baby) that necessitates an individual's absence for 1 to 3 months is a dilemma. The time-limited nature of such an interruption generally should not necessitate removal from the group.

This situation does raise the thorny issue of the fee, however. Should patients be expected to pay for sessions they cannot attend for realistic and external reasons? On the other hand, should the therapist be expected to suffer a loss of income due to reasons quite beyond his or her control? Groups usually assume (or wish) that the therapist will not charge for extended absences of this sort. However, we believe the group agreements apply and that members should be charged for all sessions in which they maintain their membership, even if they are unable to attend. This serves many therapeutic purposes, including countering the wish that the therapist be the all-giving "good breast" that takes care of members in trouble. It also safeguards the therapist's income, which allows ultimately for more economical fees in groups. Further, it protects therapists from the Solomonic position of having to decide which absences the patient should and should not charge patients for. Finally, this approach protects the patient from the anger of the therapist whose income is adversely affected by repeated absences. Nonetheless, the decision to charge or not charge for missed sessions is ultimately a personal one for each therapist to make. There is no right way to handle this delicate situation. In many clinics and hospitals, missed sessions are not considered services rendered and it is illegal to charge for them. What is vital is that each therapist have a consistent approach and abide by it. Further, for the therapist to be able to deal with fees constructively, the therapist must be convinced this is truly in the service of the patient.

More problematic is the dilemma created by a new life situation (e.g., a new job) that necessitates continuing intermittent absences or regular lateness. The rule of thumb is that members should be asked to leave the group when ongoing regular attendance is not possible. This should not be precipitous and can be discussed and learned from over many weeks. Also, the therapist needs to exercise common sense in invoking this action. If an individual has been a productive and active member of a group for a long time and gets a new job (perhaps as a result of work done in the group) that makes him or her come to group 10 minutes late each week, the therapist must determine (1) if this lateness is really unavoidable or if it is an acting out of resistance and (2) if it (once it is clear that is really unavoidable) interferes with the ability of the group to do productive work. While we would never accept into a group new members with an atypical agreement (e.g., that they will routinely come 10 minutes late), the situation is different when it arises for an existing member. In any case, it is important that the issue be raised openly in the group and that the members be given ample opportunity to express their feelings about it.

Another type of situation that raises the question of permanent removal from a group occurs when a member is continually unable to manage his or her feelings without putting them into actions. For example, in some groups there are monopolizers, individuals who simply seem incapable of shutting up. They are clearly anxious and fearful of strong affect being evoked, and they are often narcissistic and have no sense that others might have needs, too. Another example of a patient whose behavior raises the possibility of eviction is the malicious or bullying member who continually intimidates other members; clearly, this type of patient makes the establishing of an atmosphere of safety harder to attain. Yet another example of a member who acts rather than talks is the patient who has relationships with group members outside the limits of the group sessions; this is in complete defiance of the group agreements. Often these are seriously character-disordered individuals who are frightened of group intimacy and use pairing as a protection. In each of these cases the therapist may *wish* to evict the disturbing force, but that would put the therapist in exactly the same position as these troublesome patients; that is, the therapist would be acting rather than feeling and understanding.

In fact, all the behaviors mentioned in the preceding paragraph can be handled (with difficulty, it must be acknowledged) through the usual processes of confrontation, clarification, interpretation, and working through. For example, the monopolizer is almost never able to accomplish this role without the complete invitation and collusion of the group as a whole. In each of these cases the disruptive behavior can be interpreted to the benefit of all, so long as the therapist does not lose patience (and therefore patients). In very rare instances, after taking into account the meaning of the disruptive behaviors and attempting to help the member desist through understanding and/or limit setting, some patients must be removed from the group (Roberts, 1991).

One of the more serious problems with acting rather than feeling occurs when sexual intercourse occurs between two members. Sexual relations between members, whatever the specific meaning of the action to the couple, evoke in other members powerful feelings of envy, frustration, rejection, and distrust. If the involved couple is unable to discuss and explore their relationship openly in the group, one or both individuals might be asked to leave.

Nonpayment of fees is yet another breach of the group agreements that can lead to eviction. Patients who do not pay their fees are usually communicating a powerful message. Their behavior can represent a

statement about how much the therapy is worth, a wish to be special
and treated for free, a means of dealing with anger toward the therapist, and so on. Whatever the specific meaning, it is a powerful and
important dynamic that requires open exploration in the group. Typically, therapists are reluctant to address issues of fees since we seem
to harbor some countertransferential feelings about charging for the
work we do. This is a problem particularly for group therapists, who
must deal with the affects about fees in a public setting.

> Money is a taboo subject but at the same time a royal road to unconscious
> material including primitive affect, aspects of personality, and dimensions of
> orality and anality, especially greed, depletion, and withholding. Interper-
> sonal transactions around money in group highlight favoritism, sadism,
> masochism, secrecy, seduction, protection, and corruption. Lifting the taboo
> against discussing money unleashes material that may be potentially upset-
> ting for the leader as well as group members. Issues previously condensed
> into the topic of money and then split off from other parts of the self are
> now re-owned and their relevance appreciated in sectors of life other than
> sole financial ones. (Gans, 1992, p. 134)

Obviously, a member's failure to pay fees should first be broached
as an important communication that patient, group, and therapist attempt to understand. However, if the nonpayment continues, there remains no recourse other than to have the nonpaying member leave
treatment. It should be noted that this is not really an instance of the
therapist banning a member. Rather, this is an instance of the member
putting in motion a dynamic that necessitates the eviction; that is, the
member has chosen to leave.

CLINICAL EXAMPLE

Leonard consistently underpaid his bill so that his overdue balance slowly but surely mounted. The behavior seemed impervious to discussion
and exploration. When the therapist questioned the meaning of the behavior, Leonard was "hurt" and professed to be doing the very best he
could. The other members began experiencing rage at Leonard, in part
because of his behavior with his bill and in part because that behavior
was replicated in his group interactions, where he did not really give what
he owed to the others. When all dynamic techniques failed, the therapist
ultimately had to indicate firmly that unless Leonard paid his bill in full
within the next month, he would have to leave the group. Leonard was
clearly startled and humiliated by this unexpected and unusual statement
from the therapist. However, the ensuing week Leonard walked into the
group and threw a check for the full amount at the leader. He was then

sullen for several weeks in the group, and he occasionally fell slightly behind on his bill again. His sense of embarrassment and hurt over the confrontation continued for many, many months, but the limit setting was
clearly useful to him and to the group to move past an impasse. It took
Leonard 2 years before he was able to be insightful about the etiology
of his withholding the money.

Too Little Progress in Therapy

In some cases it gradually becomes clear to the therapist, and usually
to the group and the particular patient as well, that the group is simply not working. For whatever reasons, sometimes an individual simply cannot or will not use the group for therapeutic purposes. This
may be the result of improper diagnosis or assignment to an inappropriate group, or it may be the result of character style and resistance.
Whatever the reason, it becomes apparent that the patient is wasting
his or her time and money by continuing in the group. In this case it
is appropriate for the group therapist to note this reality and to suggest the possibility of the patient terminating the group and moving
to a different mode of treatment. The decision to stop the treatment
should represent a joint decision and should come as a result of dialogue between the patient, the therapist, and the group. In many cases
this is sufficient to jolt the patient into a new period of productive use
of the group; however, in other cases the patient terminates and the
group is left to mourn a failure.

It is an error to assume that a silent member is a member making
no progress. Individuals use groups in very different ways, and for some
the opportunity to sit silently is a therapeutic one. Pines (1991) has noted
that some long-term members of groups, defined as those who remain
in treatment from 5 or more years, are experienced as permanent group
residents. Therapists may rely on these patients or may wish that they
would terminate, but Pines suggest that these patients often use the group
to sustain themselves.

Too Much Progress in Therapy

Sometimes an individual makes such substantial progress that he or
she no longer fits in the group. This applies only to groups of highly
disturbed patients. When one member has clearly progressed beyond
the developmental level of the other group members, this should be
noted and discussed in and with the group. This is not a situation where
a member is barred from a group, rather it is a graduation. The departure of a member, especially one who is exceedingly helpful and in-

sightful, is difficult for the group. However, the process can be therapeutic if it is openly discussed and negotiated in the group.

The decision to remove a member from a group is a very serious one. It is recommended that the group therapist seek consultation from a trusted colleague prior to such an action in order to ensure that the therapist is not acting out.

USING THE GROUP THERAPIST'S AFFECT

Therapists' own inner feelings and experiences offer very important clues to what is happening in a therapy group. Freud (1910, 1915) recognized that patients, with their intense transferences, touch unconscious responses in the therapist. Classically these inner reactions have been labeled *countertransference*. More recently, the concept of countertransference has been expanded to include all the therapist's emotional reactions both conscious and unconscious, which are evoked by the patient (Roth, 1980). Freud's narrow definition brought precision but overlooked the obvious reality that therapists are filled with affect while sitting with patients. Under Freud's definition, therapists were often left feeling that their affective responses represented something harmful in the therapy. The broader definition frees therapists to use their inner responses in the service of understanding. It also places the therapist under the mandate to carefully assess personal feelings for traces of old-fashioned countertransference.

There are multiple sources for therapist affect. What is most productive in the therapy are those feelings in the therapist which are *evoked* by the patient. We suggest using the criteria presented in Figure 10.1 in order to assess the sources of the affects therapists experience.

As you can see from the figure, there are three potential sources of therapist affect: (1) the therapist himself or herself, (2) the relationship between therapist and group member, and (3) the patient. As with the leadership dimensions presented earlier (see Chapter 8), these distinctions are heuristic. In fact, human relationships are far too complex to be so neatly compartmentalized. However, it is helpful to conceptualize the sources of therapist affect in this manner in order to assist therapists in gaining the most information from those feelings.

Sources of Therapist Affect

The Therapist

The goal of therapy is to facilitate the exploration of the patient's inner world. When we are filled with feelings stirred by our own history and

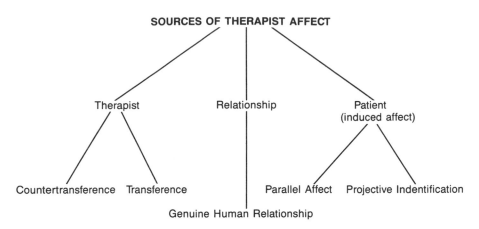

FIGURE 10.1. Criteria for assessing sources of therapist affect.

inner life old-fashioned countertransference feelings, the therapy is not facilitated; and, indeed, our ability to understand and hear our patients is almost always clouded.

If therapists find themselves preoccupied with powerful feelings, including love, hate, or envy, because the patient is reminiscent of an important and ambivilently held figure from their past, it is their responsibility to work through that feeling. In extreme cases this would be cause for reentering therapy or even referring the patient to another therapist.

All feelings generated from the therapist are not countertransference. (In fact, modern definitions of countertransference tend to include all emotional reactions of therapists to patients.) Therapists also experience affects in response to the patient's transference or character style. These feelings are not classical countertransference because they are preconscious or conscious. Moreover therapists typically bear certain transferences more easily than others: For some therapists the experience of being adored is difficult whereas being hated is easy; for other therapists the opposite is true. Therapists need to assess their inner reactions to ensure that they are not acting on the induced feelings. We do not want to communicate to our patients that certain transferences or character traits are acceptable while others are not.

The first place to look when a therapist experiences powerful affect is to the self. This is in order to protect our patients from the untoward effects of therapist countertransference in the treatment. Groups often offer consultation to the therapist in such situations, recognizing and speaking of the therapist's powerful reactions and noting that the reactions seem unique to the therapist.

The Genuine Human Relationship

Over the course of time in therapy we develop genuine human relationships with our patients. This does not imply that we act on them, of course. But it does mean that sometimes we are filled with affect triggered by the relationship itself. When a patient suffers a serious loss, we feel sad. When a patient enjoys a monumental triumph, we feel pride and pleasure. This is not usually the source of therapist affect but is a potential source.

Induced Affect

The most intriguing source of therapist affect is the patient. There are two separate sources of affect in the therapist that is generated by interaction with the patient. They are not easily recognized, in contrast to the therapist's emotional responses to the patients' transference or character style.

The first is parallel affect. That is, sometimes therapists will identify a strong affect in themselves and will come to realize that they are experiencing what the patient is experiencing. This is most powerful when the affect has not been verbalized by the patient.

CLINICAL EXAMPLE

The group therapist was trying to attend to the complaints of a group member. The member was speaking of her dissatisfaction with her life, her sense that she has not accomplished what she had expected by this time in her life. However, the therapist was overcome with a feeling of fatigue. She noticed that she was drifting into a fantasy that she was a surgeon. Rather than immediately cutting off the fantasy in order to attend to the group, the therapist recognized that she *was* indeed attending to the group and that her fantasy might inform her more about the group process. She continued the fantasy and found herself enjoying the life of a very successful surgeon, one whose successes were immediately and obviously apparent.

The therapist then understood that the patient had not been particularly successful at *verbally* communicating her despair and dissatisfaction but that she had quite successfully communicated it at a metacommunicative level. The therapist was experiencing affect parallel to that of the patient—a sense that she was not successful enough, that she had followed the wrong career path, that somehow she had missed the essence of life. One important clue for the therapist in understanding that these affects related to her patient was the fact that these feelings did not have any conscious place in her life. At a conscious level the therapist was very happy in her field and rather awed by the professional status she had attained.

Using her own affective life as a guide the therapist responded to the patient, "It is as if you have missed the boat and life is passing you by?" The patient immediately burst into tears. At the same moment, the other group members, who until this point had been somber and rather disconnected, came alive and began actively interacting with the woman.

There were two levels of communication from this patient. On the one hand she had developed a characteristic style of relating that seemed not inviting of interest or participation by others. It was typical that when she spoke others appeared bored. On the other hand she was somehow communicating her despair and unhappiness. Eventually she came to understand that her character style was related to the punishment she received as a child whenever she voiced her needs.

The second patient-induced source of therapist affect is projective identification (Klein, 1946). In this very important defensive operation, the patient projects the undesirable and unacceptable affects about the self into the therapist. The therapist contains and experiences these affects. If projection identification were at work in the example, the therapist might experience the same sense despair mentioned earlier. However, in this instance it is *not* the same affect the patient is feeling. Rather, the therapist is experiencing the affect the patient cannot tolerate. Further, the therapist is induced to respond in ways that are familiar to the patient from the past, thereby completing a life script that the patient expects to occur. Were projective identification at work in the earlier example, the patient may have rejected unacceptable feelings of self-doubt, holding instead to a counterphobic sense of confidence. This, in turn, protects the patient from identifying with a parent who was viewed as inept and defeated. The patient views herself as superior to this parent and thus to much of the world. In the therapy the identical relationship is established as the therapist begins to feel incapable when with this particular patient.

CLINICAL EXAMPLE

Sam was a quarrelsome and critical patient. He accused the therapist of charging exorbitant fees, of not paying close enough attention, of having poor taste in office furniture. Not surprisingly, the therapist soon became filled with rageful feelings toward Sam. The other group members also found Sam problematic. He was critical with them as well and never seemed to be satisfied with any of their efforts on his behalf.

The therapist allowed the rageful feelings to build and paid them heed.

He recognized a wish to slap Sam across the face and tell him, "You should be grateful for all I have given you." The therapist was shocked at that atypical response to a patient but then associated to the patient's history. Sam had been placed for adoption on counsel of the state, who had taken him from parents deemed to be unfit. He had been adopted by a cool, passionless family, very different from Sam's natural stance. Further, the only affect Sam reports his mother having displayed was anger. The therapist hypothesized that Sam was disowning the rageful parts of himself which wished to strike the therapist, and before that his adoptive parents. How could he be rageful at those who had saved his life? Thus, those unacceptable feelings were repressed and found expression only in projective identification.

The therapist finally commented to Sam, "How awful it must have felt to have wanted to strike those who had given you a home." This was a shocking comment to the entire group since Sam had never alluded so such feelings. The data for the intervention came solely from the therapist assessment of his affective reaction to Sam. Sam immediately accepted the comment, probably the first time he had uncritically accepted anything the therapist had to offer. The group was instantly more empathic to Sam and began to understand why he had developed a personal style which kept people at such distance."

It is exceedingly difficult for therapists to sort out the origins of their very strong feelings while leading a group. One way we have found that may help is to follow the following steps. First try to determine if the feelings are countertransference or responsive to the patient's transference. If that does not yield an answer, then question whether the feelings flow from the human relationship with the patient (or the group). From there ask if the feelings are invoked by the patient through either parallel affect or projective identification. We find the latter to be the usual sources of therapist affect.

Groups are particularly powerful places to use therapist affect in the service of clinical work because the members offer a source of validation. For example, projective identification is a very defensive operation which powerfully influences the feelings of others. Indeed, if projective identification is at work it is likely that the great majority of the group members will be experiencing the same affect as the therapist. Parallel affect is less powerful in its effect on others and there may be considerable diversity among group members in responses to this mechanism. Specific personal responses to the transference of another to us is quite unique and we cannot look to the group for validation.

Therapy groups evoke powerful feelings in all who sit in them, including the therapist. Classic notions of countertransference alert therapists to the possibility that unresolved issues in their own lives might keep them from hearing and understanding their patients or groups properly. However, that concept is too restrictive and threatens to close off from therapists a potentially valuable source of data. Modern practitioners of dynamic theory are very cognizant of their inner responses to patients.

11

Special Technical
Considerations: II

In this chapter we address a number of special ways in which patients communicate about themselves, ways that are either handled in unique ways in groups or demonstrate themselves uniquely in groups. These special forms of communication are (1) dreams, (2) projective mechanisms, (3) contagion of affect, and (4) nonverbal communication.

DREAMS IN GROUP PSYCHOTHERAPY

Background

Freud was not the first to consider dreams as important communications. The Talmud states, "A dream that has not been interpreted is like a letter that has not been opened." Freud's genius was that he was the first to interpret dreams rigorously, scientifically, and systematically. As with much of his work on unconscious material, Freud gained a foothold in working with dreams by postulating that they are a valid psychic communication that *can* be understood. His major contributions were developing a way of understanding the covert meaning from the manifest content and recognizing that dreams often represent wish fulfillment. Dreams, therefore, became a valuable window into the unconscious of Freud's analytic patients. Group therapists, following this lead, expanded the intrapsychic focus to include interpersonal and group-as-a-whole processes. Just as Freud began with the hypothesis that dreams depict something about the analytic situation, so do group therapists begin with the hypothesis that dreams reported in group sessions often depict something about the group itself. Some authors have found the use of dream material in groups so powerful they have established groups specifically and exclusively to deal with dream material (Shuttleworth-Jordan, Saayman, & Faber, 1988).

Any groupwide conflict or shared anxiety may be vividly portrayed in the manifest dream or exposed through the members' associations (Klein-Lipschutz, 1953; Whitman, 1973). Problems of joining and trust may be themes of dreams graphically presented in the first stage of group formation whereas rebellion, power, and autonomy may be portrayed at later stages (Battegay, 1977). Some conflicts may have been dimly recognized or consciously avoided only to reappear directly or thinly disguised in the manifest dream content (Edwards, 1977; Wolf & Schwartz, 1962). Transferences or attitudes toward the therapist also may be brought to light via dreams. Conversely, the dreamer may be informing the therapist about a countertransference affecting the whole group. Dreams also convey valuable information about the relationships among members; there are often direct references to the group or to specific members (although not necessarily those with whom there is conflict). It is also true that dreams reported in groups can provide access to an individual member's resistances, wishes, transferences, and conflicts.

Clinical Illustrations

The New Member

A chronically depressed man, in the middle of a lengthy and painful divorce, entered an ongoing therapy group in order to learn more about himself and his troubled relationships with women. The night following his first group session, he dreamed that he was in line waiting to be seated in a restaurant. As he was waiting, a group of people pushed by him and were seated by the maitre d'. He turned around and left the restaurant, reversing a sign on the front door to indicate the restaurant was closed.

From the perspective of group development, the oral imagery of the restaurant is consistent with the dreamer's position as a new member and reflects one of the themes of initial participation in the group: "Will I get enough?" Such imagery is typical of early group participation and does not automatically indicate major personal conflicts at an oral dependent level of development.

From the group-as-a-whole perspective, the dream represents the newcomer's perception that the old members are favored by the therapist, as depicted by the maitre d'. The dream indicates the newcomer's concern that he will not be able to join fully. From the interpersonal perspective, the dream reveals a chronic defensive pattern—withdrawal and retaliation—that this patient invoked to manage rejection and pain. Finally, from the intrapsychic perspective, there are suggestions of a transference to the therapist and of ego distortions, which are represented in the maladaptive manner in which an ambivalence about nurturance and dependency is handled.

Sequential Dreams

A woman entered a group in which continuing and vociferous conflict among several members dominated her first meeting. At her second meeting she reported a fragment from a dream she had the night of the first meeting. "I was driving a truck. Instead of going forward, it went backward into a very tight place."

The old members quickly recognized the dream's group-level meaning: the new member had felt stymied by the group conflict, unable to move forward on her own issues and backed into a corner. The therapist wondered whether the heated conflicts had been exaggerated in order to frighten off the new member, and he was concerned that perhaps he had brought in the member at an inopportune time.

In her third meeting the woman presented two additional dream fragments from the intervening week. "I was in a crowd of friendly people, and all of a sudden I gave birth to a baby!" She immediately associated to the group and to her new perception that the group seemed much friendlier in her second meeting. She said, "The baby is me. The group is a new beginning." She then moved to her next dream, beginning, "Now for the one in which I die." She dreamed that she was in a group of people, some of whom she recognized from work. Suddenly a man got up and shot her in the head. She associated to a man she had felt angry with and said that this dream had nothing to do with the group. Later in the session, however, she added an omitted detail: In the dream, immediately before she had been shot one of the bystanders had said,"It's what you deserve." This was the same phrase she herself had used earlier in the meeting. The repetition of the phrase helped her overcome an initial resistance to connecting the dreams to the feelings evoked in the treatment and recognize her fears in the here-and-now group interaction.

This woman's dreams, reported in two successive meetings, illustrate a common pattern for new members: At first she felt somewhat overwhelmed by the group. When she felt safer, she could conceive of attaining her wishes. Only then could she expose her underlying fear of being attacked and wounded by one of the veteran members.

Related Dreams

Sometimes various members of a group will have dreams that, taken together, provide important information about a common group stress.

A woman reported a recent dream: "I was looking for the therapist at his university office, but he was busy with other students and did not have time for me." She reported feeling "stunned and devastated." In the associations that followed, a man reported a dream he had recently: "I was taking a test in mathematics and an English professor, who was trying to help me, suddenly disappeared and was unavailable." Then he spontaneously remembered a recurrent dream from his early childhood: "I was riding in a streetcar and my mother was waiting for me at the end of the line. Just as I arrived she flew off and someone said she was a witch." Finally, a second woman reported a dream, which she termed a nightmare. "My daughter was inhabited by the devil, and I was trying to exorcise it but I couldn't do it." She awoke in a highly anxious and frightened state.

This fascinating sequence of dreams was reported in the first meeting following a series of canceled sessions due to the therapist's absence. It illustrates the interconnectedness of dreams by different members, each portraying the dreamer's response to the common stress of the therapist's absence and the canceled sessions. The representation of the unavailable therapist as a too-busy professor in the first dream is echoed in a second as a disappearing professor and in the third as the disappearing mother/witch. The last reference reminded the second woman of her dream involving exorcism, and it was through that association that she could begin to identify herself with the child who needed the devil removed.

The dream content also shows the reverberating theme of the therapist's other interests taking precedence over his interest in the members. One member's dream portrays him as too busy with others, another as not qualified to teach a course (an English professor in a mathematics course) as well as being unavailable, and another as a mother who turns into a witch.

A Group Resistance

Many times, dreams reported in groups represent information about resistance to the group treatment.

A woman reported a dream "about the group": "I was in some sort of bus. Every time the bus came to a dangerous area, we would skirt it or avoid it. This occurred several times in the dream. I thought the bus had passed my stop, but a man who was a cooking expert and

teacher got on the bus, and it seemed to head back to the right desti-
nation."

The dreamer initially spoke of how she habitually avoided all conflict, often by not knowing what she felt. But she implied others had
joined her, since she directly identified the dream as being about the
group. Her interpretation of the dream was that the "cooking expert"
was the group therapist. Analysis of the dream elements by the group
highlighted and confirmed the manifest content that the bus was in
fact controlled by the passengers, and the teacher was not the driver.
Through this the members were able to begin to acknowledge how they
had all been contributing to the avoidance of the "dangerous" sexual
feelings in the room.

The Grave Digger

Despite the emphasis on group process, it should be remembered that
dreams are also communications about the inner states of individuals.

A longtime group member had spent most of his therapy minimizing the impact of his self-righteous intellectualizing on others. His interpersonal life was characterized by a great deal of acrimonious arguing,
which his group interactions paralleled. During one session in which
the therapist again pointed out to this man that members were trying
to tell him how painful they felt his comments to be, he suddenly reported a dream: "I was digging around uncovering corpses. They were
all in brown bags so that you didn't smell them or see them, but it was
still pretty disgusting. I came across one corpse, and for no apparent
reason I just cut off its head." He reported awaking both shaken and
disgusted.

The patient's understanding was that the head belonged to a particularly obnoxious, pompous, self-righteous colleague. The therapist,
after eliciting the associations of others, suggested that this dream might
represent the patient's efforts to get rid of a particularly distasteful part
of himself. He immediately agreed, saying that as he was reporting the
dream he realized that he was talking about how the group must perceive him and how he always anticipated criticism as he spoke. His dream
clearly conveyed this patient's dawning awareness of something wrong
within himself as well as with the interpersonal impact he made.

Techniques of Dream Interpretation in Group Therapy

Some groups avidly report and analyze dreams while other groups seem
never to relate dream material. More often that not, this is a function
of the therapist's interest in dreams. Group therapists can dramatically

affect the reporting and analyzing of dreams simply by showing interest. Ignoring dreams results in extinguishing their presentations.

Freud understood dreams to be a coded representation of important affect or inner conflict. To the degree that dreams reflect important unconscious material they are *always* coded. Thus, the manifest meaning of the dream is not the most significant meaning. Indeed, the most obvious parts of dreams are quite often distractions from more unsettling material. The classic tool for breaking the dream code is free association. Ideally, it becomes a group norm for all members to associate to a dream, since the collective associations may constitute a multidimensional report on the state of the group as well as of the individuals within it. Thus, the therapist should subtly discourage members from trying to understand or interpret the dream of a colleague and should, instead, encourage them to associate to it as if it had been their own. As illustrated in the foregoing examples, some of the associations may be other dreams or even interpretations of them. While the interpretations may be either accurate or inaccurate, they represent data about the contributor's personal conflicts. The therapist should not rush to make an interpretation but should, instead, wait to elicit associations from the dreamer and from the other members.

Since feelings are usually the least disguised elements of dreams, the therapist helps the members learn to explore the affect in dreams. Members frequently assist one another in overcoming resistance to full exploration of dreams by sharing openly their own feeling responses. Usually the affects can be linked to shared feelings, and in this manner the therapeutic value of the dream is enhanced.

We do not recommend a rote practice of asking each member to respond to a dream. Rather, the flow of group associations helps clarify the dream's unconscious components. Thus, abrupt changes in topic that may appear to avoid material are usually an associative path that further elaborates or clarifies the latent meanings in the dream.

CLINICAL EXAMPLE

As a group was busily discussing their feelings about one another and about group interactions, one woman protested that she had not felt what others had been feeling. She angrily said that she experienced the therapist as pressuring the members to express feelings and that she was unable to do so. She then reported a dream, which she presented as an afterthought and which to her had no obvious connection to the conversation that had gone before: "I dreamed there was an old black lady working on a man's head. I was behind a screen and couldn't see very well.

Someone asked me to move something to the other side of the screen, but I wasn't able to do it." The dreamer immediately associated the black lady in the dream to the group therapist (a white male), "who works on heads." Then she felt confused and said, "I can't see what this dream is about, and most of the time I can't see what this group is about."

The associative process seemed to abruptly shift as a man began to talk to the dreamer about their accidental meeting outside the group sessions. He said that he was frightened by her, since she had seemed seductive at that meeting and thereafter. A raging argument ensued regarding who was trying to seduce whom. As the discussion continued and the feelings subsided, the therapist asked about the man's initial comment that he was frightened. The woman was startled and then acknowledged that she had never heard him say he was afraid, saying "I didn't know he was afraid. I just knew I was afraid and had to protect myself by attacking him."

This particular dream, and the ensuing process, added more data to a growing awareness on the part of the dreamer that she could not hear others' anxieties and fears. And her associations revealed much more: For example, the dreamer identified the therapist as a black woman, but other data suggest that the patient herself was also represented by the black woman. She worked on the man's head with her seductiveness, but she did not know what she was doing because she could not see. On the basis of data from prior group meetings, the following interpretation is likely: This patient controlled through seductiveness, she was unable to recognize others' anxious responses, and when confronted about her blindness she reacted with anger and started a fight. Further analysis of the dream might also have produced results for the male patient, since he exhibited similar characteristics, having demonstrated seductive behavior when he felt insecure about himself in previous sessions.

Dreams can serve a great many needs and might contain important dependent, competitive, exhibitionistic, or narcissistic wishes on the part of the dreamer. Other members might respond to a dream by ignoring it and the dreamer or by presenting dreams in a competitive fashion. A plethora of dreams can be presented in order to avoid or resist other, more powerful, feelings. This is often the case when the therapist finds that the group is flooded with dream material and great blocks of time are devoted to hearing and analyzing dreams. Dreams are so filled with potential meaning that therapists have the difficult job of deciding how much time can profitably be spent analyzing dreams without losing sight of the ongoing in-group process.

SCAPEGOATING

The term *scapegoat* comes from the biblical story of Aaron confessing all the sins of the children of Israel over the head of a goat, which was then sent into the wilderness symbolically bearing those sins (Leviticus 16). Thus, the origin of the term indicates the function — to protect the tribe, family, or group. Allport (1954) hypothesized that prejudice, at root, is societal scapegoating to provide a sense of solidarity among the majority. In group therapy scapegoating refers to the focusing of hostile, sadistic, and hurtful attention on one particular individual. Scapegoating serves a symbolic value similar to that in the biblical story; that is, an individual is scapegoated in order to protect the group. Toker (1972) has suggested that "the scapegoat is frequently essential for the adequate functioning of a group (whatever the nature of the group) in that he provides an area into which aggressions can be channeled and focused without presenting a threat to the psychic integrity of the individual or a threat to the stability and unity of the group itself" (p. 232). Bion (1960) also noted that fight–flight groups are prepared to sacrifice individual members in order to protect the group. Scapegoating encompasses intrapsychic, interpersonal, and group-as-a-whole mechanisms (Scheidlinger, 1982).

Not all painful confrontations are manifestations of scapegoating. Indeed, some of the most important growth experiences are forged in strong, painful, and difficult interactions between members. Groups offer unique opportunities for receiving feedback about the less desirable aspects of one's personality. Therapists must be able to distinguish between scapegoating and strong but ultimately helpful confrontations. Scapegoating, if left unanalyzed, can be hurtful to the individual and the group. The key is to determine if the challenged patient is being hurt rather than helped and that the motivation of the confrontation is to inflict pain rather than to provide information. Since scapegoats often "volunteer" for that job, there is often a countertransference feeling in the therapist that the scapegoat "deserves" the attack.

Central to understanding scapegoating is the concept of projective identification (Fairbairn, 1952a; Guntrip, 1969; M. Klein, 1946). As stated in the previous chapter, projective identification is a defensive maneuver in which individuals project into others those traits or aspects of self-representations, and their associated affects, that are unacceptable as one's own. Implied in this process is a splitting of good and bad selfobject representations and a blurring of ego boundaries, which is consistent with the developmental level or the regressive state of the projector. The notion of projective identification has been used by some authors (Grotstein, 1981) to include the projection of *object representations* (and superego), which does not involve blurring of boundaries and is a more mature defense utilized by higher-functioning individuals. The regressive interpersonal and intrapsychic pressures of joining and belonging to a group accounts for the splitting and projection that takes place for these latter patients (Scheidlinger, 1974).

The projection is not random but, rather, is directed to a willing recipient, an individual who in some substantial way demonstrates a willingness to accept the unacceptable qualities. The projector, in attempting to "change" the other, also maintains contact with the hated and dreaded parts of the self, which require continued projection. This continual involvement with the other is the essential clue to the process of projective identification (Guntrip, 1969). Thus, projective identification refers to a two-party phenomenon that involves both projection and an acceptance of the projected traits and therefore represents both intrapsychic and interpersonal processes.

CLINICAL EXAMPLE

In the process of working through a therapist's departure from the group, coinciding with the end of training, the members expressed considerable sorrow but not anger. Jane, who had always been outspoken, created a scene at one of the hospital clinics, which included a shouting match between herself and a technician and ended with Jane's bursting into tears. Following the incident, she was called by a representative of the hospital patient relations unit in an attempt to mollify her. Jane angrily reported the entire event to the group, having erroneously interpreted the phone call as a threat that she would be banished from the hospital. Jane's tirade went on for some time. The members remained silent, waiting for the therapist to respond. It appeared that Jane had become the carrier of the group anger, even in the displacement. The underlying fears of retaliation for expression of their anger was apparent in Jane's tears. In this instance, Jane could have served as a potential scapegoat if the therapist indeed had not understood the displacement and the members' anxiety; Jane would have been chastised as the angry one.

Pure projection should be differentiated from projective identification. In pure projection the subject takes an unacceptable quality and disowns it by attributing it to another person. Simple projection is a one-person system, in which the other person is an unknowing and unwilling party to the projections. An example of projection occurred when Sally, a member of the therapy group discussed in the last clinical example, recognized that Jane was angry but chose not to comment. Later Sally said that she thought Jane would be disorganized by her anger just as she (Sally) was when she became angry. Sally was projecting her belief that anger leads to disorganization onto Jane.

Scapegoating may at times feel like pure projection in that it seems that the scapegoat is an unwilling victim. However, closer examination will indicate that scapegoats indeed play a part in their fate. In fact, as Jane's behavior illustrates, they "volunteer" for the role by engaging in behaviors that draw the group's fury, thereby setting in motion familiar patterns. Scapegoats often played similar roles in their original families.

Therapists are not immune to becoming the objects of projective identification and scapegoats themselves. Levine (1979) suggests group therapists are particularly subject to scapegoating when they defensively refuse to understand the members' attempts to wrest power and control. More often, therapists are not scapegoats *per se* but, rather, containers for negative transferences. Patients usually are the target of scapegoating.

Garland and Kolodny (1973) suggest four fundamental forms of scapegoating in groups: ostracism, institutionalization, encapsulation, and inclusion through introspection. Ostracism is the most immediately malevolent form of scapegoating since it often results in the scapegoat leaving the group. In ostracism the scapegoat is placed in an accustomed role as the different one, the troublesome one, the group buffoon, and so on. This is commonly the experience of borderline individuals, who demonstrate object hunger, demandingness, and difficulty in sharing. The recognition of these universal wishes are defended against in higher-functioning individuals, whose defenses against these unacceptable feelings are threatened by the borderline patient. As a consequence, the others attempt to rid themselves of these affects and drives by projecting them into the scapegoat. The result is that the scapegoat not only feels the wishes more intensely but also feels more isolated. Under such circumstances the scapegoat may have the feeling of being in an all too familiar position and may drop out.

The encapsulated scapegoat is allowed only limited participation in the group. An example of this form of scapegoating involves the member who becomes tearful and very emotional in the first group meeting. Group members generally are not prepared to tolerate or explore intense feelings so quickly, and they find ways of isolating the tearful person in order to contain their own affects. The members act as if the "offending" member should be punished. The final form of scapegoating consists of involving the scapegoat in active, intrusive introspection, a hostile dedication to finding out what makes him or her tick. In the case of the aforementioned tearful member, others may grill the individual inquiring, "What is wrong? Why are you so upset? Why can't you manage things differently?" Such questioning further isolates the scapegoat.

The analysis of scapegoating entails helping the entire group understand that the scapegoat role is unconsciously considered crucial to the emotional survival of the group. One of the characteristics of scapegoating is emotional contagion, a phenomenon in which affects spread with lightening rapidity through the members, which magnifies the scapegoating process (W. Stone, 1990). Emotional contagion involves regression of affect. Affects are no longer used as signals but are stimuli to action or other defensive responses (Krystal, 1974). Since the scapegoated individual often suffers great pain, it is advisable for the therapist to proceed as quickly as possible to the task of understanding the function of the scapegoating in terms of its role in protecting the group in order to diminish the danger of unnecessarily hurting the patient. Scapegoating is a difficult problem for therapists. It represents a group-as-a-whole process. If the therapist moves to protect the patient, the rest of the group may perceive this as favoritism or interference with their justified criticism, thus making the plight of the scapegoated member even worse.

The therapist, understanding the projective processes, attempts to help the attacking members look at their own insecurities, which are triggered by the visage or behavior of the scapegoat. By helping the attackers realize that it is not the behavior of the scapegoat that is so troubling but their own feelings aroused by the scapegoat, the therapist is often able to help members modify their behavior. Scapegoating ends when the members own their projections and more clearly see their feelings in the scapegoat. Sometimes a comment by the therapist such as "The group is making John work very hard tonight" or "John seems to be voicing a difficult feeling that others may feel" can begin the process of stopping the scapegoat phenomenon.

EMOTIONAL CONTAGION

Emotional contagion is not only a mechanism by which affect spreads around a group; it is also a way of communicating in groups. Because emotional contagion is such an effective communicator, it is against the law to falsely shout "Fire!" in a movie theater since the ensuing panic can be disastrous; fear becomes amplified as patrons in the crowded theater almost instantly share in the feeling. Affects likewise spread with lightening rapidity throughout a therapy group (W. Stone, 1990). The precise dynamism enabling the wildfire spread of affective states in emotional contagion is unknown. According to Freud (1921), "There is no doubt that something exists in us which, when we become aware of signs of an emotion in someone else, tends to make us fall into the same emotion; but how often do we not successfully oppose it, resist the emotion, and react in quite an opposite way?" (p. 89). Freud posited suggestibility as the basis for contagion but considered this phenomenon as "an irreducible, primitive phenomenon, a fundamental fact in the mental life of man" (p. 89). Recent infant research lends support to Freud's hypothesis, as observations have demonstrated that the newborn infant is exquisitely responsive to emotional communication (Stern, 1985). It appears that these responses are genetically predetermined and are evidence of subcortical rather than cortical functions.

One form of affect contagion is scapegoating; another is so-called manic behavior. In this circumstance affective shifts are sudden and intense.

CLINICAL EXAMPLE

Members of a group responded to a therapist's announcement of a forthcoming vacation with an initial sense of loss and dread. The mood shifted dramatically to one of excitement and pleasure following the suggestion that the members get together for a picnic during the doctor's absence. The detailed planning for food, games, and whom to include in the outing took up much of the meeting. The therapist's efforts at examining the meaning of the discussion fell upon deaf ears, as the patients enthusiastically pursued their planning.

Although patients with developmental arrests are more prone to such responses, all individuals are susceptible to the forces of contagion. Yalom (1985) has observed that some individuals reject membership in a group because they fear that they will be affected by the illness of others. Some patients prematurely terminate from their group as a result of intensely affective meetings and their fear of overstimulation.

Therapists are not immune to the communication of affects. Indeed, countertransferences generally are the consequence of affect communication. In the classic conceptualization, countertransference is described as the therapist acting on feelings from the past that are reactivated by the patient in the present. A simple and commonplace illustration of the potency of affect communication is the therapist's experience of smiling or laughing during a group interaction, and later realizing that he or she would probably not have had such a response if the same type of exchange had occurred in a dyadic setting.

NONVERBAL COMMUNICATION

A great deal of highly significant communication takes place nonverbally. Some is conscious and obvious, and some is unconscious and subtle. Every therapist is familiar with the communication of the depressed individual who enters the therapy room very slowly, with head down and eyes averted; sits slouched in a chair; and does not speak. Other seemingly ordinary behaviors, such as smiling, frowning, crossing legs, nodding the head, or selecting a particular seat in the group circle, have both conscious and unconscious determinants.

Birdwhistle (1970) demonstrated that body motion is a powerful cultural tool for communication. Through nonverbal channels individuals find out who they are relative to others. They make contacts and convey and receive messages through these channels. Signals are given that regulate the flow of information and the intensity of affects. Berger (1969), in discussing nonverbal communications, noted that they function in "the establishment, maintenance, and regulation of interpersonal relationships" (p. 30). We will examine two important modes of nonverbal communication in group psychotherapy—seating arrangements and body language—and then consider the therapeutic use of the data they generate.

Seating Arrangement

There are no stereotypical meanings to seat selection. The role of therapist's helper is often signaled by a member's selection of the seat immediately to the therapist's right (the right-hand man), but that seat may also be selected by a patient attempting to avoid eye contact with the therapist. A member in conflict with the therapist might select a seat directly opposite him, but the same seat might be selected by a patient desiring to get the best possible view of the therapist. A rebellious or competitive member might sit in a chair that members have accepted as belonging to the therapist. What is important is for the members to become curious about the particular meaning that might underlie the choice of particular seats. Understanding the nonverbal communications is facilitated by the therapist's sitting in the same chair each session. If the therapist sits in a different chair each week it becomes more difficult to ascertain the meaning of seating patterns relative to him or her. The members choose seats for conscious and unconscious reasons, and many choices are made primarily in relation to the therapist.

Members also indicate their feelings about one another in their seating choices. Sexual attraction may be communicated by "couples" sitting beside each other each week. Groups working on male–female competition may arrange themselves with the men on one side of the group and the women on the other. Racial issues are frequently expressed as black and white patients sit on opposite sides of the circle.

The chairs themselves can be utilized in nonverbal communication. Members sometimes move their chairs outside the circle when they are frightened, anxious, and angry. Conversely, members will move their chairs slightly forward when they desire attention or experience closeness.

There seems to be no diagnostic predictive value in how rigidly members remain in the same seats week after week. Rather, this seems to be a function of group norms and personal character style. Some groups have a norm that each chair is designated for a specific group member while other groups change chairs regularly. These differences in style do not correlate with pathology.

Body Language

There is no doubt that body language communicates a great deal about affective experience. A blush, sweating, knuckles whitening on a chair— all are clear messages of physiological and physical responses to affect. Because our culture places considerable emphasis on eye contact, persons who do not maintain eye contact while talking are often evidencing the presence of considerable affect. Head nodding not only signals agreement but also encourages another to continue.

In some instances body language communicates something quite different from the conscious experience or feeling of the individual. A member may complain that another has taken up too much time only to be confronted by the observation that he or she had been nodding in agreement all the while the monopolizer had been talking.

Scheflen (1964) examined nonverbal communication via careful study of videotapes. He found that body positions may be open or closed to include or exclude others. He also pointed out that body language itself can convey mixed messages, as when the upper body is open (arms at sides) and the lower body is closed (legs crossed). Scheflen further described how subtle head nods or body shifts signal a wish to end a conversation.

In another study Scheflen (1965) observed unconscious communication of quasi-courting behavior in psychotherapy sessions. He noted preening behaviors, such as hair stroking, rearranging clothes, or adjusting makeup, as standard courting behaviors in women; other characteristic body motions include prolonging a gaze, exposing a thigh, placing a hand on a hip, or protruding a breast. Men may adjust their ties, pull up their socks, or smooth their hair. Scheflen states that in most cases disqualifiers, such as not completing the messages or verbally noting that others are present, accompany such courting behaviors in groups. The timing and patterns of such behaviors are valuable data in understanding the groupwide or individual conflicts. If messages are given in an ambiguous fashion, or out of the initiator's awareness, the potential for interpersonal difficulty is considerable.

Therapeutic Management of Nonverbal Communication

Upon observing emotionally important nonverbal communication, the therapist faces several conceptual and technical choices. First, the therapist should try, if possible, to link the observation to the here-and-now transactions in the group. Second, the therapist needs to remember that most nonverbal communications are unconscious and must be treated respectfully. If too abrupt or direct a confrontation is made, the individual confronted may react with denial, upset, anger, embarrassment, or hurt. This response is related not only to the content of the material but also to the therapist's having observed and made public that which was out of the patient's awareness and control. Such a move by the therapist is often experienced as a narcissistic injury, may generate iatrogenic resistance, and does little to advance the work of the group. However, tactful identification of nonverbal behavior in the context of a positive therapeutic alliance can bring into focus certain identifiable personality traits.

CLINICAL EXAMPLE

A woman explained that she had been much more open with her friends recently, a change she attributed to the learning she had experienced in the group. One friend had told her that she often led with her chin, which was a gentle way of telling her about her aggressive communicative style. The patient told of this encounter with pleasure and warmth, indicating considerable growth from her prior habitual defensive provocativeness. Later in the session she began to confront one of the other members, while simultaneously fiddling with her sweater and pulling it over her chin. When the therapist pointed out that she was covering her chin, she laughed and was able to explore her inner sense that she was acting very aggressively and was expecting retaliation. The nonverbal behavior had communicated her anxiety.

As patients gain some experience with the examination of nonverbal clues, they will imitate and identify with the therapist, widening the scope of the group analytic process. It is not unusual in a group that has been functioning for a number of months for patients to comment to one another about a facial expression, a clenched fist, the tapping of feet or fingers, or a look in someone's eye. They also learn to recognize that shifts in body position are important communications. Even when the behaviors are conscious gestures, members may not appreciated the force of their message and the extent of the underlying feelings until the behaviors are pointed out.

In this chapter we have examined some special ways in which group members regularly communicate unconscious aspects of themselves. In the next chapter we will turn our attention to the problem patient, as exemplified by certain personality types. Such individuals often engage in combined individual and group treatment or require medications, two treatment strategies that will also be explored in Chapter 13.

12

Special Technical
Considerations: III

Borderline and narcissistic patients have received extensive attention in the current psychotherapeutic literature. They warrant special attention here because of the unique ways in which groups can help them and because of the technical considerations therapists must take into account when treating them in groups. Since there is no unanimity in definition regarding these patients, some depth of description of them is needed before suggested techniques for treating them in groups are presented. Due to their volatility and difficulty maintaining object constancy, these individuals also are candidates for combined individual and group treatment. Moreover, due to their tendency to experience crises, medications are often useful to stabilize affective or cognitive disruptions. The concomitant use of medications for many patients in group treatment has become common practice, and this strategy will be examined in the next chapter.

THE BORDERLINE PATIENT

No integrated diagnostic schema exists for diagnosing borderline personality disorder, and efforts to categorize these individuals are based on descriptive, dynamic, or combined criteria. In general, patients with borderline disorder have, according to the American Psychiatric Association's (1987) *Diagnostic and Statistical Manual of Mental Disorders* (3rd ed., rev.), or DSM-III-R, "a pervasive pattern of instability of self image, interpersonal relationships and mood, beginning in early adulthood and present in a variety of contexts." Their interpersonal relations may be characterized as unstable, intense, or withdrawn. They may have outbursts of anger directed at others or the self. Their mood is equally unstable, though a chronic depressive element is frequently present. They have neither a consistent and clearly formed identity nor an ability to develop long-range goals or plans. At times of stress, often related to separations, these patients may develop brief psychotic episodes.

Dynamic formulations about borderline conditions have focused on early developmental deficits in which internal object relations have not stabilized or separation-individuation tasks have not been mastered (Masterson, 1976, p. 3). Kernberg (1975) assumes the fundamental defect is present in the ego capacity to integrate self and object representations. The internal objects remain split into all-good and all-bad entities. When equilibrium is disturbed, the aggressive drives overwhelm the "good" internal objects, and anxiety becomes paramount. Projective mechanisms serve to protect the good internal object. With such developmental deficits, these patients have little or no capacity to maintain satisfactory and consistent internal objects (Adler & Buie, 1979). The immature ego development interferes with the capacity to tolerate or integrate ambivalent feelings, and as a result, defensive splitting maintains perceptions of others as all good or all bad. It is no wonder that the variability of these patients' pathological configurations, differing ego capacities, and defenses creates problems in making an accurate diagnosis and formulating a satisfactory treatment plan. As if that were not complicated enough, feminist theorists are raising questions about possible gender bias in this diagnosis since the vast majority of patients diagnosed as borderline are female (whereas most patients diagnosed as narcissistic are male).

The interpersonal difficulties of these patients are usually apparent from the moment they enter a group (Roth, 1979). They are particularly frightened by intimacy, closeness, and feelings of contamination or annihilation by others. In order to maintain their precarious inner balance, they consciously and unconsciously resist joining the group, and this resistance is often manifest through violations of the group agreements. Tardiness, absence, and a variety of self-protective responses are quickly apparent under the stress of entry into the group. Some borderline patients blame their referring therapist for their very presence, a solution that allows them to be present without being engaged. Under this condition—and there are many variations on this theme—they can observe and test the safety of the situation. Others, upon entering, soon conclude that they have nothing in common with their fellow members, or complain that the discussions are irrelevant to their needs. They criticize the therapist for all sorts of shortcomings, sometimes very perceptively tuning in on the clinician's errors or empathic failures. In their criticisms, they may gather allies among other members, recreating their world of all-good and all-bad objects.

Another subgroup of borderline individuals enters the group exhibiting domineering and overtly controlling behaviors. The familiar roles of monopolizer or help-rejecting complainer place them at the center of attention, thereby partially gratifying exhibitionistic needs. Moreover, the hostility they generate is quite familiar to them and serves to protect them from the greater dangers of intimacy. Such behaviors make these patients particularly prone to being scapegoated in that other members project their own exhibitionistic wishes into these developmentally arrested individuals, and the borderline members, for their part, are adept at using projective identification in order to protect themselves from recognizing their own affects (Ogden, 1979).

Despite these difficulties and confusions about borderline patients, there seems to be considerable agreement about the particular advantages of group therapy for them. Horwitz (1980) has suggested three elements of group membership that are advantageous for these patients: (1) transference diffusion, which especially diminishes the negative destructive feelings about the therapist; (2) social and emotional distancing, which allows the patient to withdraw and thereby regulate the intensity of affective involvement without immediate sanctions; and (3) social pressure, which helps regulate reality testing. We would suggest that these advantages are relative since transference in groups can be intensified as well as diffused, and emotional distancing is often more difficult than in dyadic treatment.

There is some question as to whether technical modifications are necessary in the treatment of the borderline patient. In part the answer is related to group composition. One approach is to include one or two such patients in a group where others have reached higher developmental levels (Horwitz, 1977a). Under these conditions borderline patients seem to be able to learn from exploration or interpretation, and little modification in technique is necessary (Hulse, 1958). Another approach is to form homogeneous groups (Roth, 1980). There are certain advantages when all the patients are struggling with issues at the same developmental level. Diversity still remains, since individuals bring their own particular history and interpersonal style to bear on group interactions.

As mentioned earlier, borderline individuals utilize splitting of objects as a major defense. Kibel (1991) proposes that this characteristic defense can be used to therapeutic advantage by structuring the group so that the patient's image of the group as a whole is benign. This approach is based on outcome results with borderline patients treated at the Menninger Foundation (Horwitz, 1974), where the finding was that the development of the therapeutic relationship was of greater significance than the development of insight. Within this supportive frame, it is presumed that these patients expose their aggressively linked internal object relationships where they can be modified through partial identifications with others who have expressed similar aspects of themselves and have not been traumatized as a result. Moreover, borderline individuals, a significant proportion of whom have experienced physical or sexual abuse or have witnessed domestic violence, may alter or partially replace the images and experiences they harbor of their family (Herman, Perry, & von der Kolk, 1989).

When working with a borderline patient, it is important for the therapist to set realistic goals. Establishing a therapeutic alliance may be an appropriate intermediate, if not final, goal for some of these individuals. Attainment of that goal implies an ability for the patient to see both positive and negative aspects of other individuals and to experience them as separate, with their own wishes and needs. Further, it represents a significant advance in the ability of borderline patients to negotiate more mature object relatedness. Therapists must pay attention to the communications inherent in all their behaviors with regard to these patients (Glatzer, 1978; W. Stone & Gustafson, 1982). Feldberg (1958) maintains that the therapist has to be more active with borderline patients than with neurotic patients. Interpretation may have to be supplemented by other technical measures, such as universalization, confrontation, and drawing attention to similarities among individuals (Roth, 1979). These technical strategies, in the context of a supportive group, allow for more gratifying interpersonal relationships, which proceed along the path of identification to internalization of more benign internal object relations (Kibel, 1991).

Two particular strategies aid this process. Because many borderline individuals do not recognize the impact of their behaviors on others, they are surprised, hurt, and defensive when feedback is given. By empathizing with their surprise, the therapist can make emotionally meaningful contact with confronted individuals. This strategy, which differs from the usual strategy of focusing on helping the patient hear the interpretation, thereby reinforces the benign safety of the group atmosphere.

The second strategy uses interpretation aimed at having the greatest impact on the other members, not the borderline patient. For instance, a group therapist might normally draw attention to the fact that a member attacks others when he or she is anxious or frightened. However, if this interpretation were made to a borderline patient, it would likely be met with denial. When the relevant interpretation can be offered to healthier members, the borderline patients can observe those members begin to appreciate the sequencing of anxiety and attack. This facilitates the borderline patient gaining perspective and becoming less likely to withdraw or counterattack. The result is not only a safer group environment for all the members but also a wonderful laboratory for the borderline patient, who has been able to observe the transactions with interest and safety.

In treating the borderline patient in groups with less disturbed patients, the therapist must balance the unique needs of the borderline patient against the needs of the group as a whole. For example, borderline patients often barrage therapists with questions, insisting that they have a direct answer. The basis for this behavior can be multidetermined: The behavior may be an enactment of the patient's sense of entitlement, fear of being ignored, low frustration tolerance, or wish for contact. Whatever the specific etiology of often obnoxious behavior by these patients, therapists are reminded that these individuals *are* trying to gain and sustain relationships. By answering their questions directly, the therapist may soothe the borderline patients temporarily but may set these patients up for the ire of the other members for having received this special attention. By not answering the question directly, borderline patients are protected from intense sibling rivalry but are left unprotected from the intense reactions to not having their needs met. Therapists must quickly assess the pros and cons of providing an answer when borderline patients begin to question them, since any choice includes assets and liabilities in the treatment.

Many of the ego deficits and problems in maintaining a sense of identity are evident as borderline patients join a group.

CLINICAL EXAMPLES

Despite having agreed to the usual group agreements, one patient announced during his first group meeting that he would commit himself to remaining for only six sessions. At the end of his 6-week period, he extended his commitment for another 6 weeks. That was followed by yet another 6-week commitment. Only then could this patient feel safe enough to publicly commit himself to remaining in the group for as long as it took to work on his problems. Not only was this patient severely cautious, but his style was provocative and evoked criticism and resentment from the others. This only served to reinforce his reluctance to join fully because of his conviction that others would not like him. (This is yet another example of how projective identification serves to "train" the world to behave as expected.)

A borderline patient maintained her distance by angrily insisting that others reveal all the intimate details of their lives, all the while remaining resolutely mute about her own life. Her rationale was that she could feel safer and closer if others were willing to be vulnerable in her presence, but the actual effect was that others had no interest in being close to her. Nonetheless, the patient was able to persist in this stance for a number of years before consistently being able to examine her in-group behaviors.

The marked emotional volatility of borderline patients often startles the therapist and the other members.

CLINICAL EXAMPLES

A woman had seemed quite cooperative and insightful when the therapist focused an interpretation on her behavior. However, 30 minutes later she angrily screamed at him, "You're ignoring me!" when focusing on interactions between other members. The patient's difficulty in being able to share the therapist and maintain an inner representation of him as interested and concerned contributed to her outburst.

A borderline man was told by a fellow member, "You just interrupted someone again." He denied that he had done so and refused to even consider it a possibility, even though in the previous meeting he acknowledged that both inside and outside the group others had made that observation to him. His defiant stance enraged his group colleagues. Nonetheless, later in the meeting he turned to his original confronter and pleaded, "Let's be friends." He was unable to hear the response that friendship must be based on give and take and could not just be willed.

The fluctuation from an angry pout to a pleading request for friendship illustrates the borderline patient's emotional instability, need for contact, and lack of awareness of others' responses to the interaction. Borderlines are particularly successful in gaining relationships; they are very difficult to ignore!

The therapist is often the focus of attention for the borderline patient, and the task of maintaining balance in the face of incessant demands or angry outbursts is difficult. One female borderline patient had the disconcerting habit of turning her chair so that she only talked to the therapist and only made contact with him; the therapist felt riveted to her and could not disengage himself from her. Another patient unfalteringly insisted that the therapist follow up any clarification or interpretation with direct advice about how to change his behavior or how to make him feel his feelings.

The result of these and many other behaviors is that therapists find themselves on emotional roller coasters. They may be overstimulated or upset by the defensive maneuverings of these patients. This might be reflected in their dreams or in a feeling of dread before a session (Roth, 1980). A consultation with a colleague or an ongoing formal or informal opportunity for ventilation, processing, or supervision can be invaluable for the therapist trying to maintain his or her equilibrium in the face of these emotion-laden transactions.

The borderline patient's capacity to utilize group therapy most effectively is often enhanced by the concurrent use of individual therapy (Rutan & Alonso, 1982; Slavinska-Holy, 1983). The individual therapy format offers the opportunity for these patients to gain some perspective on the overstimulation they often experience in the group, whereas the group offers them the protection of peers as they explore their powerful transferences to individual therapists.

So how should one treat borderlines in group therapy? Indeed, *should* borderlines be treated in groups? If one holds to the fundamental psychodynamic principles, borderline patients are no different than any of the rest of us. They are trying to avoid pain and gain relationships. They have just developed a uniquely nettlesome defensive structure that works all too well. That is, like a skunk in the forest that "stinks up the place" when threatened, the borderline patient has the capacity to make people not want to be around them, even as they yearn for nothing more than to be the center—and the exclusive center—of attention of those very others. And in their own unique way they do often gain a place of centrality in their relationships. Groups provide unparalleled opportunities for observing this defensive operation at work in the very interpersonal field in which it was most designed to function. For a therapist to generate special or unique treatment techniques for this population, while overtly caring and thoughtful, runs the risk of accepting the projective identifications of these patients and treating them as special.

The outcome of treatment of borderline individuals has not been sufficiently studied. Nevertheless, long-term follow-up reports of severely ill borderline patients treated with extended hospitalization and individual therapy provides hope that some of these patients can lead employed and self-supporting lives, marry, and have children. Yet a significant proportion remain superficial and avoid intimacy (McGlashan, 1986). No parallel reports are available to assess the outcome of group treatment, but anecdotal reports of clinical experience have been promising.

NARCISSISTIC DISORDERS

Throughout this book reference has been made to Kohut's (1971, 1977, 1984) contributions to the evolution of a psychoanalytic theory of the self. Of the many contributors to modern psychoanalytic theory, self psychology has been the most resistant to use in group therapy. Only recently have serious attempts been made to use this model in group therapy (W. Stone, 1992). Because we believe this theory offers much to group therapy, in this section we will briefly summarize Kohut's contributions and their application to group psychotherapy.

With a focus on the consistent use of empathy and introspection as the primary tools in understanding inner emotional states, Kohut began a reformulation of the theory of human development and placed the self at "the center of the individual's psychological universe" (Kohut, 1977, p 311).

The self, conceptually, is both a psychological structure that organizes experiences and an existential structure that is the center of independent initiative. The self is developed in the myriad interactions with "selfobjects," that is, objects (persons) available to empathically understand the self and fulfill certain psychological functions that the immature or traumatized self is unable to perform for itself. The selfobject is experienced not as a person with separate needs and wishes but only as an object to fulfill functions. Many of these functions center about the selfobject's empathic capacity to assist the self in the integration of affects (Socarides & Stolorow, 1984; Stolorow, Brandchaft, & Atwood, 1987). The need for the selfobject does not disappear but is necessary throughout the life cycle. However, the need is modified as the individual matures and the self assumes more of the self-soothing functions.

Kohut (1971) initially formulated the presence of two developmental lines: the *grandiose-exhibitionistic self,* which requires phase-appropriate "mirroring" from the selfobject in order to develop ambitions and goals, and the *idealizing self,* which requires the opportunity to merge with an idealized other in order to develop values and ideals. These two "selfs" became the foundation of the *bipolar self.* In 1984 Kohut posited the need for an *alter ego selfobject,* which was conceived of as an intermediate area between the two poles. Kohut believes that the self's need for the sameness of the alter ego would aid in the development of skills and talents.

Psychopathology, within this framework, was conceptualized as a deficit in the development of a cohesive self, not the result of conflict among id, ego, superego, and reality. This notion that psychopathology results from a deficit rather than a conflict is perhaps the major theoretical difference between self psychology and traditional psychoanalytic theory.

With the caveat that specific inner meaning of the behavioral patterns must be sought out, Kohut and Wolf (1978) classified self disorders as *narcissistic behavior* disorders, in which perverse, delinquent, or addictive behaviors are efforts to prevent the disintegration or fragmentation of the distorted self, and *narcissistic personality* disorders, in which symptoms of hypochondriasis, depression, hypersensitivity to slights, and diminished vigor are present as indicators of the injured self.

In this classification Kohut and Wolf described several personalities: (1) mirror-hungry personalities, who need confirming and admiring responses to nourish the "famished self," seldom seem satisfied, and harbor a sense of inner worthlessness beneath these surface behaviors; (2) alter-ego personalities, who appear to require another with whom they can feel identical in appearance, opinion, or values and who, like the mirror-hungry personalities, exhibit an instability and chronic disappointment with the selfobject; and (3) ideal-hungry personalities, who feel the need to idealize others, that is, to be able to merge in order to feel safe and secure.

A fourth and fifth character type, both of which involve much greater degrees of disturbance, were also identified; Merger-hungry personalities, who need the selfobject in lieu of a self structure, whose boundaries between self and others are fluid, and who envy others' separateness and are demanding of their attention, and contact-shunning personalities, who avoid social contact in anticipation of rejection or frustration and who also fear that they will be engulfed or destroyed.

The therapeutic process in dyadic treatment of all such personalities is presented in the following schema: Initially, a patient's symptoms may diminish or disappear as the symptomatic self is supported and sustained in the empathic therapeutic environment by the selfobject therapist. Through the transference, the patient gradually exposes the developmental deficit in the self and the concomitant need for a selfobject. Inevitably, a break in the empathic connection (a narcissistic injury) occurs, and the patient responds by utilizing his or her typical responses (e.g., withdrawal or anger) in order to restore a sense of cohesion. The therapist then attempts, through introspection and empathy, to understand and explain (interpret) the sequence of injury and the patient's attempt to gain restitution. In the optimal situation the patient responds with a restoration of self-coherence and, with repetition of the sequence, gradually acquires self-understanding and the capacity to soothe himself or herself. This process has been labeled *transmuting internalization.*

Group psychotherapy provides multiple opportunities for individuals to reenact selfobject (narcissistic) needs. The group format itself evokes fears of uncertainty and nonresponse from others and, as a consequence, presents a danger to the self. Almost universally, members fear the potential for narcissistic injury until some level of reliability and trust in the therapist and in the group interactions has been established. It is important, however, to distinguish between narcissistic needs present in all individuals and the emergence of coherent narcissistic transferences, which would indicate a significant disturbance of the self.

Selfobject transferences may develop either to the group as a whole or to other individuals within the group. The power of the group as a whole to function as a selfobject that, at least temporarily, could evoke a sense of well-being and self-cohesion was observable during the height of the sensitivity movement in the 1960s, when many individuals behaved as if they were weekend T-group addicts. It is our speculation that these groups provided a genuine emotional high derived from the impression of having merged with the idealized image of the group. Similarly, patients in therapy groups feel an inner sense of togetherness and cohesion when they develop an idealizing transference to the group. Fried (1973) has provided a sensitive example of an idealization in a quotation from a patient's letter: "I'm helped when I recall how blessed I was to share the love and the kindness of my friends in the group and you [the therapist]. The memories of the intimacies we shared and the openness of our feelings helps keep me together" (p. 165). The development of a stable and reliable transference to the group as a whole is extremely valuable in helping some individuals maintain a sense of inner cohesion (Meyers, 1978; Rutan & Rice, 1981; W. Stone & Whitman, 1977).

Many narcissistic patients exhibit considerable resistance to developing transferences. They anticipate that the selfobject will not be reliable and consequently resist acknowledging the importance of the soothing and satisfying merger with an idealized object or their inner need for an affirming or mirroring response. Among the many motives for resistance is shame. This painful affect arises from two sources: Narcissistic individuals may be consciously aware of their inner needs for selfobject responses and are ashamed of such wishes; in addition, shame may be associated with failure to achieve the standards of the idealized self (Morrison, 1990). Some individuals with self disorders are unable to delineate or differentiate among affects. What may seem to be a resistance and what might be diagnosed as a depression may instead be a developmental deficit in which the patient complains of generalized dullness or loss of vitality (W. Stone, 1990).

Subtle tests regarding the group's reliability and safety are often conducted unconsciously by narcissistic patients prior to verbal acknowledgment of their transferential needs. Often the transference is established silently and becomes manifest only when there is a perceived failure on the part of the therapist or the group.

CLINICAL EXAMPLE

Warren, a particularly articulate and gregarious member, spoke extensively of his difficulty in forming intimate relationships with women. He presented himself as a Don Juan, with many conquests and no loves. The narcissistic transference to the group emerged when he began to complain about absences by group members, which he felt ruined group cohesion. He could not verbalize precisely the inner upset he experienced, but he was vociferous in his declarations of discomfort. The transference reaction was particularly focused on one member, who often arrived late and who seldom spoke. It did not matter to Warren whether the member spoke, but his mere presence seemed very important indeed. The feelings of hurt and disorganization experienced by Warren when a member was absent were a consequence of his viewing the group as no longer being complete and therefore no longer being available as an idealized selfobject with which to merge. As Warren was gradually able to maintain his sense of inner stability, he could discuss his fears and wishes in more detail.

The group as a whole may also be experienced as a mirroring selfobject. Nonresponse from members may be followed by withdrawal or rage on the part of narcissistic patients who often have some degree of awareness that such responses are out of proportion to the stimulus but who display or talk about their inner turmoil only after overcoming an initial resistance.

CLINICAL EXAMPLE

From time to time, Sylvia would report to the group how her relationship with her boyfriend was progressing. This was reported in a dispassionate manner, with no sense of urgency. One evening she began a meeting by announcing that her relationship had abruptly ended. As the discussion of that relationship continued, it became clear to Sylvia and the group that for months she had ignored the signals that serious troubles existed between her boyfriend and herself. Sylvia stated she needed him in order to feel an inner hope that she was acceptable. As a consequence, she said she had lived a fantasy of who her boyfriend was, refusing to recognize his particular realistic strengths and shortcomings. The group criticized Sylvia extensively for her failure to "face reality" with her boyfriend and for not discussing the relationship in more depth in the group. The therapist, however, suggested that Sylvia's needs to ignore the obvious flaws in the relationship were even more important. He went on to state that it was understandable that Sylvia might have feared discussing her boyfriend in the group because it would have made her more aware of what she was avoiding. The therapist, who had a self psychology perspective, had to determine whether or not the group was functioning as a satisfactory selfobject and, if not, whether prior narcissistic injuries had significantly contributed to Sylvia's reticence. It is possible that the group represented a selfobject similar to her boyfriend, that is, a selfobject that was needed but feared and whose deficits, consequently, were denied or avoided.

Self psychology has placed the vicissitudes of the empathic connection between the individual and the selfobject in a central position. Failures in empathy are expected and, in fact, provide for growth, since the individual under optimal conditions will develop many of the functions formerly provided by the selfobject. But if the failures are too severe or too traumatic, deficits in the self develop. However, faulty empathy itself is not ultimately harmful; what is harmful is a lack of effort to be empathic. The therapist must maintain particular awareness of the vulnerability of the narcissistic individual to empathic failures and be alert to a host of subsequent responses (W. Stone, 1992; W. Stone & Whitman, 1980). For instance, rage reactions are often a result of narcissistic injury, and interpretations of the empathic failure and the resultant hurt and rage will enable the injured individual to gain perspective and potentially to increase mastery over the vulnerability of the self. By continually considering that rage is potentially a reaction to narcissistic injury, the therapist reestablishes an empathic connection and creates an environment for renewed growth.

Several difficult problems encountered in group psychotherapy can be reassessed in the light of self psychology. The so-called help-rejecting complainer probably does not exist! That is, patients who have been given that pejorative label are probably exhibiting a fundamental inability to communicate what help they desire, demonstrating the presence of an empathic failure rather than a primary need to reject all help. These patients often gain a great amount of negative attention in groups, which may be preferable to being ignored or feeling isolated. They may also fear being understood (a variant of the contact-shunning personality), and they may feel elements of rage and revenge. Thus, multiple functions are conveyed in this behavioral configuration.

Another common problem patient in therapy groups is the monopolizer, who both wishes and fears the effect of recognition and admiration. The monopolizer therefore deals with the problem by remaining the center of attention and simultaneously fending off any real intimacy through verbal outpourings. This one-way dialogue also offers protection against hearing what others feel. At the same time, the monopolizer can maintain an idealized fantasy of the group and the therapist; the nonstop talking protects him or her from hearing the members or leader speak and thus avoids shattering the fantasy. The empathic task is to recognize the manifestations of this patient's marked ambivalence.

Through focusing on empathic connectedness, the therapist can gain insight into those situations where members seem to erupt in rage or hurt for no apparent reason. In most instances these reactions follow a narcissistic injury that has gone unrecognized. One source of injury is a group-as-a-whole interpretation. The generalization inevitably inherent in such an interpretation cannot include detailed attention and understanding of each individual. This sets the stage for narcissistically vulnerable members to feel hurt and enraged. Another source is the inevitable intragroup conflict. Two individuals may demand attention and response at the same time, and a small slight or failure to fulfill the need of either may be experienced as a narcissistic injury.

Therapists should strive to create an atmosphere that enables the narcissistic transference to become manifest. This includes the difficult task of accepting patients' idealizing transference rather than prematurely pushing them to correct their distortions (Rutan & Rice, 1981). The time will come soon enough when the therapist will be viewed as unempathic or uncaring, and this will result in sufficient hurt in our patients for us to observe their characteristic response to narcissistic injury. When this happens, our narcissistic patients' responses to the group's or a specific member's failure to respond in accordance with their inner needs may be interpreted through an empathic understanding of their inner world and their characteristic interactions.

In sum, working successfully with narcissistic patients means gaining an empathic understanding of how these individuals' behavioral styles are attempts to shore up and protect their fragile sense of self.

THE DIFFICULT PATIENT, GROUP DYNAMICS, AND THERAPIST BALANCE

In this chapter we have thus far emphasized the therapeutic tasks for patients who are diagnosed as having a borderline or narcissistic personality disorder. They represent the vast majority of what are termed "difficult patients." We believe the emphasis on the diagnosis does not do justice to the therapeutic problem because the difficult patient also has the potential to create the difficult group.

The broader conceptualization of the difficult patient extends beyond the specific diagnostic taxonomy; we understand the difficulty primarily as a *relational* problem. These patients have major deficits in developing and sustaining interpersonal relationships that are satisfying to all concerned. From a dynamic perspective, the deficits are believed to arise from defective early mother–child relationships, which result in distortions of basic trust, unsatisfied dependency needs, and the development of faulty ego structures. As discussed in the previous section, monopolizes or exhibitionists may be pleased to have an audience, but their listeners are soon disenchanted with them, once they sense that they only matter as part objects or developmentally early selfobjects.

Nitsun (1991) writes about the "anti-group," which he portrays as "the destructive aspects of groups that threatens the integrity of the group and its therapeutic development" (p. 7). All patients, but especially the more regressed patients, are understandably reluctant to enter and participate in a group that does not promise the safety, exclusive attention, and warmth of the mother–child dyad. When the therapy group proves to be less than the yearned-for ideal family, as indeed it must, the resulting disappointment and rage lead to the unleashing in the group of destructive forces which Nitsun defines as "the anti-group."

The affective response of the group members to the anti-group attitude requires attention or the difficult patient will become the recipient of disowned aspects of the other members, a fate shared by the scapegoat. The most helpful therapeutic focus is often not on the particular difficult patient but on the group's response. There is an understandable but not ultimately helpful tendency for members to find the difficult patient hateful rather than recognize that such patients represent aspects of themselves. This fixes the offending patient in an historically familiar but untenable position.

One overlooked element in the interactions that invariably take place in a group with a difficult patient is the subtle violation of the group agreements. Members act upon their feelings and are reluctant to verbalize them. They withdraw from, ignore, or only speak banalities to the offending member, or they may express their frustration and rage directly rather than examine their own experience in being in the group with this difficult member. The therapist can begin to make inroads into the destructive processes by helping the members examine these responses that run counter to their agreement.

Nonetheless, there is great resistance to altering the groupwide response. Roth (1990) points out that the archaic ego of narcissistic individuals is protected by the group's use of concrete action and emotional discharge rather than examined through reflective activity. He emphasizes that there is an absence of ideas about what is happening among the members and a propensity to externalize conflict. Members of a seemingly average therapeutic group under the influence of the intense affects generated by a difficult patient resort to earlier defensive modes and affective states, and they are no longer able to observe their responses. Instead of learning there is merely repetition, which leads members in a further downward spiral of decreasing trust in the group and its processes. No new ideas emerge.

Even clinicians sometimes find their responses altered in the presence of the difficult patient. Indeed, awareness of our own violation of the agreements or of a departure from our usual mode of operating can sometimes alert us to the presence of a difficult patient in the group before we are consciously aware of this situation. Such clues as coming late, ending the session early, blocking on a patient's name in the middle of a session, and having difficulty recalling the central dynamic issues of the preceding sessions are useful indicators of the therapist's emotional state. At these times it is important for the therapist to carefully examine his or her own emotional position with the difficult group. The clinician's anxieties, sometimes expressed in dreams, can give clues to countertransferences. Resolution of those elements may assist in overcoming the anti-group atmosphere, but generally such clarification of the clinician's response, while necessary, is not sufficient.

Recognition by therapists of their countertransference responses to the anti-group atmosphere prepares them to alter the therapeutic climate. Therapeutic stalemants are freed and the group becomes more capable of serving as a corrective emotional experience.

Friedman (1988) suggests that there are three needs in the therapist that are activated in every treatment and must be balanced by the therapist. According to Friedman, understanding the following needs, which are separate from the more traditional concept of countertransference, serves to sustain the clinician in the face of difficult therapeutic challenges.

1. *To act like a therapist:* It is important in order to maintain their balance that the material therapists hear from the patients fit the treatment plan they have developed.

2. *To satisfy curiosity:* Therapists are trained to be curious. They wonder about the members' internal worlds, their interactions, and their impact on the group forces. When answers to the questions being raised

in treatment are not forthcoming this might become routine, and stultifying, both to the patients and to the clinician. Curiosity may be limited to satisfying the therapist's theory; perhaps how material fits with their notion of psychogenesis or group-as-a-whole dynamics. *"We are curious because we have ways of recognizing that we want to put into action"* (emphasis in the original; p. 106).

3. *To elicit something desirable:* In contrast to the first two balance problems, which are intellectually stimulating, this problem emphasizes the therapists "urge to ignite a satisfying interaction with the patient" (p. 108). This is an unconscious search for a relationship in the interaction with the patient.

Difficult patients are difficult, in part, because they upset the therapist's balance. A member expressed her feelings about a difficult absent member in the following manner: "He talks to the air." This woman's wish for some personal contact with the difficult patient was frustrated, and similar feelings are activated in the therapist. Meaningful interactions are limited by such patients' pathology, and as the transactions with these patients become repetitious and stereotyped, the clinician's curiosity decreases and little is available to help him or her to feel like a therapist. Appreciation of our general motivations as therapists, as sketched by Friedman, helps us maintain our balance and work with these difficult individuals and the associated distortions produced in the group.

13

Special Technical
Considerations: IV

F or many patients, including those described in the previous chapter, combining group therapy with individual therapy or pharmacotherapy or both is indicated. Whenever different treatments are combined, complications arise along with the potential gains. It is necessary in this day and age to also understand the pros and cons involved in conducting groups under strict time restrictions since the use of this variation of group psychotherapy is increasing. In this final chapter on special technical considerations we consider the following three issues: (1) combining group therapy and pharmacotherapy, (2) concurrent group and individual psychotherapy, and (3) time-limited group psychotherapy.

COMBINING PHARMACOTHERAPY
AND GROUP PSYCHOTHERAPY

The practice of including patients receiving psychotropic medications in psychodynamic groups is widespread. A survey of 148 experienced group therapists found that more than two-thirds of the respondents included patients taking medications in their typical outpatient groups (Stone, Rodenhauser, & Markert, 1991). The survey showed only slight variation in this percentage among physicians, psychologists, and social workers who lead therapy groups.

The theory to assist the clinician in conceptualizing the indications, goals, and dynamics for combination therapy is incomplete. According to the Group for the Advancement of Psychiatry (1975):

The determinants of the type of treatment offered are hardly ever very clear. To a considerable extent they depend upon the training and ideology of the manpower available for treatment. Those without licenses to use drugs, and who therefore can not prescribe them, frequently oppose their use . . . . Even among those who are reasonably well-trained in both pharmacotherapy and psychotherapy, and who feel comfortable using them, there is a conspicuous lack of reasoned comprehension for their joint use and especially their interaction. (pp. 271–272)

This should not surprise us since psychopharmacology and psychodynamic therapy are grounded in different philosophies: From the psychopharmacological point of view affect springs from biological sources and can be mediated chemically, while from the dynamic point of view affect results from psychological sources. From a medical perspective unusually high affect represents a symptom to be relieved; from a psychodynamic point of view it represents a psychological communication and an opportunity for learning.

Karasu (1982) attempted to both distinguish and relate these differences in philosophy in the psychodynamic and psychopharmacology approaches by offering two target goals: the patient's state (i.e., symptom picture), which is treated with pharmacotherapy, and the trait (the long-standing personality structure), which is treated with psychotherapy. Questions concerning the proper timing to introduce one or the other form of therapy and the dynamics surrounding their combined or sequential use have not been fully answered.[1]

Some group therapists are uncomfortable with patients receiving psychotropic medications because of their belief that dynamic considerations take precedence. They believe that an understanding of the underlying conflicts or personality deficits that result in symptom formation is interfered with by the use of medications and that removing symptoms lessens anxiety and decreases motivation for self-exploration. An additional argument is that learning under the influence of medications is not transferable to the nonmedicated state. Some therapists further maintain that reliance on medications damages self-esteem since patients cannot take credit for their gains. Other therapists tend to dismiss discussion of medication as being outside the arena of the interpersonal/intrapsychic investigations.

---

[1]There is controversy regarding the differentiation of state of trait elements of a number of psychiatric disorders — and indeed as to whether this is a valid distinction at all. The varying clinical responsiveness of certain long-standing depressive syndromes — diagnosed as dysthymia — to antidepressant medications and the exploration of "depressive personality" as an Axis II diagnosis contributes to the bluring of these elements.

On the opposite side of the controversy are group therapists who believe that excessive anxiety and mood fluctuation interfere with participation in the interactive sphere of the group and that members can learn only when these symptoms are under control. Furthermore, they believe that the dynamics that arise during group discussions about taking medication can be effectively explored. It is our belief that patients taking psychopharmacological agents can be successfully treated in groups if the therapist is alert to the impact of a member's pharmacotherapy on the group dynamics, transferences, and countertransferences.

Rodenhauser (1989) has categorized the positive and negative effects of taking medication for the treated individual and for the group across dimensions of self-control, emotional connectedness and technical/strategic aspects. The positive aspects of self-control include an increased sense of responsibility, self-confidence, energy, reduction of internal stimuli, and reduction of stigma from disturbing behaviors; on the negative side are disavowal of responsibility, "sick role" reminder, impaired cognition, affect dulling, and stigma from taking medication. The dynamics of the increased emotional connectedness that results from taking medication include validation of the self, evidence of caring, rapid symptom reduction, and instillation of hope and trust, but these elements can be inverted and produce negative effects, such as loss of personal potency and decreased motivation.

Attitudes about medicine may have considerable impact on the group dynamics. In groups containing highly disturbed individuals, there is the potential for emotional contagion in which fears of overidentification with the medicated member evoke self-protective responses such as withdrawal, scorn, and hostility. Concern about taking drugs may turn to an oversolicitousness that covers negative attitudes. Regression may occur when members identify with the medicated patient's wishes for a magical (drug) cure, thereby creating a dependent group; in fact, there may be subgrouping and splitting between those who do take medication and those who do not. Group dynamics may reflect a patient's reluctance to explore the meaning of and reason for taking an antianxiety medication, a reluctance that may parallel the patient's resistance within the group.

CLINICAL EXAMPLE

Quietly, at the end of a session, the patient asked the therapist to refill his medication, which he took before making public presentations at work. The patient's shame in not being able to contain his anxiety emerged in his softly spoken request. The timing of the request effectively prevented immediate discussion of the topic. The patient, who was generally very

passive and quiet in the group, reenacted his problem of speaking before
a crowd by requesting his medication in an unobtrusive fashion. In the
following meeting the members did not mention the medication until the
issue was addressed by the therapist, who noted the possible dynamic
meaning of the manner in which the prescription had been requested.
At that time a variety of uncomfortable affects emerged around the medicated patient's request and the members' own attitudes and passivity in
exploring the problem, which highlighted the group's participation in
avoiding exploration of this facet of the patient's personality.

In sum, in considering whether or not a patient should use medication, we return to a point made earlier regarding the place of affect
in psychotherapy: The goal in dynamic therapy is to stimulate and encourage as much *useful* affect as possible. When patients experience
such high degrees of affect that their day-to-day lives and their therapy
are compromised, medication should be considered. Too often, medication is conceived as permanent or not considered at all. Patients receiving antidepressants generally decrease or stop their medications after
their mood disorder has become sufficiently stabilized. Other patients
can be helped to use their medications primarily to forestall crises or
to help in times of predictable distress (e.g., anniversaries of losses, repeti-
tively difficult times of the year).

Metaphors and Transferences

As in a discussion of any other topic, patients may use their medication as a reality issue or as a metaphor for their experience in the group
(Zaslav & Kalb, 1989). Clues to their use of metaphors are apparent
in the responses of the others. A preoccupation within the group with
problems of side effects (e.g., sleepiness and fatigue with an antidepressant or dry mouth as an anticholinergic effect from a variety of medications) may represent anxiety about the power of the therapist (who
may not necessarily be a physician) or feelings about the group as a
whole. Discussions about medications often become major preoccu-
pations in members with early developmental conflicts as a way of testing
the safety of the group atmosphere and, at an unconscious level, the
limits of what can be discussed. Similar discussions may appear during times of boundary changes such as vacations or other interruptions.
The meaning of the medication then becomes linked with the harm
that is being done to the members. Sometimes the discussion contains
a covert request for medication to replace the group, suggesting that
medication may serve as a transitional object. A discussion of medications may reveal patients' hopes about the efficacy of psychotherapy

or of their own efforts. It may convey messages about members' concepts of authority and control, which is implied in the term *compliance* (Zaslav & Kalb, 1989), which refers to the willingness of the patient to use the prescribed drugs appropriately.

Clinicians often are hard-pressed to maintain their therapeutic stance and may be inclined to prematurely cut short discussions of medications. One way to check for countertransference would be for therapists to compare their reaction to a discussion of medication for a medical illness (such as insulin for diabetes) to their reaction to a discussion of psychotropic medications. In most instances, a therapist would listen for the feelings or the metaphor embedded in the former but might have a certain impatience in response to the latter. Certainly, a discussion of any illness may be a communication about the psychotherapy, but there often seems to be a differential response to discussions of psychotropic as compared to other drugs. Moreover, psychiatrists and nonprescribing clinicians may have different countertransference problems. The physician may feel compelled to attend solely to the medical content of the issue and may feel unprofessional if he or she assigns process meaning to the group discussion. Nonprescribing clinicians may feel ignorant or helpless when their patients discuss medications and may thus either feign knowledge they do not in fact have or adopt a position hostile to the taking of medication.

The response of group members to an individual's discussing medications may also be a clue to the therapist's countertransference. Is the therapist pleased when members do not respond, thereby suppressing the discussion? Conversely, is encouragement or participation in the discussion by others annoying? Such reactions on the part of the therapist may provide important information about groupwide affects as well as that countertransference.

It behooves all clinicians to be aware of the usual side effects of medications and to recognize that some comments may reflect a patient's realistic effort to obtain information about the therapeutic impact or side effects of a drug. Clues to other meanings can be obtained from the context in which the discussion arises. When the therapist is not a physician, metaphorical communication is more likely, but the possibility still exists that the patient is seeking information from others in the group who may be taking the same medication or may have taken it in the past.

Too little attention has been given to the impact of a member or members in a group being on psychotropic medication. As with all other group issues, exploration of the meaning of the of medication for the individual and for the group can provide information about ways patients communicate and protect themselves from uncomfortable affects.

We have found no salient reason to exclude individuals using psychotropic medication if they are group appropriate, except for the therapist's personal preference.

CONCURRENT AND INDIVIDUAL THERAPY

There is growing interest in the advantages that may accrue when patients are seen in individual and group therapy concurrently (Rutan & Alonso, 1982, 1990; Battegay, 1972; Gans, 1990; Bernard & Drob, 1985; Wong, 1990). Each modality offers something that the other does not. In individual therapy there is the opportunity to focus precisely and in detail on the history, transferences, and associations of a single patient. In group therapy patients are seen in their interpersonal fields, and their characteristic relational and defensive styles are available for direct observation. Therapists who have seen patients in both modalities are accustomed to finding new information in each setting. A morose, depressed patient in dyadic therapy might demonstrate a social aptitude in the group setting that the individual therapist would not have predicted, and a quiet, seemingly uninvolved group patient might relate a panorama of vivid reactions to and feelings about the group in the safety of a dyadic therapy.

A variety of issues must be addressed when considering concurrent therapy (Rutan & Alonso, 1982). For example, when should the patient see the same therapist in both individual and group therapy (combined therapy), and when should the patient see different therapists (conjoint therapy)? When should group therapy be added to individual therapy, and when should individual therapy be added to group therapy? How would these additions be best accomplished? For which patients is concurrent therapy indicated, and for which patients is it contraindicated?

Group Therapy Added to Individual Therapy

Patients in individual therapy sometimes experience difficulty generating sufficient associational material to fuel their individual therapy effectively. Groups evoke many feelings and memories for these patients, and these affects and memories can then be used productively in both settings.

There are patients for whom the dyadic transference is insufficient to help them resolve their interpersonal problems; for such patients a group can assist them with relating to both sexes, different ages, and multiple personality styles. The group format not only provides patients with an opportunity to experience a much wider range of interpersonal options, but it represents a situation that is more easily generalized to life.

Group therapy also benefits those patients who, in the course of their individual therapy have made significant strides toward understanding the roots of interpersonal problems and now need a laboratory in which to cement their gains or to further explore these issues.

In situations where a therapist becomes locked into a countertransference struggle with a patient, the addition of a group can often resolve the difficulty and thus save the individual therapy.

Individual Therapy Added to Group Therapy

The patient who is unable to express himself in the group is often assisted by individual therapy. This patient needs to be distinguished from the patient who refuses to relate in the group. Both can be helped to use the group more productively by supplemental dyadic therapy, but the latter type of patient should be helped to own the hostile aspects of his or her stubbornness as part of the referral.

The patient who in the course of group therapy has identified a specific area that may require more intensive treatment to work through can use individual therapy. For instance, patients who hear about sexual abuse in group sessions and gradually become aware that they too were molested may need individual sessions to adequately explore their experience. This situation generally is a result of effective work in group therapy; provided that individual therapy is understood as supplementing and not replacing the group, we do not view it as a resistance.

Some patients find the interpersonal setting of the group too frightening and need the presence of an individual therapist to help them remain in the group. Individual therapy can assist such patients by exploring the roots of their fears about group membership, thus allowing them to continue in the group.

When group members undergo an external crisis, such as a death in the family, short-term individual therapy is often a useful tool to help them through the time of crisis. A variation on this situation is the developmentally immature member who may react to a crisis, such as the simultaneous termination of several members or the expression of strong affect in the group, with a request for individual treatment. These members, who seem unable to directly address their tension within the group, usually attribute their difficulty to external sources, and seem temporarily unable to integrate the transferential implications of their external conflict, can be successfully managed with several individual sessions. They regain their balance through individual contact with the therapist and the opportunity to discuss their difficulties.

Conjoint Therapy

Conjoint therapy, an arrangement in which the patient is seen in group therapy and individual therapy by two different therapists, is a common therapeutic practice. In many instances patients are referred for group treatment by a clinician who wishes to continue the individual therapy. If the patient is deemed appropriate for group work, it is necessary for the group therapist to obtain the patient's permission to communicate with the individual therapist. Because conjoint therapy provides a fertile ground for splitting, it is important for the two therapists to keep in communication about the patient. It is not unusual for therapists who do not even know each other to begin working with the same patient in this dual mode of treatment. It is important to gain the patient's agreement for the two therapists to communicate, so that there will be no secrets between them. We believe that accepting a patient referred to group therapy who refuses to give permission for the group therapist to speak with his or her individual therapist is contraindicated. This patient, who has already indicated that there is an unshareable "secret" life, would be entering the group with a less stringent agreement regarding openness than others. On the other hand, a different complication arises if it is the individual therapist who maintains that confidentiality of the dyadic treatment cannot be violated. In this case the group therapist needs to assess the *patient's* willingness and ability to speak in group sessions about what is important in the dyadic treatment. If the individual therapist considers an impermeable membrane between group and individual to be important but the patient does not, the patient may be accepted for group therapy. This is not an easy decision, and some group therapists routinely refuse to accept patients into a group when the individual therapist will not agree to communicate since there is built-in split between the group and the individual therapist, and since the unwillingness by the individual therapist to share information promotes secrets and suggests that an antigroup bias may exist. We believe patients can be accepted in group therapy under these conditions, though they are not ideal, *if* the individual therapist's position is based on a theoretical conviction about the absolute privacy of communication in individual therapy rather than on a conscious or unconscious derogation of group therapy. In these cases the group therapist should tell the patient, "You will have a somewhat more difficult job than others who are in individual therapy. I will not be able to assist by collaboration with your individual therapist. Therefore, we will rely on you to ensure that the important material from your individual sessions comes to the group as well." It is also important that the group therapist not engage in splitting (the unconscious mechanism of viewing the world as "good" and "evil" in order to avoid being ambivalent). The decision to completely protect the confidentiality of individual sessions, while not one with which we agree, is nonetheless an honorable and defensible one.

Combined Therapy

Combined therapy refers to the practice of seeing one's own patients in both individual and group therapy. This is an extremely powerful therapeutic format, but it requires that the patient and therapist reach agreement regarding the interface between the two therapies. Controversy exists as to the limits of confidentiality, with one side proposing a strict boundary between the two treatments (Wong, 1983) and the other maintaining that "the patient's contract should include explicit agreement that the therapies are not separated by a boundary of confidentiality" (Rutan & Alonso, 1982). While either position is defensible, we opt for the latter since the former inevitably implies that there are some subjects that are just too powerful to be related in groups and runs the risk of patient and therapist having a "secret" from the group. Nonetheless, it is acceptable practice if a therapist prefers, to maintain confidentiality between group and individual therapy. It is most important that the therapist be consistent in whatever approach is taken.

Obviously, all of a patient's communications have relevance in both individual and group therapy. Nonetheless, some material clearly relates to one modality more than the other. Patients sometimes find it easier to speak in individual therapy of difficult material that belongs in group therapy, and vice versa. In such instances the therapist is faced with a delicate situation. On the one hand, the therapist wants to hear the material and to help the patient understand it; and on the other hand, the therapist does not want to collude with the patient in withholding material from the primary therapeutic modality.

It is useful for therapists to remember that patients are free to talk about whatever they choose in either modality. Our role is not to punish them for choosing the "wrong" setting. However, it is certainly appropriate to explore with the patient why the particular setting was chosen.

CLINICAL EXAMPLE

In his individual session John mentions that he is furious with Sally, a fellow group member. He also reports that he cannot tell Sally directly of his anger because he is fearful she will be devastated; nor is he convinced he can control his sadism toward her. Furthermore, he asks that the therapist not speak of this in the group.

The therapist is faced with a difficult problem. He does not want to forestall John's talking about his important feelings, and yet he does not want to enter into a collusion with John to keep secrets from the group. The therapist uses the individual time to explore John's powerful reaction to Sally, and says, "She is very important to you." At the end of the session the therapist states, "You have some important things to discuss with Sally and the group."

In the following group session John does not mention his feelings toward Sally. In the ensuing individual session the therapist notes this John did not speak with Sally and the focus of this individual session is on why John feels incapable of sharing these feelings in the group. Ultimately John links his feelings toward Sally to his ambivalent feelings toward his alcoholic mother. On the one hand he is furious with mother; on the other hand he pities her and does not wish to cause her more pain. Typically, he speaks privately with his father about these difficult feelings. The therapy parallels that situation, and John's wish to speak with the therapist privately about his feelings toward Sally replicates his private conversations with father.

When John understands the etiology of his reactions, he speaks to Sally in the group. To his surprise she is able to hear him and respond. He further learns how angry he has been with his father for colluding with him to make mother the identified patient in the family.

Though it is less frequent, it is not unusual for patients to mention in group something the need to explore more completely in the individual therapy. Lipsius (1991) refers to this as "background use," where the patient sets the stage for further discussion of important material later.

Whether material is presented in either group therapy or individual therapy with an intent to avoid it in the other therapeutic arena, the therapist should neither force the patient to reveal the material in the primary modality nor collude to keep the material from that modality. (This is true in conjoint as well as combined treatment.) Rather, the therapist should patiently work toward understanding *why* the patient feels the need for secrecy. Secrets are ultimately much less interesting than the reasons why the patient feels the need for secrecy, and it is usually much more productive to explore the fantasies about why the material cannot be shared in the primary modality. Nevertheless, occasionally the therapist will decide to bring material from one arena into the other. This must be done delicately and in full recognition of the fact that even if this is part of the therapeutic agreements the patient may experience this as a breach of confidentiality.

It is not uncommon for patients in combined treatment to make references in the group session to material from their individual sessions. Many times such comments are very meaningful to the current group interaction, and therapists must bear the burden of hearing their words or their meaning altered. Attention to the here and now of the communication assists therapists in maintaining narcissistic balance. In such circumstances therapists may compare the patient's perceptions with their own. On occasion the patient may be conveying information about a countertransference response of the clinician in the safety of the group. A premature confrontation of the patient's "distortion" may disrupt the treatment relationship. There are occasions in which the patient's distortion is grossly inaccurate, and the therapist may, following self-scrutiny, provide the correct information. To mention material from one therapeutic setting in the other is not breaking confidentiality since the boundary of confidentiality surrounds both therapeutic venues.

For some primitive patients the dissonance raised by two different types of therapy is more than they can integrate. This is less a factor of a particular diagnostic category and more a function of the individual's particular strengths and weaknesses. Some severely disturbed borderline patients can be greatly assisted by combined therapy whereas others inevitably utilize splitting and perceive one therapist or therapy as all good and the other as all bad. With the more primitive patients, careful attention must be paid to the benefits or liabilities of having the same therapist in both individual and group therapist roles. For some the consistency of the therapist makes the divergent experiences tolerable while for others the forced sharing within the group sessions of the individual therapist is more than they can tolerate. Again, in consultation with the patient, these decisions must be made on a case-by-case basis.

When individual and group therapy are used concurrently, it is important that neither be viewed as superior to the other. Rather, they are adjunctive to one another. There will be times during the therapy when the patient will give more weight to one or the other, and that is to be expected. In the usual course of events, patients gradually put more and more emphasis on their therapy group, and the individual therapy commonly ends before the group therapy is terminated.

When individual therapy and group therapy are viewed as cooperative by therapist and patient alike, they present a very powerful therapeutic modality for use with a wide variety of patients.

TIME-LIMITED PSYCHODYNAMIC
GROUP PSYCHOTHERAPY[2]

In this era of managed care, PPOs, HMOs, and the like, many therapists whose natural predilection is to run long-term, character-changing groups are finding themselves compelled to run time-limited, often symptom-focused groups (Sharfstein & Goldman, 1989). This implies that they must forgo their psychodynamic principles in favor of cognitive, behavioral, or more active techniques in order to accomplish anything in the time designated, but in fact it is quite possible to use psychodynamic principles in time-limited groups. (We much prefer the term *time-limited therapy* to *short-term therapy*. The former suggests the importance of reduced time as a dynamic in the treatment modality while the latter merely implies a comparison with a longer course of treatment.)

Indeed, Freud was originally a short-term therapist. When Freud began he practiced hypnotherapy, and the goal of the treatment was to remove symptoms. Even in his use of psychoanalysis, he did not work with his patients for the length of time used for present analyses. For example, Freud analyzed Ferenczi three times—once in 1914 and twice in 1916—comprising a *total* of less than 9 weeks!

With the discovery of transference, and as free association and dream analysis became the hallmarks of psychotherapeutic technique, the ending of treatment became more vague. Now the goal of psychotherapy was no longer the removal of the symptom but, rather, an *understanding* of the function of the symptom. This inevitably lengthened the process of therapy, though the case can be made that it *reduced* the ultimate treatment time required, since making the symptom's function conscious reduced the possibility of it's returning in another form that would require further therapy. The concept of transference reduced the role of suggestion by the therapist, which was replaced by the less active role of exploration. That is, the interaction between patient and therapist decreased as Freud and his followers refined techniques that fostered transference. The result was that therapy took longer and longer—so much longer that Freud wrote (1937) "Analysis Terminable and Interminable" (and this at a time when analyses took approximately 6 months to a year). As the divergence between long-term and short-term therapy widened, certain characteristics began to dominate each. Long-term therapy became less focused, depended on the meanderings of free association, and attended to underlying character style. Short-

[2]For a more complete study of various modes of time-limited therapy see Groves (1992).

term therapy became more focused, with a concern for continually monitoring progress. Long-term therapists became less interactive with their patients, while short-term therapists became more so.

However, *brevity, focus,* and *therapist activity* are axes about which there is great debate even among time-limited therapists (Groves, 1992). A final parameter of disagreement among short-term therapists is *patient selection*. We will look at each of these variables in a moment. First, let's review the history of time-limited therapy.

History

World War II, with the sudden emergence of thousands of soldiers and civilians with mental health crises, created the fertile ground from which flourished many therapeutic modalities, including group therapy and short-term therapy. The great need, combined with the shortage of trained professionals, led to the examination of ways in which to make the therapeutic process more effective.

In 1944 Grinker and Spiegel, working with soldiers, and Lindemann, working with survivors of the Coconut Grove fire, rediscovered the active short-term therapies that Ferenczi and Rank (1925) had advocated.

In more modern times Sifneos (1971) and Mann (1973) in Boston, Malan (1976) in London, and Davanloo (1979, 1980) in Montreal were probably the first to systematically apply psychodynamic principles to time-limited therapy. It is interesting to note that each of these practitioners suggests that the time-limited format holds more promise for healthier patients.

Sifneos (1971) contrasts anxiety-suppressive and anxiety-provoking therapies. In anxiety-suppressive therapy, where treatment is restricted to 4 to 10 meetings, the goal of treatment is to impart better coping skills, reduce anxiety, and diminish symptoms. Sifneos advocates the use of anxiety-suppressive therapy with more disturbed patients. With both therapies he recommends that the focus of the work be quite narrow, with the therapist acting in the role of "teacher." In an anxiety-provoking time-limited model Sifneos maintains that transference is "forced" and that anxiety is used as a curative lever. In this model the dynamic goals of self-understanding and character change apply. The number of sessions may be anywhere from 12 to 20. Sifneos believes that only the healthiest 2% to 10% of patients can use the anxiety-provoking model.

Malan (1976) sets a firm termination date (allowing between 20 and 30 meetings) in order to arouse anxiety and promote regression and dependency. Using object relations theory, he aims interpretations at patients' interpersonal style, not their defenses. Malan suggests that his model, in which the therapist acts a "doctor," works best with relatively healthy or mildly character-disordered individuals.

Davanloo (1979, 1980) uses a much more aggressive approach, vigorously attacking the patient's defenses in a calculated effort to elicit anger. Here the therapist plays the role of "critic." Whereas Sifneos uses anxiety as a therapeutic agent of change, and Malan uses dependency, Davanloo relies on anger. He suggests between 1 and 40 sessions as an acceptable treatment duration and he believes that only the healthiest 30% to 35% of our patient population can respond to his techniques. Patients accepted into treatment with Davanloo must respond positively in their first meeting.

Mann (1973), like Malan, relies on an immutable termination date to promote affect. Furthermore, he has an inflexible number of meetings for all patients—12. No time-limited model requires more of the therapist than Mann's since he attempts to widen the scope of the therapeutic venture as much as possible. For Mann the goal of time-limited therapy is to help patients identify the central issue that lies beneath their symptoms. Mann is also the clearest about using time as the agent of change. He essentially allows patients to believe that their problems can be resolved in the 12 weeks allotted, and then analyzes their reactions as it becomes clear that this hope will not be met. The range of diagnostic categories from which Mann is willing to accept patients is broader than that for any of the other time-limited therapists. The therapist's role in this model may be described as "empathic helper."

None of these theorists have applied their work to group therapy. Budman and Gurman (1988), who have attempted to apply time-limited theories to work with groups, propose an "IDE focus," which refers to the interpersonal, developmental, and existential vantage points. Because these authors maintain that most change in group therapy occurs at the beginning, they attempt to provide a powerful model for change to occur in a few weeks. Unlike some time-limited therapists, Budman and Gurman do not prohibit patients from returning for several courses of time-limited treatment.

Likewise, MacKenzie (1988, 1990, 1993) has developed specialized techniques for employing group psychotherapy in a time-limited mode. For MacKenzie time-limited groups can accomplish a variety of goals: "psychoeducation, crisis management, or support and groups that are designed for active intrusive interpersonal work" (1993, p. 425). However, careful selection of patients is necessary and depends on the goals of the group. MacKenzie's approach is quite structured and the leader assumes an active role.

Advantages and Disadvantages
of Time-Limited Group Therapy

Time-limited groups offer some unique advantages. For example, groups formed homogeneously around particular symptoms, demographics, or crises typically attain cohesion much more quickly than do heterogeneous long-term groups. The patients begin with the realistic assumption that the other members, who share with them the common identity around which the group was formed, will understand their situation. Further, the commonality of members allows for easier discussion during the formative stages of the group. The accent on universality enhances that major curative factor in groups, and it, in turn, reduces a sense of shame.

The limited duration of the group also offers some protection, since members know the end is in sight. Within the allotted amount of time members can come together around their commonality (and they may even have time to begin to note their diversification within that commonality). Finally, the forced ending promotes work on such issues as individuation, grief, and unfulfilled hopes.

Pressure for time-limited therapy derives from the increasing cost of medical care. Invoking draconian measures to curtail the rise at times results in many patients being referred to time-limited groups who do not fit the usual criteria for time-limited interventions. One model that may apply to such individuals has been described by Hardy and Lewis (1992). Working with patients, many of whom were recently discharged from a psychiatric hospital, Hardy and Lewis helped the patients focus on limited goals that could be attained in 12 weeks. Following this 12-week group experience the patients met with the group therapist individually to determine if they had reached their goals. If they had not, they could reenlist for another time-limited group to try to achieve those goals. If the patients felt they had attained their goals, they were given the option of selecting a new goal and joining another time-limited group to work on that goal. Some patients were reported to have enlisted in more than six successive time-limited groups. This is one of a number of models of "intermittent" treatment that are emerging to meet the needs of our changing treatment environment.

There are also some distinct disadvantages to time-limited groups. For one thing, groups formed around symptoms tend to promote the unfortunate tendency for patients to see themselves solely in terms of their symptom. More and more in our society individuals are identifying themselves with their symptoms. Patients report, "I am an adult child of alcoholics," or "I am an eating disorder." These patients do not conceive of their symptoms as compatible with the self and as

TABLE 13.1. Dynamic Theories of Time-Limited Therapy

Therapist	Number of sessions	Focus of therapy	Role of therapist	Therapist behaviors	Patient selection guidelines
Sifneos: Anxiety-suppressive therapy	4–10	Narrow; on crisis, coping (conscious)	Teacher	Clarifies, supports, decreases transference	Less healthy but able to recognizes psychological origin of problem
Sifneos: Anxiety-provoking therapy	12–20	Very narrow; oedipal conflict; unconscious grief; transference	Teacher	Interprets transference and resistance; idealizing transference becomes ambivalent	Very rigid standards; top 2%– 10% of clinical population
Malan	20–30 (with a fixed termination date)	Narrow; implicit (therapist finds it); unconscious	Doctor	Promotes "insight"	Relatively healthy; mild character pathology
Davanloo	1–40 (25 ca.)	Broader; resistance; use of aggression	Critic	Confronts resistance especially around anger	Top 30%– 35%; must respond in first trial
Mann	Exactly 12	Broadest; "central issue"; time itself; termination	Empathic helper	Focuses on separation and stage where parent failed	Broader selection

Note. Adapted from Groves (1992, pp. 38–39). Copyright 1992 The Guilford Press. Adapted by permission.

representing a defense to protect against deeper, more character-based pain. Although groups composed along symptoms are powerful in helping patients work on those symptoms, one must keep in mind that the "adult child of alcoholics" and the "eating disorder" are ultimately more alike than different inasmuch as both are struggling with ways to manage powerful and unacceptable affects.

It is our conviction that all homogeneously formed groups *should* be time-limited. No matter how much time-limited groups might contribute to the notion that "I am my symptom," this is not nearly so much a problem in those groups as in long-term groups that are formed homogeneously. Not only does the homogeneity itself restrict the group experience, but members may later resist dealing with a new member who presents with the common symptom. For example, a long-term eating disorder group would essentially preclude men. Furthermore, after the group matures and has stopped focusing exclusively on eating disorder issues, it becomes very difficult for new members with eating disorders to join (Riess & Rutan, 1992). It should be added that the time limit for homogeneous groups can productively be quite a long one. It can often be useful to have a time limit of a year or even more. We believe that homogeneous groups are best served if the members understand at the outset that the group has a definite termination date.

14

Termination in
Group Psychotherapy

Termination of psychotherapy is an extremely complex process. It is further complicated in therapy groups. In dyadic therapy the leave-taking is between two individuals, and it can be modified to suit the situation. In terminating individual therapy there is usually the recognition, barring unusual circumstances, that the patient has the option of returning to the therapist in the future, if needed, and it is occasionally useful to terminate the therapeutic relationship gradually, by meeting less and less often and thus giving the patient the opportunity to "try it out" before a final termination occurs. In groups, however, the leave-taking is more public and more complicated because the member is leaving many individuals, not just one. Furthermore, terminations from groups tend to be final. That is, when a patient terminates group therapy, it is unlikely that the group will remain unchanged should the patient need or desire further treatment. Finally, it is more difficult in groups to modify terminations to suit the needs of individual patients because this flexibility would adversely affect the therapeutic effectiveness of the group, whose members need continuity and consistency of format in order to accomplish their work.

HISTORICAL REVIEW
OF THE CONCEPT OF TERMINATION

The criteria by which to judge the time to terminate therapy have varied. In the earliest days of psychoanalysis, when Freud and Breuer were involved in hypnosis, termination was based on the topographic theory of mental functioning. According to this theory, therapy was finished when the unconscious was made conscious. This goal implied the lifting of repression but did not address the possibility of evaluating changes in psychic structure.

The theoretical picture was altered by Freud's discovery of transference neurosis. Transference, as one element of repetition compulsion, implies the existence of a stable, organized mental agency with characteristic defenses. As a result of this perspective, a new criterion was added in order for treatment to be considered complete: the transferential attachment to the analyst had to be resolved. Such resolution was seen as a concomitant of change in mental structures. However, Firestein (1976), in a study of successful training analyses, found that simply reentering the interview situation reawakened the old transferences, though in mild and manageable form. This study suggests that even in a healthy population, transference neurosis is by no means obliterated or eliminated.

Further modifications in termination criteria followed the development of ego psychology. Successful psychotherapy was correlated with the emergence of higher-level defenses, greater appropriateness in the use of defenses, greater flexibility in defensive style, and improvement in the ego's capacity for autonomous functioning. The outgrowth of this shift in perspective to the level of ego functioning led directly to questions of internalization and structuralization, that is, to an interest in how new or regained ego capacities are integrated into the mental apparatus.

Another important contribution to the conceptualization of termination came from the object relations school, which postulated that the primary human drive is to find objects (relationships). Criteria for termination were associated with the individual's capacity to develop object constancy, the ability to hold a reliable internal image and memory of others. This capacity was operationalized through examination of the patient's ability to find and form meaningful relationships with appropriate persons and to tolerate ambivalent feelings.

The work of Kohut (1971, 1977) suggested yet another set of criteria for termination. Viewed from the perspective of self psychology, the individual in therapy develops a reliable capacity to experience others as separate individuals who have their own needs and wishes and are not present solely to fulfill a missing function of the self. Self psychologists believe that the attainment of appropriate goals, ambitions, pride, and self-esteem is the result of maturation of infantile grandiosity and that the acquisition of appropriate values and ideals results from maturation of infantile idealization. Closely linked to these steps is increased empathic capacity.

CURRENT CRITERIA
FOR APPROPRIATE TERMINATION

Advances in theory are largely reflected in our understanding of preoedipal, borderline, and narcissistic character formations. There is some disagreement among those writers who discuss termination criteria for patients with preoedipal pathologies, in contrast to patients with classical oedipal conflicts. The classical criteria for termination for all pathologies have included the following:

- The transference neurosis and resistances have been analyzed, with the resulting development of a more mature superego and ego ideal.
- Defenses have become freer.
- Drives are discharged in a more socially acceptable manner.
- The patient has internalized the therapist's analyzing capacity.

Blanck and Blanck (1974) have summarized termination criteria that seem most applicable to those patients with earlier developmental deficits and arrests:

- Identity, differentiation between self and object representations, and the capacity to retain the representation of the object independent of the state of mind have been attained.
- Higher levels of integration have been reached, indictaing that structuralization has proceeded.
- Object relations approach object constancy.
- A more competent defensive capacity has been acquired.
- The ego exercises more and more of its own functions.

Kohut (1971) suggested that in disorders of the self the development of a stable, cohesive self may be sufficient for the individual to restart the thwarted growth process and spontaneously move through oedipal developmental stages. In a more controversial formulation, Kohut (1971) also emphasized the development of structures in either the grandiose or idealizing axis to compensate for major organizational deficits in the opposite axis.

TERMINATION IN GROUPS

All of the aforementioned criteria are adequate means of judging the therapeutic process. More often than not, therapists will utilize a variety of criteria chosen according to their theoretical orientation.

In addition, we tie judgments about the suitability of termination to the original group agreements, in which patients agree to remain in the group until they resolve the problems they bring to the group. This is a complicated judgment because many original problems have not been "cured" or eradicated but may have been resolved to the satisfaction of the patient. One example is the patient who comes to treatment in order to counter a terror of success. In the course of therapy the patient may discover the roots of that terror and may overcome the perpetual self-sabotaging of success but may still lack success. Yet it may be goal appropriate for the patient to terminate before some ideal success is attained. Another example is the patient who comes with the specific goal of gaining the interpersonal attributes necessary to form a loving relationship, marry, and become a parent. Such a patient might terminate when he or she has been able to form a stable and successful loving relationship even though that is only the first step in the original design.

Almost universally, patients discover *more* problems in the course of their therapy. Is termination appropriate if the patient resolves the problems that brought him or her but not the other problems that became apparent during the treatment?

Some patients enter treatment with a curative fantasy (W. Stone, 1983) that is an organized wish for what they hope to gain in therapy. It cannot be expressed through a set of agreements because the curative fantasy contains both conscious and unconscious elements; instead, it is expressed in the process of the treatment. These patients use the intragroup relationships to strengthen a sector of their personalities. When this has been accomplished, some of these patients terminate, leaving the therapist bewildered. Although they seemingly have not fulfilled the agreements, they depart quite satisfied.

The most important single criterion for determining the appropriateness of termination has to do with the question "Has this patient gained the most that can be gained from continuing to meet with the group at this time?" This means that for different patients the answer will be quite different and that the group agreements function as a rough guideline for termination. Patients may use the agreements in a positive fashion, but they may also defensively invoke the agreements as a rationale for leaving. Under the latter circumstance the therapist must work with the resistance to further therapy.

When individuals decide to stop treatment, they terminate from the real and the fantasied relationships with their colleagues, therapist, and the group as a whole. This is an active process, and the form it takes depends on the group norms, which define the way terminations are managed, and on a person's prior experiences with separations.

Typically, three major affective components are evoked by termination: feelings about death and mortality, feelings about separation
and/or abandonment, and hope (a new beginning). The degree to which
each or all of these components are emphasized in particular terminations is a function of the individual and the prior group process. Though
these dynamics and affects interact during the process of termination,
we will attempt to separate them for heuristic purposes.

GROUP DYNAMICS
IN THE TERMINATION OF INDIVIDUALS

Many different kinds of terminations occur in groups. Most members
terminate successfully, but some members quit prematurely and others
leave for external reasons or with significant but incomplete gains. Some
people quit with advance notice, others just disappear.

Because life is filled with good-byes, the capacity to bear the affect surrounding loss is necessary if one is able to have intimacy in relationships. Each and every termination from a group offers all the
members another opportunity to learn more about the experience of
saying good-bye. Since loss and death are such painful experiences, members often resist experiencing the emotions surrounding terminations.
Because they try to avoid their affects, their responses are either totally
hidden or are expressed metaphorically.

The therapist, functioning in the role of norm setter, must help
draw the members' attention to the feelings surrounding loss. The therapist's attitude and willingness to confront these feelings increases the
members' capacity to study their inner worlds. The therapist also tries
to establish norms regarding proper termination procedures, including appropriate notification of the group and setting a termination date
far enough in advance to allow for sufficient exploration of the feelings evoked by the leaving.

Not all patients terminate in the same way, and not all terminations have the same impact on groups. We will now turn our attention
to some common forms of termination.

Early Terminators

When termination occurs within the first few weeks of an individual's
membership in a group, the group's response usually reflects the level
of group development. There is little sense of belonging in new groups,
and members have had little time to learn about the internal state of
the early terminator. Further, before group cohesion has occurred, mem-

bers are unconsciously reluctant to speak (or even think) of how devastating it is to the group to have someone leave so abruptly because such an acknowledgment precludes the possibility that *they* will flee. What the members do know is that someone is missing, but the dynamics mobilized around that event usually remain unspoken or receive only cursory attention. Often the response is to ignore or condemn the dropout. When several members leave, there emerges a concern about the continued existence of the group; members become preoccupied with the future, asking about newcomers and the future plans of the therapist. The therapist has the task of balancing the discussion of the group's future with the more immediate feelings of discouragement and despair.

Some Group Dynamics in Premature Quitting

Exclusive attention to an individual member is often insufficient for understanding a threatened or actual premature termination. Powerful regressive forces are activated in group formation, and the interplay between these forces and the individual is generally what prompts a person to drop out. For instance, people do not suffer with problems of intimacy in isolation; pressures for intimacy and closeness may be frightening forces that prematurely propel some individuals out of groups. Group norms for instant intimacy are most likely to produce premature terminations. Furthermore, when a group does not recognize the frail but courageous efforts of certain members to become more engaged, the resulting painful narcissistic injury is covered in either a raging, stormy departure or a perplexing, sudden, unannounced disappearance (W. Stone, Blase, & Bozzuto, 1980). Other group processes that contribute to early departure are scapegoating, avoidance of in-group conflict, and insistence on immediate and intense expression of feelings (Bernard & Drob, 1989; Connelly, Piper, DeCarufel, & Debbane, 1986).

Premature Leaving in New Groups

Prematiure quitting presents a particular therapeutic problem in new groups because there is insufficient group development to allow the generally unacceptable affects in the remaining members to emerge and be examined in an accepting atmosphere. These affects include both guilt and envy. Guilt is almost universal. It may arise from the belief that not enough was done to prevent the dropping out or that one's hostile feelings or behaviors toward the departed member were responsible for the leaving. In the forming phase members maintain their distance, attempt to gain control, or actively push others away, and many of these behaviors evoke fear or hostility that is not modified through understanding. Thus, when an individual leaves, the remaining members may feel guilty because of their rage—whether or not it was expressed—and from their relief and pleasure that the member is gone.

Envy is also a powerful and frequently expressed feeling. Since it can be assumed that there is a part of every member that wishes to avoid belonging to a group and experiencing the difficult task of growing, all reamining members feel envious of the departed member. This feeling is often covered by a reaction formation, with those remaining avowing their increased dedication to and optimism about the group.

Contributing to the difficulty in exploring feelings about the early dropout is the remaining members' competitiveness. To each of them leaving represents a victory in that there is one less person with whom to vie for the group's attention or with whom to compete for the therapist's favor. Because these feelings are usually experienced as shameful, they are likely to remain hidden in a new group.

The absence of overt affect about an early dropout should not be mistaken for a genuine lack of interest in the event. Sometimes no mention is made of an early dropout until someone else leaves, and then a flood of previously unexpressed sentiments emerge. It is not at all unusual for a significant discussion of an early departure to occur months later, evoked by something in the current process of the group. The therapist must attempt to tactfully help the newly forming group explore their reactions to an early dropout, even in the face of considerable resistance.

Premature Leaving in More Mature Groups

In more mature groups the departure of a recently added member stimulates many of the same feelings and dynamics found in new groups. In this case, however, the affects will be more available for discussion and exploration. In addition, the therapist may be the object of anger for having selected such an individual, since the old members are acutely aware of the disruptive effect of having someone enter and depart so quickly. In the process of group development they have acquired the capacity to explore their affects in the here and now of meetings and are in a position to retrospectively examine some of their own fears of joining and their wishes to flee. Compared to members of a newly formed group, they may be more empathic toward the departed member and more introspective about the processes that may have contributed to the quitting. This, of course, does not mean that all new members will remain in an established group, only that members of mature groups will have more access to the feelings evoked by the departure and more capacity to utilize those feelings for learning. Established groups are in fact not damaged or slowed down nearly as much by the premature departure of a new member as are the less mature groups.

INCOMPLETE TREATMENTS

Individuals who leave a group further along in the therapeutic process may stop for reality reasons, or they may have achieved symptomatic relief and wish to settle for that. Despite gains, these who have achieved only symptomatic relief demonstrate continuing deficits in interpersonal or intrapsychic maturity. In groups that have reached a more advanced level of development, the remaining members are usually ready to explore their feelings of hurt, disappointment, and rage at the one who left without finishing his or her work. Angry reactions to the loss of members are much in evidence in such groups, and considerable therapeutic gain is possible for members as a result of freeing up angry affects.

Beneath the anger is often a deep-seated feeling of personal or groupwide failure to help or more deeply engage the departing member. These painful affects, along with the associated depressive feelings, also can be examined in a therapeutically productive fashion. They are more readily available when the termination is forced by external factors because such terminations carry with them the added dimension of the lost opportunity. In a truncated way, forced terminations reawaken old experiences of death and of separations that occurred without the participants' volition.

Incomplete treatments provide an opportunity to examine motivations and actions as the members try to discriminate between terminations that are the result of fate or external factors and those that at first *seem* to be the result of external factors but are later understood, upon closer examination, to be the final product of resistance to or acting out against the therapy. If there is sufficient time—and if the departing individual has not burned all his or her bridges—this examination may even prevent the premature leaving.

In attempting to help departing patients examine the unconscious aspects of leaving, the therapist might review their initial complaints and symptoms with the idea of seeing how the present wish to stop treatment might be a continuation of a behavioral pattern. On the other hand, the leave-taking may be the result of newly exposed conflicts or of interpersonal clashes within the group that are fueled by historic conflicts. The therapist might state quite directly that the work of therapy is incomplete and that this is not the most propitious time to terminate.

Of course, this should always be done with tact and empathy and in full recognition of the fact that patients are free agents. On occasion, however, a forthright statement about the incomplete therapeutic work will encourage a redecision. In some instances the entire process is an unconscious test of the therapist or group, a test designed to discover whether or not the therapist or group cares enough to fight to have the patient stay.

To focus solely on the individual in question is usually insufficient to understand fully what is occurring. It is useful to encourage the patient to be curious about why the decision to leave occurs at a particular point in the group's life. By understanding the decision to leave in the context of the group process, the tendency to focus solely on the departing member is diminished. This not only provides the member with a more complete understanding of the impetus for wishing to leave, but it also makes it easier for the him or her by offering a face-saving reason to remain in the group.

One additional very important groupwide component is part of every premature termination: There are some members, focusing only on the gains and overlooking the continuing difficulties of the departing patient, who are initially in complete agreement with the decision to leave. Thus, the resistance to continuing treatment or exploring the conflict may be a groupwide resistance. In these circumstances an exploration of the resistance in the members who sided with the announced departure should take place so that the potentially departing member may have sufficient distance to assess his or her own resistances.

Finally, such premature terminations highlight the very real limitations of control and power one person has over another. The opportunity for the remaining members to discover and deal with that reality can be a very maturing experience and can be distinguished from a neurotic feeling of helplessness or giving up. To believe genuinely that a member would be in error by terminating at a particular point in time and to make every effort to communicate that conviction to the member and still have the termination occur is to face both the real and existential limitations of life.

THE COMPLETED TREATMENT

Successful terminations from groups are usually moving and powerful experiences for all concerned. Unlike terminations from dyadic therapy, terminations from groups are witnessed, felt, and shared by a number of people.

The optimal process for termination is set forth in the original group agreements (Chapter 7). The agreement to "remain in the group until the problems that brought you have been resolved" implies a great deal about what constitutes appropriate termination; that is, patients are expected to stay until a particular goal or set of goals has been achieved. Furthermore, at the time of negoitiating the agreements, the procedure for termination is explained; prospective members are told that they should terminate when they have finished their work and that they should accomplish the termination by announcing their decision in a group meeting, after which they should continue to attend the group for as long as it takes to discuss the idea and to deal with the important process of saying good-bye. The therapist should help the departing patient set a termination date far enough in advance for the *group* to deal with and learn from the related feelings. Generally, the process will be facilitated if the departing member has had the opportunity to observe a spectrum of terminations before saying his or her own good-byes.

In most successful terminations, the therapist and many of the members will sense that a termination is coming. The quality of the interactions, along with reports of improved functioning outside the group, provides ample data upon which to build an awareness that the work is approaching a conclusion. One hallmark of a successful termination is the agreement of almost everyone in the room that the time is right (though many may be bitterly disappointed or angry about it.)

When a member announces plans to terminate, major emotional responses are inevitable. Each patient has the right to determine when termination is in order. Termination is not the result of a group vote. Nonetheless, successfully terminating patients will allow and encourage input from their colleagues about the advisability of termination, and they will examine this decision as they have learned to examine all important decisions. Some terminating members will announce steadfastly, "I have decided to terminate," and will state the date of the last meeting they will attend. Others invite more groupwide participation in the decision. The approach can be appropriate or inappropriate, depending upon the individual and the situation. Sometimes an individual will make a hard-and-fast decision, including the date of the final meeting, as a way of avoiding the power of the feelings regarding separation and loss. On the other hand, an individual who desires to forestall the inevitable leaving will appear to require groupwide approval of the decision to terminate, thereby delaying the implementation of a decision that has inwardly already been made. The important point is to make every possible effort to allow sufficient time and opportunity to explore the relevant affects that lead to and result from the decision of a member to terminate.

No stereotypical rule governs the length of time the termination process should take, but the most common error is allowing too little time to experience and learn from the feelings. Therapists and patients alike are hesitant about fully facing the feelings evoked by important good-byes. Time is needed for the group to come to grips with the idea of the termination. We prefer to have the discussion of the idea of termination precede the setting of an actual departure date. After the discussion a departure date should be set far enough in the future to allow for full exploration and elaboration of the event. As a rough guideline, this entire process might take one month for each year that the patient has been in the group.

Following an announcement of the intention to terminate, members generally respond with important derivative material, frequently by associating to other important losses. This should not be viewed as a resistance to dealing with the leave-taking but, rather, as an integral part of mourning. By associating to powerful previous good-byes, the other patients are communicating how deeply this loss will be felt. The current loss also provides an opportunity for a more complete grieving of earlier, insufficiently mourned losses. As the actual departure date approaches, the group will deal more and more directly with the here-and-now feelings about saying good-bye to the departing individual.

In the termination process an appraisal of the departing member's growth, changes, and unresolved conflicts is commonly undertaken. Previous intragroup conflicts, incompletely resolved, will often resurface. Regression takes place, often affecting many in the group, and the emotional responses may include intense efforts to dissuade the member from leaving. Sometimes the terminating member succumbs to the pressure, or to his or her ambivalence, and considers not stopping therapy. Again, envy of the success of a colleague may be in evidence, but often reaction formation clouds the feelings by overidealizing the terminating member. These regressions are usually short-lived, with all members realizing the archaic nature of their responses. Indeed, the members gain satisfaction from recognizing that they can experience old feelings and conflicts and rapidly regain their balance.

It is important to appreciate that not all the pressures to prevent or delay a departure are transferential. In the place of a senior, mature, and contributing member, the group will gain a neophyte who will initially take much more than he or she gives. Furthermore, there are also real relationships between human beings that will be missed.

Once a definite date for leaving is set, the departure becomes a reality. The termination date should not coincide with another disruption, such as the group therapist's vacation or the addition of a new member. Each major disruption requires careful attention, and to confuse the successful termination of a member with another disruption diminishes the poignancy of the loss for the group members. Maintaining continuity in the face of loss furthers appropriate grieving.

Setting the final date underlines the group's awareness that the individual in question will soon be leaving and will ultimately be replaced by someone else. The focus on the future also concerns the departing member, and members will often ask, "What will you be doing on this night in the future?" and "What will it be like in group without you?" Members also turn their attention to their own futures, often wondering how many more months or years will be required before they too can successfully leave the group. In this process they may review their progress, and under the influence of the positive atmosphere they may work on their problems with new resolve.

As the final session approaches, it is usually increasingly difficult for the members to tolerate the feelings; thus, there is frequently a proposal made for action—a social gathering or the purchasing of a group gift to commemorate the termination. These discussions can generate considerable enthusiasm, and much energy and effort can go into the planning of a "last supper." It is difficult under these circumstances for any single member to refuse to join in, and great therapeutic skill is required to handle these situations. When confronted with such plans for action, therapsits should tactfully remind the members that the agreement is to share feelings verbally rather than to act on them. Furthermore, such proposals attempt to set a norm that homogenizes all terminations, thereby diminishing the often painful reality that people are missed and mourned differently. Moreover, there is always—in addition to the genuine wish to send the successful patient of with good cheer—the opposite envious or angry side.

CLINICAL EXAMPLE

The therapist entered the office for the final group meeting with Zelda, a patient terminating quite successfully after many years. To his surprise and dismay, the therapist found that the room resembled a New York deli, with cold cuts, potato chips, wine, and all the utensils spread around in a decorative fashion. The group was in a festive mood, each member sitting with a plate brimming with food. The therapist was instantly greeted by Mildred, who offered to pour him some wine and make him a sandwich.

The therapist was confronted with a delicate therapeutic task. Clearly, great effort had gone into this lavish display, and the members obviously felt they were honoring the termination of Zelda. They had no conscious awareness of the denial implied in their party atmosphere. For the ther-

apist to focus only on the resistant elements of the "celebration" would
have been to miss part of the point. On the other hand, to have participated in the party would have been an even more serious error since doing so would have meant altering the fundamental agreements.

In this instance the therapist simply noted, "The group certainly seems
to be celebrating Zelda's departure," and placing the glass of wine that
he had been handed on an end table beside his chair, he said, "But I think
there are a wide range of feelings to be expressed and explored on such
an important evening." As the members realized that the therapist was
not going to eat or drink, the plates and glasses slowly were placed on
the floor or on tables. Mildred was the last to give up the hope that this
last meeting with Zelda could be given over to eating and drinking and
laughing. She angrily accused the therapist of being a "spoilsport" and
wondered, "What shall I do with all this food I brought?" A prolonged
and painful silence followed, punctuated by tears as various members began to experience Zelda's loss. Suddenly Mildred burst into tears, saying
"My God! I'm doing what I did at my mother's funeral. I catered that
affair; I fed everyone. I never left myself time to cry."

Endings evoke very important feelings, and therapists should resist
the temptation to alter the fundamental operation of the group when
terminations occur. On the other hand, they must be able to respond
creatively and not stereotypically. When a terminating member brings
a gift, for example, there is no simple rule about whether to accept
it. For some patients, the gift represents their continuing worry that
without a physical reminder the group and the therapist will not remember them. If the therapist judges this to be the impetus, the gift usually
should be tactfully interpreted and not accepted. In other cases a gift
simply represents a wish to give something to commemorate the experience and accompanies feelings amply expressed verbally as well;
in this case *not* accepting the gift might well result in a final narcissistic injury.

It is a rather common occurrence at termination that members will
exchange addresses and telephone numbers with the aim of remaining
in touch with the departing member. Sometimes members will inquire,
"Is this a breach of our agreements?" We believe that the agreements
hold only for members who are in the group and that what transpires
between members and ex-members is not included. That is not to imply, however, that this wish to continue a relationship should not be
explored like any other wish. Sometimes the wishful intention represents
an avoidance of the termination and an unwillingness by a member
to acknowledge a loss.

No separation or loss is complete. We all carry the images and memories of the departed individual and of his or her interactions with us, and the hope to say a complete and final good-bye is a fantasy. Successful terminations are painful and joyous occasions mixed together, and the therapist should make every effort to help the members explore all aspects of this very important experience.

THE TERMINATION PROCESS
FOR THE DEPARTING MEMBER

Individuals terminate from groups in a wide variety of ways. Some simply never return, disappearing without even a good-bye. But when individuals remain in groups for any protracted period of time, it is more likely they will engage in at least some formal leave-taking.

Terminations from groups are somewhat different from terminations from individual, or dyadic, therapy. In groups there is less time, because of the presence of the other members, for a detailed discussion of all the associations and memories that are stirred in the terminating patient by the leaving. Although, as in all human endeavors, there is a wide range of individual responses, individuals terminating from groups seem to experience less regression than do those terminating from dyadic therapy.

In successful terminations from a group there is a useful tendency on the part of the departing member to reminisce aloud about the treatment. Indeed, therapists can facilitate reminiscing if this does not occur spontaneously. The rich and varied interactions that occurred between members and leader are remembered and discussed. Typically, departing members review incidents that illustrate their developing ego capacities and their abilities to manage conflict and tolerate affects. Although they may also discuss areas that require further attention and conflicts that remain unresolved, they convey an ability to master rather than be dominated by these incompletely resolved problems. As one departing member said, "I still get extra angry, but now I can stop it and try to work it out rather than just blame the other person." Another said, "I still tend to take care of people too much, but I don't let myself be used all the time anymore." The goal is not perfection but the capacity to recognize, accept, understand, and forgive one's weaknesses and vulnerabilities and to own and recognize one's strengths.

Departing members may give credit to others who were able to see things well before they could see them for themselves. Moreover, they may comment on the unique opportunities the group afforded them to genuinely understand someone else. During the development of a group there is a growing feeling of mastery in members as they learn about one another and appreciate what is going on beneath surface appearances. In other words, members who terminate groups success-fully no longer take the position of an external observer of the other members. They have developed or expanded the capacity to empathize, and for many patients this is a highly significant step.

Finally, almost all those who terminate indicate that they will miss the camaraderie, affection, and work of the group. They often wonder aloud if they will be missed or remembered. Since the group has be-come an important part of their lives, it is natural for them to specu-late on whether the remaining members and therapist will think of them, recall their contributions, and in some fashion indicate that they have made an enduring impact upon someone.

WHOLE GROUP TERMINATIONS

As time-limited group therapy becomes more and more prominent, an entire group must struggle with termination at the same time. Homogeneous groups, organized around a particular symptom, crisis, demographic variable, or diagnosis, are often closed to new members time-limited. On occasion, entire groups terminate owing to life events for the therapist (Chapter 10).

Though many patients in time-limited groups achieve their goals and are ready to stop at the specified time, this is not the universal sit-uation. The dynamics that ensue are the reverse of those in effect when individuals prematurely drop out of groups. This time the group is quit-ting too soon. The entire termination process is complicated because the overt and covert resentments about the loss are difficult to elicit when the group's ending was originally agreed upon. Kauff (1977) described the group fantasy of the destructive witch/mother in forced whole-group terminations or transfers. This reawakening of primitive fantasies surrounding the termination is consistent with the patients' deep-seated fears that their basic needs will remain unmet.

As time-limited groups reach the midpoint of their life expectan-cy, themes of good-bye, separation, and loss become more and more dominant. The therapist has the important and difficult task of keep-ing the group's attention on the impending termination. There is a great temptation, aided and abetted by the patients, to discount the impor-tance of the approaching ending. The process of exploring the forth-coming separation and loss is complicated by the fact that members have more therapeutic work to do. Thus, a balance needs to be struck between these two elements. Usually, through clarification of metaphors such as death, divorce, and graduation, the therapist can help the patients understand how they are managing their feelings about the group's demise. As the ending approaches, certain patients may demonstrate a high rate of absenteeism. At the end of each meeting for the last 4 or 5 weeks, the therapist may, as a reminder, announce to the group the number of meetings that remain.

As in other effective terminations, initially the members of a time-limited group will typically resonate to the theme of saying good-bye and will deal with issues from their own personal histories. This is often a time when some excellent work is done on unresolved grief. As the end point gets closer and closer, the group begins dealing with the here-and-now good-byes to the various members, to the leader, and to the group itself.

It is almost never in the best interests of the members of time-limited groups to alter the agreed-upon ending date. Inexperienced therapists occasionally take a vote of the members about whether or not to continue. In the usual scenario a substantial portion, if not all, of the members vote to continue the group, but those who felt coerced may quit immediately or soon after the original deadline. In the diminished group, morale is undermined and effective therapy ceases. If a group was formed with the agreement that it would terminate on a specific date, it should do so. In time-limited groups the therapist should help members evaluate the need for continued therapy, but members should understand that they have fulfilled their group agreements and have no responsibility for joining another group. Members wishing to continue therapy may opt to join a *new* group, perhaps even an open-ended one. Ideally, that group should begin a month or so after the ending of the time-limited group.

TERMINATION AND THE GROUP THERAPIST

The therapist is by no means immune to the effects of members' departures. Just as there are reverberations among the members of themes of separation and loss, so too are memories and affects of these themes stirred in the therapist, potentially producing powerful countertransferences. Therapists may find numerous reasons to interfere with a patient's departure, paralleling their own separation problems. Similarly, they may be uncomfortable with the wide range of intense affects evoked by terminations and therefore may avoid interpreting the resistance and acting out that are part of termination.

In the case of premature terminations the therapist may suffer the narcissistic hurt of not having been successful or loved. This is much more likely when a therapist is conducting just one group. There is no question that it would be exceedingly difficult for a dyadic therapist to gain therapeutic distance and perspective if he or she had only one patient. Likewise, the feelings of hurt, failure, or discouragement when someone leaves a therapist's only group can be intense. Such situations are always powerful, but if the therapist has other groups that are going well he or she is somewhat protected from severe narcissistic injury. Whenever a therapist's personal issues with loss keep him or her from fully exploring the issues of termination, patients lose opportunities to grow.

In especially difficult groups the therapist may harbor the fantasy that if one member quits, the others will also and thereafter he or she will not be burdened with the problem group. Unfortunately, this occasionally comes to pass, particularly for neophyte therapists and those who have not had the experience of successful terminations. As with those who learn long-term individual psychotherapy, only a few trainees in group therapy have the good fortune to be in a training placement long enough to experience the successful conclusion of an intensive therapy.

When there is a successful termination, the therapist has the narcissistic gratification of a job well done. At the conclusion of successful dyadic psychotherapy, the therapist often has the opportunity to state quite openly some of what the treatment experience has been like from his or her point of view. In a group the emotional connection from the therapist to the patient is no less powerful, but other patients are privy to and are participating in the good-bye. For some members the overt statement of caring from therapist to departing patient would be overstimulating, but most patients are significantly helped by observing the genuine relationship that has developed between the therapist and the terminating patient.

In sum, therapists should feel free to state the same things to terminating group patients that they would state to terminating individual patients. However, they should be acutely aware of the impact of such statements on the remaining patients. Termination represents the completion of the therapeutic process. It is our hope that the ideas presented in this book will facilitate the successful termination of many group patients.

References

Abse, D. W. (1974). *Clinical notes on group analytic psychotherapy.* Charlottesville: University of Virginia Press.

Ackerman, N. (1949). Psychoanalysis and group therapy. In J. Moreno (Ed.), *Group therapy* (Vol. 8, Nos. 2–3, pp. 204–215). Boston: Beacon House.

Adler, G., & Buie, D. H. (1979). Aloneness and borderline pathology: The possible relevance of child development issues. *International Journal of Psycho-Analysis, 60,* 83–96.

Agazarian, Y. M. (1989). Group-as-a-whole system theory and practice. *Group, 13,* 131–54.

Agazarian, Y. M. (1992). Contemporary theories of group psychotherapy: A systems approach to the group-as-a-whole. *International Journal of Group Psychotherapy, 42,* 177–203.

Allport, G. (1965). *The Nature of Prejudice.* Cambridge, MA: Addison-Wesley.

Alonso, A., & Rutan, J. S. (1990). Common dilemmas in combined individual and group treatment. *Group, 14,* 5–12.

Alonso, A., & Swiller, H. I. (1993). Introduction: the case for group therapy. In A. Alonso & H. I. Swiller (Eds.), *Group therapy in clinical practice* (pp. xxii–xxiii). Washington, DC: American Psychiatric Press.

American Psychiatric Association. (1987). *Diagnostic and statistical manual of mental disorders* (3rd ed., rev.). Washington, DC: Author.

Arsenian. J., Semrad, E. V., & Shapiro, D. (1962). An analysis of integral functions in small groups. *International Journal of Group Psychotherapy, 12,* 421–434.

Ashback, C., & Schermer, V. L. (1987). *Object relations, the self and the group: A conceptual paradigm.* New York: Routledge & Kegan Paul.

Astrachan, B. M. (1970). Towards a social systems model of therapeutic groups. *Social Psychiatry, 5,* 110–119.

Bach, G. R. (1954). *Intensive Group Psychotherapy.* New York: Ronald Press.

Bader, B. R., Bader, L. J., Budman, S., & Clifford, M. (1981). Pre-group preparation model for long-term group psychotherapy in a private practice setting. *Group, 5,* 43–50.

Battegay, R. (1972). Individual psychotherapy and group psychotherapy in combination. *Acta Psychiatrica Scandinavica, 48,* 43–46.

Battegay, R. (1977). The group dream. In L. Wolberg & M. Aronson (Eds.), *Group therapy, 1977: An overview* (pp. 27–41). New York: Stratton Intercontinental Medical Book.

Benne, K., & Sheats, P. (1948). Functional roles of group members. *Journal of Social Issues, 4,* 41–49.

Bennis, W. G., & Shepard, H. A. (1956). A theory of group development. *Human Relations, 9,* 415–437.

Berger, M. M. (1969). Notes on the communication process in group psychotherapy. *Journal of Group Process and Psychoanalysis, 2*,(1), 29–36.

Bernard, H. S., & Drob, S. (1985). The experience of patients in conjoint individual and group psychotherapy. *International Journal of Group Psychotherapy, 35,* 129–146.

Bernard, H. S., & Drob, S. L. (1989). Premature termination: A clinical study. *Group, 13,* 11–22.

Binstock, W. (1979). The psychodynamic approach. In A. Lazare (Ed.), *Outpatient psychiatry: Diagnosis and treatment* (pp. 19–70). Baltimore: Williams & Wilkins.

Bion, W. R. (1960). *Experiences in groups.* New York: Basic Books.

Birdwhistle, R. L. (1970). *Kinesics and context.* Philadelphia: University of Pennsylvania Press.

Birk, L. (1974). Intensive group therapy: An effective behavioral-psychoanalytic method. *American Journal of Psychiatry, 131,* 11–16.

Blanck, G., & Blanck, R. (1974). *Ego psychology: Theory and practice.* New York: Columbia University Press.

Borriello, J. F. (1979). Group psychotherapy with acting-out patients: Specific problems and techniques. *American Journal of Psychotherapy, 33,* 521–530.

Bowlby, J. (1973). *Separation: Anxiety and anger.* New York: Basic Books.

Bratter, T. E. (1981). Some pre-treatment group psychotherapy considerations with alcoholic and drug-addicted individuals. *Psychotherapy: Theory, Research and Practice, 18*(4), 508–515.

Brenner, C. (1988). Working through, 1914-1984. *Psychoanalytic Quarterly, 56,* 88–108.

Brown, D. (1992). Bion and Foulkes: Basic assumptions and beyond. In M. Pines (Ed.), *Bion and group psychotherapy* (pp. 192–219). London: Tavistock/Routledge.

Brown, D., & Pedder, J. (1979). *Introduction to psychotherapy: An outline of psychodynamic principles and practice.* London: Tavistock.

Budman, S. H., Demby, A., Redendo, J. P., Hannan, M., Feldstein, M., Ring, J., & Springer, T. (1988). Comparative outcomes in time-limited individual and group psychotherapy. *International Journal of Group Psychotherapy, 38,* 63–71.

Budman, S. H., & Gurman, A. S. (1988). *Theory and practice of brief therapy.* New York: Guilford Press.

Butler, T., & Fuhriman, A. (1980). Patient perspective on the curative process: A comparison of day treatment and outpatient psychotherapy groups. *Small Group Behavior, II,* 371–388.

Chiang, E., & Beck, B. L. (1988). The effects of therapist turnover in a training group: The core group phenomenon. *International Journal of Group Psychotherapy, 12,* 127–134.

Christ, J. (1975). Contrasting the charismatic and reflective leader. In Z. Liff (Ed.), *The leader in the group* (pp. 104–113). New York: Jason Aronson.

Cohen, Y. A. (1961). *Social structures and personality.* New York: Holt, Rinehart & Winston.

Comstock, B. S., & McDermott, M. (1975). Group therapy for patients who attempt suicide. *International Journal of Group Psychotherapy, 25,* 44–49.

Connelly, J. L., Piper, W. L., DeCarufel, F. L., & Debbane, E. G. (1986). Premature termination in group psychotherapy: pretherapy and early therapy predictors. *International Journal of Group Psychotherapy, 36,* 145–152.

Cooper, A. M. (1987). Changes in psychoanalytic ideas: Transference interpretation. *Journal of the American Psychoanalytic Association, 35,* 77–98.

Cooper, L., & Gustafson, J. (1979a). Toward a general theory of group therapy. *Human Relations, 32,* 967–981.

Cooper, L., & Gustafson, J. P. (1979b). Planning and mastery in group therapy: A contribution to theory and technique. *Human Relations, 32,* 689–703.

Davanloo, H. (1979). Techniques of short-term dynamic psychotherapy. *Psychiatric Clinics of North America, 2,* 11–22.

Davanloo, H. (1980). *Short-term dynamic psychotherapy.* New York: Jason Aronson.

Day, M. (1981). Process in classical psychodynamic groups. *International Journal of Group Psychotherapy, 31,* 153–174.

Demarest, E. W., & Teicher, A. (1954). Transference in group therapy: Its use by co-therapists of opposite sexes. *Psychiatry, 17,* 187–202.

Dohrenwend, B. P. & Dohrenwend, B. S. (1974). Social and cultural influences on psychopathology. *Annual Review of Psychology, 7,* (No. 25), 417–452.

Durkin, H. E. (1964). *The group in depth.* New York: International Universities Press.

Durkin, H. E. (1981). The technical implications of general system theory for group psychotherapy. In J. Durkin (Ed.), *Living groups* (pp. 171–198). New York: Brunner/Mazel.

Durkin, J. E. (1981). Foundations of Autonomous Living Structures. In J. Durkin (Ed.), *Living groups* (pp. 24–59). New York: Brunner/Mazel.

Edwards, N. (1977). Dreams, ego psychology, and group interaction in analytic group psychotherapy. *Group, 1,* 32–47.

Eisenthal, S. (1979). The sociological approach. In A. Lazare (Ed.), *Outpatient psychiatry: Diagnosis and treatment* (pp. 73–115). Baltimore: Williams & Wilkins.

Eliot, A. O. (1990). Group coleadership: A new role for parents of adolescents with anorexia and bulimia nervosa. *International Journal of Group Psychotherapy, 40*(3), 339–352.

Ethan, S. (1978). The question of the dilution of transference in group psychotherapy. *Psychoanalytic Review, 65,* 569–578.

Evans, N. J., & Jarvis, P. A. (1980), Group Cohesion: A review and evaluation. *Small Group Behavior, 11,* 359–370.

Ezriel, H. (1973). Psychoanalytic group therapy. In L. Wolberg & E. Schwartz (Eds.), *Group therapy 1973* (pp. 183–210). New York: Stratton Intercontinental Medical Book.

Fairbairn, W. R. D. (1952a). *An object-relations theory of the personality.* New York: Basic Books.

Fairbairn, W. R. D. (1952b). *Psychoanalytic studies of the personality.* London: Tavistock.

Feldberg, T. M. (1958). Treatment of borderline psychotics in groups of neurotic patients. *International Journal of Group Psychotherapy, 8,* 76–84.

Ferenczi, S., & Rank, O. (1925). *The development of psychoanalysis* (C. Newton, Trans.). New York: Nervous & Mental Disease Publishing.

Firestein, S. (1976). Termination in psychoanalysis. *Journal of the American Psychoanalytic Association, 24,* 3–10.

Foulkes, S. H. (1948). *Introduction to group-analytic psychotherapy.* London: Heinemann.

Foulkes, S. H. (1961). Group process and the individual in the therapeutic group. *British Journal of Medical Psychology, 34,* 23–31.

Foulkes, S. H. (1964). *Therapeutic group analysis.* London: Allen & Unwin.

Foulkes, S. H. (1973). The group as the matrix of the individual's mental health. In L. Wolberg & E. Schwartz (Eds.), *Group therapy 1973* (pp. 211–220). New York: Stratton Intercontinental Medical Book.

Foulkes, S. H. (1975). *Group analytic psychotherapy: methods and principles.* London: Gordon & Breach.

Foulkes, S. H., & Anthony. E. J. (1965). *Group psychotherapy: the psychoanalytic approach* (2nd ed.). Baltimore: Penguin Books.

Frank, J. D. (1957). Some determinants, manifestations, and effects of cohesiveness in therapy groups. *International Journal of Group Psychotherapy, 7:* 53–63.

French, T. M. (1952). *The integration of behavior* (Vols. 1 & 2). Chicago: University of Chicago Press.

Freud, S. (1905). Fragment of an analysis of a case of hysteria. In J. Strachey (Ed. & Trans.) *The standard edition of the complete psychological works of Sigmund Freud* (Vol. 7, pp. 1–122). London: Hogarth Press, 1957.

Freud, S. (1910). The future prospects of psychoanalytic theory. In J. Strachey (Ed. & Trans.), *The standard edition of the complete psychological works of Sigmund Freud* (Vol. 11, pp. 139–151). London: Hogarth Press, 1957.

Freud, S. (1913). On beginning the treatment. In J. Strachey (Ed. & Trans.), *The standard edition of the complete psychological works of Sigmund Freud* (Vol. 12, pp. 121–144). London: Hogarth Press, 1958.

Freud, S. (1914). Remembering and repeating and working through. In J. Strachey (Ed. & Trans.), *The standard edition of the complete psychological works of Sigmund Freud* (Vol. 12, pp. 145–156). London: Hogarth Press, 1958.

Freud, S. (1915). Observations and transference love. In J. Strachey (Ed. & Trans.), *The standard edition of the complete psychological works of Sigmund Freud* (Vol. 12, pp. 157–171). London: Hogarth Press, 1958.

Freud, S. (1921). Group psychology and the analysis of the ego. In J. Strachey (Ed. & Trans.), *The standard edition of the complete psychological works of Sigmund Freud* (Vol. 18, pp. 69–143). London: Hogarth Press, 1955

Freud, S. (1937). Analysis terminable and interminable. In. J. Strachey (Ed. & Trans.), *The standard edition of the complete psychological works of Sigmund Freud* (Vol. 23, pp. 209–253). London: Hogarth Press, 1964.

Fried, E. (1954). The effect of combined therapy on the productivity of patients. *International Journal of Group Psychotherapy, 8,* 76–84.

Fried, E. (1970). Individuation through group psychotherapy. *International Journal of Group Psychotherapy, 20,* 450–459.

Fried, E. (1971). Basic concepts in group psychotherapy. In H. Kaplan & B. Sadock (Eds.), *Comprehensive group psychotherapy* (pp. 47–71). Baltimore: Williams & Wilkins.

Fried, E. (1973). Group bonds. In L. Wolberg & E. Schwartz (Eds.), *Group therapy 1973: An overview* (pp. 161–168). New York: Stratton Intercontinental Medical Book.

Fried, E. (1982). Building psychic structures as a prerequisite for change. *International Journal of Group Psychotherapy, 32,* 418–422.

Friedman, L. (1988). *The anatomy of psychotherapy.* Hillsdale, NJ: Analytic Press.

Frost, J. C. (1990). A developmentally keyed scheme for the placement of gay men into psychotherapy groups. *International Journal of Group Psychotherapy, 39*(2), 155–168.

Fulkerson, C. C. F., Hawkins, D. M., & Alden, A. R. (1981). Psychotherapy groups of insufficient size. *International Journal of Group Psychotherapy, 31,* 73–81.

Gans, J. S. (1990). Broaching and exploring the question of combined group and individual therapy. *International Journal of Group Psychotherapy, 40,* 123–137.

Gans, J. S. (1992). Money and psychodynamic group psychotherapy. *International Journal of Group Psychotherapy, 42,* 133–152.

Gans, R. (1962). Group co-therapists and the therapeutic situation: A critical evaluation. *International Journal of Group Psychotherapy, 12,* 82–87.

Ganzarain, R. (1991). The "bad mother-group": An extension of Scheidlinger's "mother-group concept." In S. Tuttman (Ed.), *Psychoanalytic group theory and therapy* (pp. 157–173). Madison, CT: International Universities Press.

Garland, C. (1982). Taking the non-problem seriously. *Group Analysis, 15,* 4–14.

Garland, J. A., & Kolodny, R. L. (1973). Characteristics and resolution of scapegoating. In S. Bernstein (Ed.), *Further explorations in group work* (pp. 67–68). Boston: Milford House.

Gauron, E. F., & Rawlings, E. I. (1975). Procedure for orienting new members to group psychotherapy. *Small Group Behavior, 6,* 293–307.

Getty, C., & Shannon, A. M. (1969). Co-therapy as an egalitarian relationship. *American Journal of Nursing, 69,* 762–777.

Gibbard, G. S., & Hartman, J. S. (1973). The oedipal paradigm in group development: A clinical and empiral study. *Small Group Behavior, 4,* 305–354.

Giovacchini, P. (1979). *Treatment of primitive mental states.* New York: Jason Aronson.

Glatzer, H. T. (1953). Handling transference resistance in group therapy. *Psychoanalytic Review, 40,* 36–43.

Glatzer, H. T. (1978). The working alliance in analytic group psychotherapy. *International Journal of Group Psychotherapy, 28,* 147–162.

Glatzer, H. T. (1989). Working through in analytic group psychotherapy. *International Journal of Group Psychotherapy, 19,* 292–306.

Greenberg, J. R., & Mitchell, J. A. (1983). *Object relations in psychoanalytic theory.* Cambridge, MA: Harvard University Press.

Greene, L. R. Rosenkrantz, J., & Muth, D. Y. (1986). Borderline defenses and counter transference: research findings and implications. *Psychiatry, 49,* 253–264.

Greenson, R. R. (1967). *The theory and practice of psychoanalysis.* New York: International Universities Press.

Grotjahn, M. (1975). The treatment of the famous and the "beautiful people" in groups. In L. Wolberg & M. Aronson (Eds.), *Group therapy 1975: An overview* (pp. 76–82). New York: Stratton Intercontinental Medical Book.

Grotstein, J. (1981). *Splitting and projective identification.* Northvale, NJ: Jason Aronson.

Group for the Advancement of Psychiatry Committee on Research. (1975). Pharmacotherapy and psychotherapy: Paradoxes, problems and progress. *GAP Report, 9,* 271.

Group for the Advancement of Psychiatry Committee on Therapy. (1992). *Psychotherapy in the future.* Washington: American Psychiatric Press.

Groves, J. E. (1992). The short-term dynamic psychotherapies: An overview. In J. S. Rutan (Ed.), *Psychotherapy for the 1990s* (pp. 35–59). New York: Guilford Press.

Grunebaum, H., & Kates, W. (1977). Whom to refer for group psychotherapy. *American Journal of Psychiatry, 132,* 130–133.

Guntrip, H. (1969). *Schizoid phenomena, object-relations, and the self.* New York: International Universities Press.

Gustafson, J. P., & Cooper, L. (1979). Unconscious planning in small groups. *Human Relations, 32,* 1039–1064.

Gustafson, J. P., Cooper, L., Lathrop, N. C., Ringler, K., Seldin, F. A., & Wright, M. K. (1981). Cooperative and clashing interests in small groups: Part I. Theory. *Human Relations, 34,* 315–339.

Gustafson, J. P., & Cooper, L. (1992). After basic assumptions: on holding a specialized versus a general theory of participant observation in small groups. In M. Pines (Ed.), *Bion and group psychotherapy* (pp. 157–175). London: Routledge.

Guttmacher, J. A., & Birk, L. (1971). Group therapy: what specific therapeutic advantages? *Comprehensive Psychiatry, 12,* 546–556.

Hardy, J., & Lewis, C. (1992). Bridging the gap between long and short-term group psychotherapy: A viable treatment model. *Group, 16,* 5–17.

Herman, J. L., Perry, J. C., & van der Kolk, B.A. (1989). Childhood trauma in borderline personality disorder. *American Journal of Psychiatry, 146,* 490–495.

Hill, W. & Grunner, L. (1972). A study of development in open and closed groups. *Small Group Behavior, 4,* 355–381.

Horwitz, L. (1974). *Clinical Prediction in Psychotherapy.* New York: Jason Aronson.

Horwitz, L. (1977a). Group psychotherapy of the borderline patient. In P. Hartocollis (Ed.), *Borderline personality disorders* (pp. 399–422). New York: International Universities Press.

Horwitz, L. (1977b). A group-centered approach to group psychotherapy. *International Journal of Group Psychotherapy, 27,* 423–440.

Horwitz, L. (1980). Group psychotherapy for borderline and narcissistic patients. *Bulletin of the Menninger Clinic, 44,* 181–200.

Hulse, W. (1958). Psychotherapy with ambulatory schizophrenic patients in mixed groups. *Archives of Neurology and Psychiatry, 79,* 681–687.

Johnson, D., & Howenstein, R. (1982). Revitalizing an ailing group psychotherapy program. *Psychiatry, 45,* 138–146.

Kadis, A. L. (1956). The alternate meeting in group psychotherapy. *American Journal of Psychiatry, 10,* 275–291.

Kadis, A. L., Krasner, J. D., Winick, C., & Foulkes, S. H. (1963). *A practicum of group psychotherapy.* New York: Harper & Row.

Kanas, N., Deri, J., Ketter, T., & Fein, G. (1990). Short-term outpatient therapy groups for schizophrenics. *International Journal of Group Psychotherapy, 39,*(4), 517–522.

Kaplan, S. R., & Roman, M. (1961). Characteristic responses in adult therapy groups to the introduction of new members: A reflection on group process. *International Journal of Group Psychotherapy, 11,* 372–381.

Karasu, T. B. (1982). Psychotherapy and pharmacotherapy: Toward an integrative model. *American Journal of Psychiatry, 138,* 1102–1113.

Katz, G. A. (1983). The non-interpretation of metaphors in psychiatric hospital groups. *International Journal of Group Psychotherapy, 33,* 56–68.

Kauff, P. F. (1977). The termination phase: its relationship to the separation-individuation phase of development. *International Journal of Group Psychotherapy, 27,* 14–22.

Kauff, P. F. (1979). Diversity in analytic group psychotherapy: The relationship between theoretical concepts and technique. *International Journal of Group Psychotherapy, 29,* 51–66.

Kauff, P. F. (1993). The Contribution of analytic group therapy to the psychoanalytic process. In A. Alonso & H. I. Swiller (Eds.), *Group therapy in clinical practice* (pp. 3–28). Washington, DC: American Psychiatric Press.

Kelman, H. (1963). The role of the group in the induction of therapeutic change. *International Journal of Group Psychotherapy, 13,* 399–451.

Kernberg, O. F. (1975). A systems approach to priority setting of interventions in groups. *International Journal of Group Psychotherapy, 25,* 251–275.

Kernberg, O. F. (1976). *Object relations theory and clinical psychoanalysis.* New York: Jason Aronson.

Kibel, H. S. (1991). The therapeutic use of splitting: The role of the mother-group in therapeutic differentiation and practicing. In S. Tuttman (Ed.), *Psychoanalytic group theory and therapy* (113–132). Madison, CT: International Universities Press.

Klein, E., & Astrachan, B. (1971). Learning in groups: A comparison of T-groups and study groups. *Journal of Applied Behavioral Science, 7,* 659–683.

Klein, M. (1946). Notes on some schizoid mechanisms. *International Journal of Psycho-Analysis, 27,* 99–110.

Klein, R. H., & Carrol, R. A. (1986). Patient characteristics and attendance patterns in outpatient group psychotherapy. *International Journal of Group Psychotherapy, 36,* 115–132.

Kleinberg, J. L. (1991). Teaching beginning group therapists to incorporate a patient's empathic capacity in treatment planning. *Group, 15,* 141–154.

Klein-Lipschutz, E. (1953). Comparison of dreams in individual and group psychotherapy. *International Journal of Group Psychotherapy, 3,* 143–149.

Kohut, H. (1971). *The analysis of the self.* New York: International Universities Press.

Kohut, H. (1977). *The restoration of the self.* New York: International Universities Press.

Kohut, H. (1984). *How does analysis cure?* Chicago: University of Chicago Press.

Kohut, H., & Wolf, E. S. (1978). The disorders of the self and their treatment: An outline. *International Journal of Psycho-Analysis, 59,* 413–425.

Kris, E. (1956). The recovery of childhood memories in psychoanalysis. *Psychoanalytic Study of the Child, 2,* 54–88.

Krystal, H. (1974). The genetic development of affect and affect regression. *Annual of Psychoanalysis, 2,* (pp. 98–126).

Lang, E., & Halperin, D. A. (1989). Coleadership in groups: Marriage a la mode? In D. A. Halperin (Ed.), *Group psychodynamics: New paradigms and new perspectives* (pp. 76–86). Chicago: Year Book Medical Publishers.

Lasch, C. (1979). *The culture of narcissism.* New York: Norton.

Lazare, A., & Eisenthal, S. (1979). A negotiated approach to the clinical encounter. II: Attending to the patient's perspective. In A. Lazare (Ed.), *Outpatient psychiatry: Diagnosis and treatment* (pp. 141–156). Baltimore: Williams & Wilkins.

Lazare, A., Eisenthal, S., & Frank, A. (1979). A negotiated approach to the clinical encounter. II: Conflict and negotiation. In A. Lazare (Ed.) *Outpatient psychiatry: Diagnosis and treatment* (pp. 157–171). Baltimore: Williams & Wilkins.

Leary, T. F. (1957). *Interpersonal diagnosis of personality.* New York: Ronald Press.

LeBon, G. (1920). *The crowd: A study of the popular mind.* New York: Fisher, Unwin.

Leighton, A. H. (1959). *My name is legion: Stirling county study of psychiatric disorder and sociocultural environment* (Vol. 1). New York: Basic Books.

Leszcz, M. (1992), The interpersonal approach to group psychotherapy. *International Journal of Group Psychotherapy, 42,* 37–62.

Levine, B. (1979). *Group psychotherapy: Practice and development.* Englewood Cliffs, NJ: Prentice-Hall.

Lieberman, M., Yalom, I. D., & Miles, M. D. (1973). *Encounter groups: First facts.* New York: Basic Books.

Lipsius, S. H. (1991). Combined individual and group psychotherapy: Guidelines at the interface. *International Journal of Group Psychotherapy, 41,* 313–327.

Loewald, H. W. (1973). On internalization. *International Journal of Psycho-Analysis, 54,* 9–17.

Long, K., Pendleton, L., & Winter, B. (1988). Effects of therapist termination on group process. *International Journal Group Psychotherapy, 38,* 211–222.

Lundin, W. H., & Aronov, V. M. (1952). The use of co-therapists in group psychotherapy. *Journal of Consulting Psychology, 16,* 77–84.

MacKenzie, K. R. (1987). Therapeutic factors in group psychotherapy: A contemporary view. *Group, 11,* 26–34.

MacKenzie, K. R. (1988). Recent developments in brief psychotherapy. *Hospital and Community Psychiatry, 39,* 742–752.

MacKenzie, K. R. (1990). *Introduction to time-limited group psychotherapy.* Washington, DC: American Psychiatric Press.

MacKenzie, K. R. (1993). Time-limited group theory and technique. In A. Alonso & H. I. Swiller (Eds.), *Group therapy in clinical practice* (pp. 423–447). Washington DC: American Psychiatric Press.

MacLennon, B. (1965). Cotherapy. *International Journal of Group Psychotherapy, 15,* 154–165.

Mahler, M. S., Pine, F. & Bergman, A. (1975). *The psychological birth of the human infant.* New York: Basic Books.

Malan, D. (1976). *The frontier of brief psychotherapy.* Cambridge, MA: Harvard University Press.

Malan, D. H., Balfour, F. H. G., Hood, V. G., & Shooter, A. (1976). Group psychotherapy: A long term follow-up study. *Archives General Psychiatry, 33,* 1303–1315.

Mann, J. (1973). *Time-limited psychotherapy.* New York: Plenum.

Marin, P. (1975, October). The new narcissism. *Harpers* pp. 44–56.

Massad, P., West, A., & Friedman, M. (1990). Relationship between utilization of mental health and medical services in a VA hospital. *American Journal of Psychiatry, 147,* 465–469.

Masterson, J. F. (1976). *Psychotherapy of the borderline adult.* New York: Brunner/Mazel.

McDougall, W. (1920). *The group mind.* New York: Putnam.

McGee, T. F. (1969). Comprehensive preparation for group psychotherapy. *American Journal of Psychiatry, 23,* 303–312.

McGee, T. F. (1974). Therapist termination in group psychotherapy. *International Journal of Group Psychotherapy, 24,* 3–12.

McGlashen, T. H. (1986). The Chestnut Lodge Followup Study: III. Longterm outcome of borderline personalities. *Archives of General Psychiatry, 43,* 20–30.

Meyers, S. J. (1978). The disorders of the self: developmental and clinical considerations. *Group, 2,* 131–140.

Michaels, R. (1981). The present and the past. *Bulletin of the Association of Psychoanalytic Medicine, 20,* 49–56.

Middleman, R. R. (1980). Co-leadership and solo-leadership in education for social work with groups. *Social Work with Groups, 3,* 30–40.

Mintz, E. (1965). Male-female co-therapists: Some values and some problems. *American Journal of Psychotherapy, 19,* 293–301.

Morrison, A. P. (1990). Secrets: A self-psychological view of shame in group therapy. In B. E. Roth, W. N. Stone, & H. D. Kibel (Eds.), *The difficult patient in group* (pp. 175–189). Madison, CT: International Universities Press.

Munzer, J. (1967). Acting out: Communication or resistance? *International Journal of Group Psychotherapy, 16,* 434–441.

Neumann, M., & Geoni, B. (1974). Types of patients especially suitable for analytically oriented group psychotherapy: Some clinical examples. *Israel Annals of Psychiatry and Related Disciplines, 12,* 203–215.

Nitsun, M. (1991) The anti-group: Destructive forces in the group and their therapeutic potential. *Group Analysis, 24,* 7–20.

Ogden, T. H. (1979). On projective identification. *International Journal of Psycho-Analysis, 60,* 357–373.

Ormont, L. R. (1967). Group resistance and the therapeutic contract. *International Journal of Group Psychotherapy, 18,* 147–154.

Ornstein, P. H. (1978). The evolution of Heinz Kohut's psychoanalytic psychology of the self. In P. Ornstein (Ed.), *The search for the self* (pp. 1–106). New York: International Universities Press.

Pine, F. (1985) *Developmental theory and clinical process.* New Haven: Yale University Press.

Pines, M. (1981). The frame of reference of group psychotherapy. *International Journal of Group Psychotherapy, 31,* 275–285.

Pines, M. (1991). Interminable patients. In J. Roberts & M. Pines (Eds.), *The practice of group analysis* (pp. 112–115). London: Routledge.

Pines, M., & Hutchinson, S. (1993). Group analysis. In A. Alonso & H. I. Swiller (Eds.), *Group therapy in clinical practice* (pp. 29–47). Washington, DC: American Psychiatric Press.

Pratt, J. H. (1969). The home sanatorium treatment of consumption. In H. Ruitenbeek (Ed.), *Group therapy today* (pp. 9–14). New York: Atherton Press.

Rabin, H. M. (1967). How does co-therapy compare with regular therapy? *American Journal of Psychotherapy, 21,* 244–255.

Redl, F. (1963). Psychoanalysis and group therapy: A developmental point of view. *American Journal of Orthopsychiatry, 33,* 135–147.

Rice, A. K. (1969). Individual, group, and intragroup process. *Human Relations, 22,* 565–584.

Rice, C. A. (1992). Contributions from object relations theory. In R. H. Klein, H. S. Bernard, & D. L. Singer (Eds.) *Handbook of contemporary group psychotherapy* (pp. 27–54). Madison, CT: International Universities Press.

Riess, H., & Rutan, J. S. (1992). Group therapy for eating disorders: A step-wise approach. *Group, 16*(2), 79–84.

Roberts, J. (1991). Destructive phases in groups. In J. Roberts & M. Pines (Eds.), *The practice of group analysis* (pp. 128–135). London: Routledge.

Rodenhauser, P. (1989). Group psychotherapy and pharmacotherapy: Psychodynamic considerations. *International Journal of Group Psychotherapy, 39,* 445–456.

Rogers, C. (1970). *Carl Rogers on encounter groups.* New York: Harper & Row.

Roller, B. (1989). Having fun in groups. *Small Group Behavior, 100,* 97–100.

Roth, B. E. (1979). Problems of early maintenance and entry into group psychotherapy with persons suffering from borderline and narcissistic states. *Group, 3,* 3–22.

Roth, B. E. (1980). Understanding the development of a homogeneous identity-impaired group through countertransference phenomena. *International Journal of Group Psychotherapy, 30,* 405–425.

Roth, B. E. (1990) The group that would not relate to itself. In B. E. Roth, W. N. Stone, & H. D. Kibel (Eds.), *The difficult patient in group* (pp. 127–155). Madison, CT: International Universities Press.

Rothke, S. (1986). The role of interpersonal feedback in group psychotherapy. *International Journal of Group Psychotherapy, 36,* 225–240.

Rutan, J. S. (1992a). Psychodynamic group psychotherapy. *International Journal of Group Psychotherapy, 42,* 19–35.

Rutan, J. S. (Ed.). (1992b). *Psychotherapy for the 1990s.* New York: Guilford Press.

Rutan, J. S., & Alonso, A. (1978). Some guidelines for group therapists. *Group, 2,* 4–13.

Rutan, J. S., & Alonso, A. (1979). Group therapy. In A. Lazare (Ed.), *Outpatient psychiatry: Diagnosis and treatment.* Baltimore: Williams & Wilkins.

Rutan, J. S., & Alonso, A. (1980). Sequential cotherapy of groups for training and clinical care. *Group, 4,* 40–50.

Rutan, J. S., & Alonso, A. (1982). Individual, group, or both? *International Journal of Group Psychotherapy, 32*(3), 3–16.

Rutan, J. S., Alonso, A., & Molin, R. (1984). Handling the absence of the leader. *International Journal of Group Psychotherapy, 34,* 273–287.

Rutan, J. S., & Rice, C. A. (1981). The charismatic leader: Asset or liability. *Psychotherapy: Theory, Research, Practice, 18,* 18.

Savaray, S. (1975). Group psychology and the structural theory. *Journal of the American Psychoanalytic Association, 23,* 69–89.

Savaray, S. (1978). A psychoanalytic theory of group development. *International Journal of Group Psychotherapy, 28,* 481–507.

Scheflen, A. (1964). The significance of posture in communication. *Psychiatry, 27,* 316–331.

Scheflen, A. (1965). Quasi-courtship behaviors in psychotherapy. *Psychiatry, 28,* 245–256.

Scheidlinger, S. (1968). The concept of regression in group psychotherapy. *International Journal of Group Psychotherapy, 18,* 3–20.

Scheidlinger, S. (1974). On the concept of the mother-group. *International Journal of Group Psychotherapy, 24,* 417–428.

Scheidlinger, S. (1982). On scapegoating in group psychotherapy. *International Journal of Group Psychotherapy, 32,* 131–143.

Schutz, W. C. (1958). *Firo.* New York: Rinehart.

Sharfstein, S. S., & Goldman, H. (1989). Financing the medical management of mental disorders. *American Journal of Psychiatry, 143,*(3), 345–349.

Sharpe, M. (1991). Death and practice. In J. Roberts & M. Pines (Eds.), *The practice of group analysis* (pp. 163–173). London: Routledge.

Shuttleworth-Jordan, A., Saayman, G., & Faber, P. (1988). A systematized method for dream analysis in a group setting. *International Journal of Group Psychotherapy, 38,* 473–489.

Sifneos, P. E. (1971). Two different types of psychotherapy of short duration. In H. Barton (Ed.), *Brief therapies* (pp. 82–90). New York: Behavioral Publications.

Sifneos, P. (1972). *Short-term psychotherapy and emotional crisis.* Cambridge, MA: Harvard University Press.

Slater, P. E. (1966). *Microcosm: Structural, psychological, and religious evolution in groups.* New York: John Wiley.

Slavinska-Holy, N. (1983). Combining individual and homogeneous group psychotherapies for borderline conditions. *International Journal of Group Psychotherapy, 33,* 297–312.

Slavson, S. R. (1950). *Analytic Group Psychotherapy.* New York: Columbia University Press.

Slavson, S. R. (1957). Are there group dynamics in therapy groups? *International Journal of Group Psychotherapy, 7,* 115–130.

Socarides, D. D., & Stolorow, R. D. (1984). Affect and selfobjects. *Annual of Psychoanalysis, 12/13,* 105–119.

Solomon, A., Loeffler, F. J., & Frank, G. H. (1953). An analysis of co-therapist interaction in group psychotherapy. *International Journal of Group Psychotherapy, 3,* 174–188.

Stein, A. (1963). Indications for group psychotherapy and the selection of patients. *Journal of Hillside Hospital, 12,* 145–155.

Stein, A. (1964). The nature of transference in combined therapy. *International Journal of Group Psychotherapy, 14,* 410–416.

Stern, D. N. (1985). *The interpersonal world of the infant.* New York: Basic Books.

Stolorow, R. D., Brandchaft, B., & Atwood, G. E. (1987). *Psychoanalytic treatment: An intersubjective approach.* Hillside, NJ: Analytic Press.

Stone, L. (1961). *The Psychoanalytic situation.* New York: International Universities Press.

Stone, W. N. (1975). Dynamics of the recorder-observer in group psychotherapy. *Comprehensive Psychiatry, 16,* 49–54.

Stone, W. N. (1983). The curative fantasy in group psychotherapy. *Group Therapy Monograph, 10.*

Stone, W. N. (1988). Transferences in groups: Theory and research. In D. Halperin (Ed.), *Group psychodynamics* (pp. 44–61). Chicago: Year Book Medical Publishers.

Stone, W. N. (1990). On affects in group psychotherapy. In B. Roth, W. Stone, & H. Kibel (Eds.), *The difficult patient in group* (pp. 191–208). Madison, CT: International Universities Press.

Stone, W. N. (1992). The place of self psychology in group psychotherapy: A status report. *International Journal of Group Psychotherapy, 42,* 335–350.

Stone, W. N., Blase, M., & Bozzuto, J. (1980). Late dropouts from group psychotherapy. *American Journal of Psychotherapy, 34,* 401–413.

Stone, W. N., & Gustafson, J. P. (1982). Technique in group psychotherapy of narcissistic and borderline patients. *International Journal of Group Psychotherapy, 32,* 29–47.

Stone, W. N., Rodenhauser, P. H., & Markert, R. J. (1991). Combining group psychotherapy and pharmacotherapy: A survey. *International Journal of Group Psychotherapy, 41,* 449–464.

Stone, W. N., & Rutan, J. S. (1984). Duration of treatment in group psychotherapy. *International Journal of Group Psychotherapy, 34,* 101–117.

Stone, W. N., Schengber, J. S., & Seifried, F. S. (1966). The treatment of a homosexual woman in a mixed group. *International Journal of Group Psychotherapy, 16,* 425–433.

Stone, W. N., & Stevenson, F. B. (1991). Seeking perspective on patients' attendance in group psychotherapy. In S. Tuttman (Ed.), *Psychoanalytic group theory and therapy* (pp. 339–356). Madison, CT: International Universities Press.

Stone, W. N., & Whitman, R. N. (1977). Contributions to the psychology of the self to group process and group therapy. *International Journal of Group Psychotherapy, 27,* 343–359.

Stone, W. N., & Whitman, R. M. (1980). Observations on empathy in group psychotherapy. In L. Wolberg & M. Aronson (Eds.), *Group and family therapy* (pp. 102–117). New York: Brunner/Mazel.

Strachey, J. (1934) The nature of the therapeutic action in psycho-analysis. In L. Paul (Ed.), *Psychoanalytic clinical interpretation* (pp. 1–41). New York: Free Press.

Sullivan, H. S (1953). *The collected works of Harry Stack Sullivan.* New York: Norton.

Swiller, H. J. (1988). Alexithymia: Treatment utilizing combined individual and group psychotherapy. *International Journal of Group Psychotherapy, 38,* 47–61.

Toffler, A. (1970). *Future Shock.* New York: Random House.

Toker, E. (1972). The scapegoat as an essential group phenomenon. *International Journal of Group Psychotherapy, 22,* 320–332.

Truax, C. B., & Wargo, D. G. (1969). Effects of vicarious therapy pretraining and alternate sessions on outcome in group psychotherapy with outpatients. *Journal of Consulting and Clinical Psychology, 33,* 440–447.

Tuckman, B. W. (1965). Developmental sequence in small groups. *Psychological Bulletin, 63,* 384–399.

von Bertalanffy, L. (1966). General system theory and psychiatry. In S. Arieti (Ed.), *American handbook of psychiatry* (pp. 705–721). New York: Basic Books.

Weiss, J., Sampson, H., & the Mount Zion Psychotherapy Research Group. (1986). *The psychodynamic process.* New York: Guilford Press.

Whitaker, D. S. (1989). Group focal conflict theory: Description, illustration and evaluation. *Group, 13,* 225–251.

Whitaker, D. S., & Lieberman, M. A. (1964). *Psychotherapy through the group process.* New York: Atherton Press.

Whitman, R. (1973). Dreams about the group: An approach to the problem of group psychology. *International Journal of Group Psychotherapy, 23,* 408–420.

Whitman, R. M., & Stock, D. (1958). The group focal conflict. *Psychiatry, 21,* 269–276.

Winick, C., Kadis, A. L., & Krasner, J. D. (1961). Training and professional practice of American group therapists. *International Journal of Group Psychotherapy, 11,* 419–430.

Wogan, M., Getter, H., Anidur, M. J., Nichols, M. F., & Okman, G. (1977). Influencing interaction and outcome in group psychotherapy. *Small Group Behavior, 8,* 26–46.

Wolf, A., & Schwartz, E. K. (1962). *Psychoanalysis in groups.* New York: Grune & Stratton.

Wolf, A., & Schwartz, E. K. (1975). The role of the leader's values. In Z. Liff (Ed.), *The leader in the group* (pp. 13–30). New York: Jason Aronson.

Wolf, E. S. (1988). *Treating the self.* New York: Guilford Press.

Wong, N. (1979). Clinical considerations in group treatment of narcissistic disorders. *International Journal of Group Psychotherapy, 27,* 325–345.

Wong, N. (1980). Combined group and individual treatment of borderline and narcissistic patients: Heterogeneous versus homogeneous groups. *International Journal of Group Psychotherapy, 30,* 389–404.

Wong, N. (1983). Combined individual and group psychotherapy. In H. Kaplan & B. Sadock (Eds.), *Comprehensive group psychotherapy* (2nd ed., pp. 73–83). Baltimore: Williams & Wilkins.

Yalom, I. D. (1966). A study of group therapy dropouts. *Archives of General Psychiatry, 14,* 393–414.

Yalom, I. D. (1985). *The theory and practice of group psychotherapy* (3rd ed.) New York: Basic Books.

Yalom, I. D., Bond, G., Bloch, S., Zimmerman, E., & Friedman, L. (1977). The impact of weekend group experience on individual therapy. *Archives of General Psychiatry, 34,* 399–418.

Zaslav, M. R., & Kalb, R. D. (1989). Medicine as metaphor and medium in group psychotherapy with psychiatric patients. *International Journal of Group Psychotherapy, 39,* 457–468.

Zetzel, E. (1956). Current concepts of transference. *International Journal of Psycho-Analysis, 37,* 369–376.

Zimmerman, D. (1976). Indications and counterindications for analytic group psychotherapy: A study of group factors. In M. Aronson, A. Wolberg, & L. Wolberg (Eds.), *Group therapy 1976: An overview* (pp. 232–242). New York: Stratton Intercontinental Medical Book.

Zinkin, L. (1983). Malignant mirroring. *Group Analysis, 16,* 113–126.

Index